T0309932

Socrates in the Underworld

Other titles of interest from St. Augustine's Press

Nalin Ranasinghe, *Logos and Eros: Essays Honoring Stanley Rosen*

Plato, *The Symposium of Plato; The Shelley Translation*. Percy Bysshe Shelley, translator

Aristotle, *Aristotle – On Poetics*. Seth Benardete and Michael Davis, translators

Aristotle, *Physics, Or Natural Hearing*. Glen Coughlin, translator

Francisco Suarez, *Metaphysical Demonstration for the Existence of God*. A.J. Freddoso, translator

Francisco Suarez, *On Creation, Conservation, and Concurrence*. John P. Doyle, translator

Zbigniew Janowski, *Augustinian-Cartesian Index*

Averroes, *Averroes' Middle Commentaries on Aristotle's Categories and De Interpretatione*. Charles Butterworth, translator

Averroes, *Averroes' Middle Commentary on Aristotle's Poetics*. Charles Butterworth, translator

Thomas Aquinas, *Commentary on Aristotle's Nicomachean Ethics*

Thomas Aquinas, *Commentary on Aristotle's Posterior Analytics*. Richard Berquist, translator

Thomas Aquinas, *Commentary on Aristotle's Metaphysics*

Thomas Aquinas, *Commentary on Aristotle's De Anima*

Thomas Aquinas, *Commentary on Aristotle's Physics*

Thomas Aquinas, *Disputed Questions on Virtue*. Ralph McInerny, translator

John of St. Thomas, *Introduction to the Summa Theologiae of Thomas Aquinas*

St. Augustine, *On Order [De Ordine]*. Silvano Borruso, translator

St. Augustine, *The St. Augustine LifeGuide*™

Henry of Ghent, *Henry of Ghent's Summa of Ordinary Questions*

James V. Schall, *The Regensburg Lecture*

Josef Pieper, *Happiness and Contemplation*

Josef Pieper, *Scholasticism*

Josef Pieper, *The Silence of St. Thomas*

C.S. Lewis, *The Latin Letters of C.S. Lewis*

Peter Kreeft, *Socratic Logic*

Seth Benardete, *Achilles and Hector: The Homeric Hero*

Seth Benardete, *Sacred Transgressions: A Reading of Sophocles'* Antigone

Stanley Rosen, *Plato's Symposium*

Stanley Rosen, *Plato's Sophist: The Drama of Original and Image*

Stanley Rosen, *Plato's Statesman*

Ronna Burger, *The Phaedo: A Platonic Labyrinth*

Socrates in the Underworld

Nalin Ranasinghe

Introduction by Peter Augustine Lawler

ST. AUGUSTINE'S PRESS
South Bend, Indiana
2009

Manufactured in the United States of America.

1 2 3 4 5 6   15 14 13 12 11 10 09

Library of Congress Cataloging in Publication Data
Ranasinghe, Nalin, 1960–
Socrates in the underworld: on Plato's Gorgias / Nalin Ranasinghe.
p. cm.
Includes bibliographical references and index.
ISBN-13: 978-1-58731-778-1 (hardcover: alk. paper)
ISBN-10: 1-58731-778-8 (hardcover: alk. paper)
1. Plato. Gorgias. 2. Socrates. I. Title.
B371.R36 2008
170 – dc22   2008009145

∞ The paper used in this publication meets the minimum requirements of the American National Standard for Information Sciences – Permanence of Paper for Printed Materials, ANSI Z39.48–1984.

ST. AUGUSTINE'S PRESS
www.staugustine.net

This book is dedicated,
with the utmost love and gratitude,
to Gudrun Krüger.

Annotated Table of Contents

Acknowledgments

Assumption College provided a faculty development grant that supported my writing of the first draft of this book over the summer of 2006.

I gladly acknowledge the collegiality and fellowship of my colleagues in the Philosophy Department at Assumption. Outside my department, Dean Mary Lou Anderson and Rick Sorenson were generous friends and trusted interlocutors. A special debt of gratitude is also owed to Dan Mahoney, without whose inspiration this project could not have been conceived or realized. Ronna Burger, Harold Brogan, Peter Lawler, Mary Mumbach, and Bainard Cowan were unfailing in their encouragement and support. And Bruce Fingerhut has always shown me the kindness and catholicity for which he is justly renowned.

Introduction: Our Hero, Socrates

Peter Augustine Lawler, Berry College

This is one of the most able, eloquent, noble, profound, and *loving* books ever written on Socrates. It restores for us the example of a moral hero who inaugurated a moral revolution in opposition to his country's post-imperial cynicism and nihilism. What Socrates discovered about the human soul remains true for us in our similarly cynical and nihilistic time. Here's the truth: "Self-knowledge is both the cure and the punishment for evil." We *are* the beings who can't help but know the truth about ourselves and be open to the truth about all things. The truth is *real;* we lack the power to command or negate it. The truth has *authority* over us; we can't live well unless we see that it is the power that allows us to perform genuinely free and deliberate acts. The truth is *attractive*; it both draws us out of ourselves and is a sort of magnet that puts our souls in order. And the truth is genuinely moral or *beautiful.*

Each of us and the *cosmos* itself "is so structured that true happiness can only result from virtue." Both intellectual and moral virtue are required to be genuinely open to the whole truth, and so the view that one form of virtue is possible without the other is mistaken. The Socrates Ranasinghe presents us with, is undeniable *personal* evidence that "philosophy still has the moral authority to sustain the soul's resilience and inspire virtue in times of moral strife and social chaos." Socrates can be *our* hero, freeing us from the cynical deceptions that seem to have given us a time without heroes.

One characteristic of our cynical and nihilistic time is that many of our scholars are certain to object that Ranasinghe's presentation of Socrates is too edifying to be true. It's easy to foresee their charge that this author doesn't have what it takes to penetrate beneath the superficial and banal pieties Plato employed to protect philosophical skepticism for moral indignation. He's suckered by Plato's *exoteric* moralism because he's not rigorous and sophisticated enough to get to the *esoteric* or genuinely philosophic dimension of Socratic dialectic. The esoteric Socratic teaching is all about rational liberation – liberation of the philosopher from moral dogma for the amoral truth about the human situation.

Socrates' true view, according to this skeptical interpretation, is that *the philosopher* is an *atheist*, and he uses morality or *ethics* to serve his selfish and hedonistic goals. From this view, the philosopher Socrates befriends the sophist Gorgias in order to learn the right sort of manipulative rhetoric that will serve him and his liberated friends. Genuine spiritual or philosophical liberation is reserved for a very few, and the liberated few are stuck with employing various sophistic deceptions to humor the moral many who threaten their private enjoyment. Plato, from this view, writes to preserve and improve upon morality not because it is true or good, but because there's no doing without it for most people.

This skeptical view that, for Socrates, *truth* and *morality* are fundamentally at odds, Ranasinghe shows, is itself based on a relatively superficial reading of the Platonic dialogues, one complacently satisfied at stopping before genuine spiritual enlightenment begins. The skeptical reading of Plato isn't *erotic* enough, because it tends to be based on the suspicion that *eros* or love itself is, deep down, an illusion. That's why, as Ranasinghe suggests, skeptical readers miss how radical Socrates' criticism of Thucydides' deterministic "realism" is.

For Ranasinghe, the deepest level of Socrates' teaching is the overcoming of skepticism and a philosophical justification of morality, a justification of our undeniable erotic impulse to have faith in *logos* as the foundation of friendship as genuine human community. Ranasinghe's reading of the *Gorgias* clearly establishes that genuine dialectic is the deadly enemy of sophistry; this means that the sophist Gorgias and the philosopher Socrates could never be friends. The pseudo-philosophical interpreters of Plato achieve their sham enlightenment by not really appreciating the radical distinction between Socratic dialectic and sophisticated manipulation. Socratic dialectic means to offer spiritual enlightenment to us all.

The deepest depth of the Platonic dialogue is a return to its surface, which is genuinely illuminating conversation about the moral or purpose-driven concerns we *really* share in common. We learn that the true purpose of the capacity for speech given to particular members of our species is neither *technical* nor *transgressive*. It is an error to view words as primarily weapons for either practical manipulation or for destroying the various articulations of the moral responsibilities given to social persons open to the truth.

Socrates finally confirms the goodness of all that we've been given as the beings with *eros* and *logos,* which means that all pretensions to solitary liberation or autonomous self-sufficiency are revealed, deep down, to be nothing but unnecessarily misery-producing illusions. Speech directed by reason and pulled toward reality by *eros* is, most of all, what keeps us from being alone. It also allows each of us to make genuine progress toward personal moral perfection. Our truth-inspired responsibilities are *both* personal and social.

"The crucial question," as Ranasinghe articulates it, "has to do with how seriously one takes Socrates' understanding of the soul as the seat of moral agency." Do we really know enough to be able to say with confidence, against the skeptics, that our perception of moral choice is real? Socrates' "knowledge of ignorance" is his awareness that omniscience is not a human possibility. We can't really resolve the question of human freedom through the study of natural science, and one condition of our freedom is our ability to know that we can't fully comprehend or control all that exists. We don't have the power, in fact, to make ourselves more or less than humans stuck between the other animals and God. Divine freedom or blind determination by impersonal necessity will never characterize us.

Do we still know enough to know that being good and being happy are really choices to open to us? Do we really know that any effort to feel good – to be happy – without really being good is bound to fail us? Socrates, Ranasinghe patiently explains, gives a *psychic* account of evil; good and evil are both profoundly *personal*.

I am evil, I can say, because I'm to blame if my soul is disordered, if I've been choosing against what I really know about myself. Evil *is* real and personal, and so it has a real and personal remedy. Telling the truth to myself as a rational and erotic being is the precondition for my choosing good over evil. That means that no radical social or technological transformation – no mega-effort to escape from the reality we've been given – can solve or even address the problem of evil. The Socratic way – the only way that respects the mystery of human freedom – is to proceed one soul at a time.

The Socratic teaching is morally demanding – the truth is we're not excused from doing the right thing by being victims or playthings of arbitrary gods or impersonal forces. But it is also reassuring. An ugly old guy trapped in an unhappy marriage turns out to be the best and the happiest Athenian of all. We can live well in the most adverse circumstances. Our happiness doesn't depend on happenstance or what's beyond our control, just as it doesn't depend on being a successful control freak.

Socrates, Ranasinghe shows, was no Stoic. The Stoics were also tough-minded men. They did their duty as rational beings in what they saw as a cold, deterministic world, and so they thought it was possible to keep one's own fate in one's own control. The Stoics actually thought life is tougher than it really is. In their self-understanding, there's no room for freedom or love or real happiness.

The world would be evil if the Stoics are right, and one appropriate response would be tight-lipped rational endurance of what can't be changed. The Stoics were unerotic because they thought the only way to think of themselves as happy is to think of themselves as *minds*, and not as whole human beings. But Socrates was actually happy in thinking about who he really is, because the pull of his *eros* was away from the illusion connecting rational self-sufficiency with happiness.

If the Stoics are right on the facts, then the Epicureans (or the Epicurean sophists) actually make more sense. The world is evil insofar as it's hostile to my very existence. Everything human is ephemeral and pointless, and so both hope and fear make me stupid. Such sophists argue that since evil isn't caused by me and can't be remedied by me, my proper response to worldly events is apathy. I might as well try to lose myself in imaginary pleasures, including taking some proud pleasure in being able to rise above the futile sound and fury that surrounds me. My personal assault on reality is, in fact, a value judgment on reality. I'm free to do whatever it takes to get me through this hell of a life.

But the truth is that I can't ever fully believe that my perception of reality is nothing but a private fantasy. I can't turn what I really know about my death into "death" or a linguistic construction amenable to reconstruction with my happiness in mind. In a certain way the Epicurean teaching is tougher than the Stoic position. Losing oneself is a full-time job; there's no real break from the pursuit of pleasurable diversions. There's no greater source of human misery, perhaps, than believing that nothing makes us more miserable than thinking clearly about what we really know. The fact that that thought is very un- or anti-erotic also helps to explain why Epicureans don't actually have much fun; they, like the Stoics, mistakenly refuse to go where their erotic longings could take them.

One of the most wonderful and genuinely useful features of this book is the large number of pointed and witty contemporary applications of the way Socrates reconciles truth, virtue, and happiness. Here's the Socratic good news for us: Our alternatives extend beyond fatalistic Stoicism (as practiced by our Southern aristocrats), emotive religion (as practiced, say, by our Evangelicals) aimed at opposing the loving will of God to scientific or empirical nihilism, and the unerotic and otherwise boring Epicureanism promulgated by our academic deconstructionists and animating the creeping and often creepy libertarianism that characterizes our culture as a whole.

Our lefty postmodernists and our right-wing free marketers, Ranasinghe shows, serve the same sophisticated cause of liberating us from any responsibility to moral truth. They think we'll be better off if we believe that what Socrates says we most need to know is unknowable, and succumb to their cynical claim that even the bonds of love are for suckers. By causing us to flee from what we really know and thus from our real potential for virtue, our sophisticates lead us to think and act as less than we really are. But it's still possible to recover who we really are; we can still imitate Socrates' ennobling example.

One reason among many Ranasinghe's Socrates is so attractive to me is that he draws him close to my moral/intellectual heroes actually alive today – Pope Benedict XVI (Joseph Ratzinger) and the great Russian writer and spiritual witness Aleksandr Solzhenitsyn. Ranasinghe says that part of his mission is to contribute to Ratzinger's effort to restore the proper place of *logos* in Christian thought. And we learn much from his Socrates to supplement both the pope's famous speech at Regensburg on *logos* and his first encyclical on love (which itself dramatically restored the place of *eros* in Christian thought). Ranasinghe shows us that the personal *eros* that animates Socrates' dialectic isn't really drawn toward the impersonal and unmovable God described by Aristotle. Through his insistence that there is support for loving moral freedom in the very ground of being, Socrates makes it clear that what we know thorough our minds both depends upon and doesn't negate the real existence of particular persons.

Ranasinghe also allows us to wonder whether even the Socrates he displays for our benefit gives a fully adequate account of the personal truth about either human *logos* or human *eros*. We wonder, for example, how Socrates could be so happy in an unhappy marriage, but we have to add that he was hardly a model of conjugal or paternal responsibility. It's not so clear that his *eros* culminates in love of particular persons – the most strange and wonderful beings imaginable.

Christians are allowed a soft dissent from the Socratic account of the cosmic order that mirrors a well-ordered soul insofar as it doesn't clearly have room for a personal God who is both Logos and Love. At the same time, Christians learn from the Socrates Ranasinghe displays that the *eros* and *logos* described by the early church fathers might be described as a correction of Socrates' thinking along lines he himself – through his erotic dialectic and his morally steadfast life – revealed. Ranasinghe does both philosophers and Christians the great service of showing the hard distinction between reason and revelation – or the liberated way of the atheistic or agnostic philosopher and the willfully obedient way of the believer in the personal God – doesn't square with what we can see with our own eyes about our souls or the cosmos. Christian philosophy or, better, philosophical Christianity need not be an oxymoron.

Ranasinghe's navigation through many scholarly and liberationist prejudices brings us toward the insight that Solzhenitsyn *is* the closest person to a Socrates in our time. Both *men* faced death with an intransigent courage in opposition to nihilistic lies. Both defend the reality of personal or psychic good and evil against the various sophisticated deterministic and social constructivist illusions that pervaded their allegedly enlightened times. Each man, through his heroic, truthful example, exposed and authoritatively discredited the tyranny beneath the democratic pretenses of his country's form of government.

Both Socrates and Solzhenitsyn claim, in Solzhenitsyn's words from his famous Harvard Address that "if man were born only to be happy . . . he would not be born to die." That means he's *both* born to die and to be happy. The secret to happiness is not his futile and degrading self-denial, but living well or morally with who he really is. What's most wrong with communism, in its ancient (as implicitly but radically criticized in the *Republic*) or modern forms (as described by Marx), is its inevitably totalitarian attempt to deny the invincible reality of personal death and personal love.

Ranasinghe leads us to wonder whether either the heroic example or account of the soul given by Socrates can quite account for Solzhenitsyn. Compared to Solzhenitsyn, it almost seems that prudent Socrates was a wimp. Although his dialectical boldness was constant, he spent only one day as an old man in open and impetuous defiance of his country's rulers, and he died comfortably in prison sipping hemlock with his friends around him. The Soviet Union's challenge to human freedom and personal truth, of course, was much more radical and far more cruel than the Athenian one. There's nothing in Plato or Thucydides that is quite as demonic as the Gulag or the ideologically inspired murder of millions. Socrates' victory over Athens was purely moral and long-term, while Solzhenitsyn actually defeated the lie of ideology as a ruling principle, not only in his country but everywhere, with stunning speed.

Still, Ranasinghe shows us that Socrates and Solzhenitsyn would agree on the relevance of the challenge of the *Gorgias* for our time. The *Republic* was the dialogue that exposed in advance the angry denial of reality that produced communist utopianism. We Americans battled with admirable responsibility against the various totalitarian forms of what Harvey Mansfield correctly identified as the "manliness run amok" (or revolutionary hatred of an erroneous perception of our real personal insignificance) in the 20th century. But the defeat of the ideological lie of communism exposed more clearly than ever the spiritual emptiness of the contemporary West. It's natural that our fascination with the just or unjust city of the *Republic* be replaced by our close attention to the *Gorgias,* the dialogue about the impossibility of either filling or negating the soul through technical manipulation.

The Cold War gave us a common purpose in defense of liberty, but now we're stuck with remembering that we have little idea of what all our power, freedom, and prosperity is for. Ours is a time characterized by the success of the technological manipulation of nature and each of us. We see ourselves as beings defined by our *interests*, and we think we display our freedom as individuals who use words to maximize our own comfort and security. We agree with the sophists that words are weapons in the service of one's own liberty, and not at all for knowing and loving a reality or real beings that exist beyond ourselves.

We can't say that all our technological progress has made us either more happy or more able to live well with what we really know. So our success must be understood, as Solzhenitsyn puts it in his 1993 Lichtenstein Address as a "trial for our free will." Our nihilistic error in understanding all reality – including our own being – as fundamentally technological has so isolated and disoriented each of us that the main fact about the human soul today is an overwhelming loneliness. The technological means for living well are useless for securing our happiness if we don't believe we have a purpose or point worthy of beings who have souls. Ranasinghe is right that we can turn to the heroic Socrates for much of what we most need to know to act as rational, moral, and loving beings with *souls* today.

We've been given the technological gift of very long lives, but the old seem to have become useless and cut off from the young. While we live alongside more senior citizens than ever before, we don't appreciate their recollections of the past or the evidence they provide of what lies ahead of us. They seem to have nothing to offer the young to guide their basically technological futures, and we no longer think of wisdom in terms of enduring problems or cultural transmission. Surely Socrates is *the* model for how to live happily as an old man without strong family ties, and he offers for us all the perennial human wisdom that is a condition for replacing the feverish techno-pursuit of happiness with happiness itself.

Friendship has been diminished in the direction of networking, and so members of the same generation also regard each other with alienation and apathy. Increasingly we see one another only as *users*. Because we don't know how to think in terms of the reality of common responsibilities, we seem to live in the most unerotic or boring of times. But our erotic longings, in truth, persist. That's why Solzhenitsyn hears just beneath the surface of our happy-talk therapeutic pragmatism "the howl of existentialism." That howl, Socrates would say, is all we have left when we've lost confidence that our real experiences can be articulated and shared. The example of Socrates intensely and happily engaged in his characteristically intensely social and morally concerned activity can help restore our confidence that, as rational and loving beings, we're made for more than instrumental relationships.

And most of all, as Solzhenitsyn says, "we lack a "clear and calm attitude toward death." Free individuals today tend to believe that being itself is identical with one's own being, and so *my* extinction is the end of *being itself.* We're the most death-haunted people ever, in part, because we spend so much time denying its inevitability. We end up dying no matter how astutely we attend to the various risk factors that surround us. We're also traumatized by death because we have so little confidence in the reality of love; the abstract individual we've constructed lacks the capability to be moved deeply by beings other than himself. Socrates' calmness in the face of death, which so astonished his friends and fellow citizens, came from never identifying being with himself, from regarding the point of his life as his responsible and loving participation in a reality beyond himself.

Ranasinghe shows us a Socrates old and beautiful, the hero most needed to remedy what ails an aging society consumed by image and vanity. He helps us to appreciate that Socrates is the anti-technological thinker most able to show us how to benefit from our technological progress. This Socrates gives us confidence that the best way to win friends and influence people is through truth and love. We can still be happy while learning how to die. My personal finitude is not only necessary but good, a small price to pay for being given *logos* and *eros,* as well as the demanding and joyful challenge of living virtuously with what I really know.

Ranasinghe is my new hero. But I haven't even begun to explain *how* he performed one of the most noble of deeds by using a single dialogue to display the riches of the Platonic presentation of Socrates. I wouldn't want to spoil the wonderful surprise you'll begin to discover by turning the page.

Prologue

Wise men speak and fools decide. Although the true subject of Plato's third longest and most serious work, the *Gorgias,* is the moral basis of politics,[1] it is best known today for a frequently anthologized speech by Callicles roundly denouncing Socrates for his political irresponsibility. As the editors of the most recent translation of the dialogue put it "the *Gorgias* most clearly shows why Athens executed Socrates."[2] While Socrates' passionate defense of reason and morality is generally scorned or ignored, the vulgar values animating Callicles' diatribe are robustly regnant in all four corners of our post-Christian world. This means that while pessimistic conservatives can join Callicles in deploring Socrates' presumptuous use of ethical principles to judge hoary tradition, libertarian realists find that Callicles' views accord well with their worship of power, markets, and money. Likewise, at the other end of our hyper-extended political spectrum, we see that just as radical leftists will be in complete sympathy with Callicles' deconstruction of the soul and praise of unbridled desire, their postmodern allies are free to marvel at how well his subversive discourse undermines the logo-centric confines of Platonic proto-fascism. But even as we cringe at the prospect of sound-bites from tightly woven texts being used to serve anti-intellectual ideological agendas, surely a sign that rhetoric rules today's academy, we wonder whether it is even more important to defend Socrates from his friends; many close readings of the *Gorgias* suggest that Plato subtly uses this text's many moral impasses to indicate the impotence and inadequacy of Socratic ethics.[3] Is the *Gorgias* ultimately no

1   *Gorgias: A Revised Text* with an introduction and commentary by E. R. Dodds, (Clarendon, 1959), p. 1.
2   *Gorgias*, trans. Arieti and Barrus (Focus, 2007), p. 1.
3   James Arieti argues in *Interpreting Plato* (Rowman and Littlefield, 1991) that Socrates comes off as "bull-headed, tricky, abusive and indifferent to reality." He concludes, "Surely Plato means for us to see in this dialogue a failure in the extreme Socratic way of life" (p. 90).

better than a flawed[4] preparation for themes better addressed in his *Republic*?[5] Does the dialogue reflect an unresolved conflict raging in Plato's own soul?[6] Is battle (*polemou*), literally the first word of the *Gorgias*, also its last word, end result, and final teaching?

Callicles' overheated harangue may be seen to radicalize a discussion between Socrates and Polus over whether shame, morality, and justice are natural or conventional. The shameless bluntness of Callicles' speech goes far beyond the blustery ire of Thrasymachus in the *Republic*; it also gives a violent version of the subtle critique of the just life made by Glaucon. Unlike Thrasymachus, who belatedly realized that his alien status in Athens demanded some caution, Callicles is portrayed as a wealthy young Athenian – one with no reason to hide his deepest beliefs from his peers. Though there are reasons to doubt whether or not he existed, the *persona* of Callicles clearly represents the mindset of nihilism very adequately indeed.[7] While he plays a role halfway between those of Glaucon and Thrasymachus in this work, which could be read as a poor-man's *Republic*, it is clear that Callicles' precociously jaded soul is far less susceptible to erotic speech than those of Socrates' interlocutors during that famous all-nighter at the Piraeus. We are led to wonder if the draconian regime of Plato's *Republic* is necessitated by the failure of the historical Socrates to adequately refute the battered realism of post-war Athens. Even if a naïve philosopher fails in his earnest efforts to educate the many, like exiled

---

4   T.K. Seung calls it "artistically, the lowest point in Plato's career." He adds: "many readers get irritated by its ungraceful construction." *Plato Rediscovered* (Rowman and Littlefield, 1996), p. 1.

5   For example, Dodds says, "here Plato's case is not yet encumbered with all the metaphysical baggage of the *Republic*"; Friedlander looks ahead "to the *Republic*, where this blueprint of the *Gorgias* is expanded": Paul Friedlander, *Plato: the Dialogues – First Period,* (Princeton, 1964), p. 267. Likewise, Terence Irwin says that "the *Republic* is a further attempt to carry out the task that is first proposed in the *Gorgias,*" *Plato's Ethics* (Oxford, 1995), p. 126.

6   See Werner Jaeger, *Paideia II* (Oxford, 1945), p. 138.

7   Roslyn Weiss, in *The Socratic Paradox and its Enemies* (Chicago, 2006), observes "although Callicles is not a sophist, he subscribes to and is a proponent of every one of the sophistic views. . . . He believes that the wise are unjust and intemperate, and the fools temperate. He thinks that the right way to be, the best way to be, is intemperate, that intemperance is the right way to happiness. He thinks that only the weak praise justice and denounce injustice, but that even they are just not because they hold justice in esteem; it is only their ineptitude that prevents them from practicing injustice successfully. In other words, from Callicles' perspective, no one does right willingly. Callicles' regards courage and intelligence as the virtues of superior men , seeing in justice, temperance and piety the impotence of the inferior masses" (pp. 69–70).

Prospero he still dreams of ruling over the city that derisively rejected him. While modern times have seen the austere model of the *Republic* literally imitated by countless reformers (from Christian Calvinists to Chinese Communists) and eagerly studied by curious intellectuals, the toothless idealism and irresponsible morality espoused by Socrates in the *Gorgias* has been ignored by politicians and disdained by scholars for millennia.

Indeed it seems incredible to suppose that the protagonist of a literary work set silently but pointedly against the backdrop of the long and brutal Peloponnesian War is serious, either in his loudly avowed contempt for the makers of public opinion or in the steadfast assertion that those who unjustly wield unlimited power are unhappier than their victims. Those students of Nietzsche among us who have absorbed Thucydides' lessons about the grim reign of *ananke* (necessity) in wartime surely know more than Socrates. The moral virtues are the orphan children of habit and hope; bred in halcyon days, they cannot but buckle and collapse under the impossible burdens placed on the soul in times of *stasis* (strife). *A fortiori*, it seems that turning to Socrates for guidance in *our* troubled post-9/11 era is the height of stupidity. If even poetry became barbaric after Auschwitz,[8] how much less credible are the rationalist conceits of philosophy today?

Surely parricidal "Platonic Irony" is employed in this work to suggest that Socratic *maieutic* wordplay is patently ineffectual before the soul-killing realities of battle, plague, starvation, and treachery? While Socrates' insistence that punishment is good is touchingly impractical, his inability to convince Callicles that self-rule is preferable to a gaudy spree of opportunism is striking. Finally, how can we not find it pathetic that the philosopher spends the final quarter of the dialogue simply talking to himself and inventing heterodox myths about an afterlife, dreaming of a world turned upside-down, where his eccentric way of thinking would be vindicated?[9] This is most manifestly a pyrrhic victory in speech rather than in deed; the earnest moral discourse of Socrates seems only to harden the heart of his scornful interlocutor. The philosopher's final recourse to a *deus ex machina* solution is all the more absurd because it comes from a man who spent his life ridiculing those who claimed to have any knowledge of divine matters. Socrates must learn to cultivate less idealistic but more effective muses. This must have been why he was

---

8   Adorno, Theodore, *"Cultural Criticism and Society,"* in *Prisms* (MIT Press, 1981), p. 34.

9   Even Hannah Arendt, perhaps the best reader of this dialogue, claimed that "when Kallikles cannot be persuaded by argument, Plato proceeds to tell his myth of the afterlife . . . with great diffidence, clearly indicating that the teller of the story, Socrates, does not take it seriously," in *Between Past and Future* (Penguin, 1968), pp. 293–94.

originally anxious to learn from that most long-lived and successful of Sophists: Gorgias.[10]

Indeed Socrates and Gorgias could be said have a great deal in common to the extent that they both disavowed any claim to be wise and even denied the accessibility of wisdom to human beings. The uncharacteristic respect that Socrates seems to show Gorgias, markedly unlike the hostility, mockery, or even contempt that he displays towards other Sophists like Protagoras, Thrasymachus, and Hippias, also seems to support this viewpoint. According to this less literal way of interpretation, even though Socrates himself was unable to make the most of this opportunity, Plato surely intended that his readers should take to heart a bitter lesson concerning the impotence of a beautiful soul brought into stark confrontation with the wicked ways of the world. Callicles' disconcertingly accurate prophecy concerning Socrates' eventual tragic fate at the hands of the very democratic jurors and orators he so despised can be regarded as an ironic Platonic signal underlining the validity of such a fashionably realistic reading of the dialogue.

My reading will take issue with the popular and plausible lines of exegesis set forth above. I will contend that the true focus of the *Gorgias* is the instrumental perversion of speech introduced by its namesake. Although the dialogue's trajectory moves away from the sophist himself, Socrates' extended debate with Callicles employs indirect communication and *reductio ad absurdum* argumentation to show the itinerant Gorgias the long-term results of his manipulative technique and moral irresponsibility – effects extending into our own times. *Gorgias* provides us with a model of reality adequate to the troubling issues raised by the manipulative power of rhetoric; it also demonstrates how philosophy still has the moral authority to sustain the soul's resilience and inspire virtue amid times of moral strife and social chaos. Perhaps the *Gorgias* could even help us escape the coils of a sophisticated marketing culture that, already having changed citizens into consumers and colleges into corporations, now threatens to turn children into clones?

More than any other dialogue, the *Gorgias* vividly depicts the great value that Socrates and Plato attached to the soul's freedom and integrity. Just as Socrates much prefers making a stronger but esoteric argument, written on the soul, to a weaker and purely exoteric triumph over his adversaries and audience, Plato always seeks to refute the best arguments that can be leveled against the position that he ultimately endorses. For these two reasons, the interpretation of a Platonic text can never be regarded as a purely intellectual

---

10   A more sober version of this claim is the starting point of a recent book, *The Unity of Plato's Gorgias* by Devin Stauffer (Cambridge, 2006). My approach presumes more enmity between philosophy and sophistry.

or technical task. Careful exegesis of the *Gorgias* reveals how it challenges us to see beyond dismissive impressions based on a superficially clever reading of this or any dialogue. While this temptation to conflate philosophy and sophistry is present in any Platonic text, the *Gorgias* in particular seems to offer various moral tests that must be negotiated before the essential contours of the work reveal themselves.

This is why, even though the *Gorgias* is much easier to read than the *Republic* (or the *Laws*), we must be forewarned that this dialogue makes very different, and more difficult, demands on its readers. I will try to show how the passionately written *Gorgias* militates against the separation of moral from intellectual virtue and requires that its readers' souls be integrated and fully engaged by the labyrinthine work before it.[11] By contrast, the *Republic* (despite its outlandishness) is more ironic, and calls for the more familiar academic virtue of impersonal theoretical speculation; otherwise its readers will fail to see that the Cave described in Book VII results directly from the very reforms prescribed in the five books preceding it! Likewise, obscure dialogues like the *Philebus* and *Parmenides* are more attractive to the typical pedagogue than the psychically intrusive *Gorgias*; scholars naturally drawn to playing language games and solving puzzles are often incapable of being spiritually and morally challenged by the text that is closest to the *Apology* in its ability to convey the bracing experience of a meeting with Socrates. Otherwise put, the ponderous procedures of the Eleatic Stranger are more familiar and agreeable to today's academics than the *ad hominem* challenges posed by Socrates. But, since Socrates did not wish to pass an inverted Turing test, and made his arguments to human souls rather than to computer chips and algorithms, we may only understand him out of the fullest exertion of our humanity.

Indeed Platonic *psychography* is more objectionable than pornography to a typical philosopher of today – whether analytic or incontinental – since all talk of the seat of moral consciousness, the soul, is viewed as being little better than antiquated babble in the modern academy. The response of Polus to Socrates' critique of Gorgias and his art showed that Plato was quite aware of this perennial possibility; yet, even though many Socratic precepts are vulnerable to ridicule from those who cannot appreciate that philosophy is erotic and moral, and neither technical nor transgressive, we should beware of gaining safety from ridicule at the heavy cost of becoming just like the persons we seek

---

11 As Seth Benardete puts it, "In the *Gorgias*, Socrates puts all his cards on the table and still has them all up his sleeve." This is because "it is one thing to know what happens when an argument of a certain kind meets a soul of a certain kind, but quite another to be able to recognize it when it happens right before one": *The Rhetoric of Morality and Persuasion* (Chicago, 1991), p. 1.

protection from (510a–e). However by recovering the foundational insight of Western Civilization, the Socratic discovery of the soul as moral substance, we stand to gain something far more precious than a new intellectual gambit or argumentative ploy.[12] Perhaps the only real cure to the nihilism that threatens to gut our hero-less civilization – destroying the hold of mimetic morality over our uncontrollable desires and apocalyptic fears – consists in both remembering and understanding the exemplary conduct of those who displayed moral integrity in the most adverse circumstances. This is why Plato's accounts of how ugly old Socrates overcame the fear of death and practiced erotic virtue to the end of his life can yet inspire honest and honorable human beings to face similar challenges in their own time.

There are very good reasons for holding that the key to understanding Socratic virtue is to be found in the *Gorgias* and not in its more famous cousin, the *Republic*; quite simply, the essence of the latter work has been shown to consist of an argument against the perverse impulse to prefer tyrannical rule over others to temperate rule over oneself.[13] Although the *Republic* does discuss the healthy soul *en passant*, the bulk of its text is devoted to showing the impossibility of solving psychic disease by political means. The *Gorgias*, however, is unique among the Platonic works in offering us *inter alia* several positive statements of a Socratic worldview. These include a list of the four principles of the cosmos, an expanded version of Socrates' defense of the soul's power to resist evil, justification for his claim to be the only practitioner of the true political art, and an account of the soul's afterlife that turns out to be the crucial transition between the Homeric and Christian views of the meaning of life and death that lies at the birth of Humanism. In other words, while numerous mis-readings and flawed imitations of the *Republic* characterize the failed enterprise of modernity, the *Gorgias* best conveys the Socratic vision of a morally governed cosmos that eventually provided both the language and concepts by which the sublime message of Christianity spread throughout the Hellenized world and gave birth to Western Civilization.[14]

Let's take a deep breath and start again. Even though the *Republic* argues subtly against the hubris of constructing a tyranny based on an artificial reality, it is striking that the monstrous regime it depicts masquerades – all too

12   To this extent, my work is animated by Pope Benedict XVI's stirring call for the Re-Hellenization of Christianity as articulated in his *Regensburg Address* – a work known to everybody and no one. See James V. Schall's *The Regensburg Lecture* (St. Augustine's Press, 2007).

13   Leo Strauss is certain that the *Republic* is "the most magnificent cure ever devised for every form of political ambition": *The City and Man* (Chicago, 1964), p. 65.

14   The history of this process is magisterially summarized in Jeffrey Hart's *Smiling through the Cultural Catastrophe* (Yale, 2001).

successfully – as the best city. However, in doing so, it pays the tribute of vice to virtue and does not deny the existence or value of objective reality. In the *Gorgias* the challenge posed is far more radical. The orators opportunistically distorted reality in a context markedly unequal to the challenge posed by their hubris. As a result of the moral havoc wreaked by three decades of bitter war, several outbreaks of the plague, the loss of its empire, and the death of over half of its adult male citizenry, far too many decent Athenians had come to despair of the meaning and goodness of reality itself.[15] This is why it is in the *Gorgias* that Plato renders his most complete account of the various constituent factors, natural and psychic, of the reality that Socrates contemplated, and dwelt and acted in. While the *Republic* traffics in the very modern categories of perfection and artifice, alternates between creating gods and defying nature, and dabbles dangerously in both exoteric predestination and esoteric atheism; it is the more postmodern *Gorgias* that looks past the over-determined space of the *Republic* and towards the gaping abysses (Pascal's infinite spaces) that separate humanity from both nature and the gods.

In the crudest terms, in an era where nihilism replaces totalitarianism as the main challenge facing humans, it is the *Gorgias,* not than the *Republic,* that will help us to gain strength from the origins of the Western Tradition. This is because while we no longer believe in artificial utopias, centuries of striving in this direction have caused grave environmental damage and insidious moral degeneration. Humanity desperately needs to become reacquainted with reality. Becoming "faithful to the earth" – as Nietzsche famously put it – is not sufficient; as suggested earlier, our disenchanted and hero-less age has to get reacquainted with both the human soul itself and the original erotic striving towards excellence and virtue that got the Western tradition under way.

Yet before we enter the text of the *Gorgias,* we must attend to various formal and historical questions that demand prior consideration. It is first worth noting that this work takes unusual liberties with time; appropriately enough, on account of its nihilistic namesake, the *Gorgias* could not have been! It has been frequently observed and well documented that the dramatic date of this dialogue cannot be situated at any point in Athenian history. A casual reference to the very recent demise of Pericles (who died in 429) is scarcely reconciled with Socrates' claim that the trial of the admirals at Arginusae (406) occurred a year ago. Also, we know that Gorgias's only attested visit to Athens was in 427, an event consistent with the earlier date, but this won't jibe with talk of Archelaus the notorious new tyrant of Macedonia, whose reign began in 413,

---

15   Victor Davis Hanson's *A War Like No Other* (Random House, 2005) gives perhaps the best and most vivid portrayal of the staggeringly unprecedented human cost of the Peloponnesian War.

and countless references to Euripides' late play, *Atiope*, from the last decade of the fifth century.[16]

The reader must also remember that Gorgias's visit to Athens occurred when Plato was only about a year old. This means that the author of this dialogue could not have seen Socrates conversing with Gorgias. Indeed the *Gorgias* describes a conversation that could never have taken place – since it deals with matters that could not have been discussed simultaneously. On the other hand, any Athenian schoolboy would have seen the significance of Gorgias visiting Athens in the early years of the war. We know that this visit was undertaken to persuade the Athenians to come to the aid of Gorgias's polis of Leontini. This successful mission marked the beginning of an Athenian involvement in Sicilian affairs that culminated in the massive and ill-fated expeditions launched against Syracuse a decade or so later. These projects literally took the lives of a generation of Athenians and drastically changed the course of Athenian history. While we will continually discover connections between the man Gorgias, the eponymous dialogue, and the war itself, we cannot forget that the backdrop of the *Gorgias* is the Peloponnesian War.[17]

It is also noteworthy that our text is titled *Gorgias* and not *Callicles;* neither can we forget that the book known as the *Republic (Politeia)* was not named after Glaucon or Thrasymachus; *this* work has to do with Socrates' efforts to heal the effects visited by the plague of rhetoric on the city. In other words while the *Republic* warns us against tyrants trying to supplant politics, the *Gorgias* depicts the contrary danger of a demagogic political regime that would transcend gods and nature and eventually leave everyone alienated from reality. Responsibility for this state of affairs is ultimately attributed to Gorgias; he valued victory over truth, answers over questions, and satisfaction over learning. Furthermore, by teaching men to use language in an opportunistic or instrumental way, he corrupted Greek culture and denied humanity the interrelated experiences of participation in the logos and the cosmos. This bellicose attitude towards life, which trickles down from speech through deeds and slowly poisons the soul itself, is subtly condemned in the *Gorgias* for being at least as much a cause as an effect of the Peloponnesian War. Socrates, by contrast, tries to maintain a reverential attitude towards language itself and all the human beings who participate in its gathering power. While

16   Seth Benardete notes that the cumulative effect of these anachronisms is that "Plato situates the *Gorgias* in wartime Athens but in such a way that we are enjoined to believe that the conversation never occurred. The *Gorgias* is of a time but not in time" (p. 7).

17   See Arlene Saxonhouse, *An Unspoken Theme in Plato's Gorgias: War* in *Interpretation* vol. 11 (2) pp. 139–69. This essay provides an excellent summary of the historical backdrop to the *Gorgias*.

manipulative discourse plagues a polity, tears people apart, and alienates them from the better angels of their own nature, shared dialogic speech plays a vital role in moving human souls towards self-knowledge, community and truth.

The spatial parameters of this dialogue are not devoid of interest or pertinence either. The conversation begins outdoors where Gorgias has been providing an impressive public exhibition (*epideixis*) of his art. It is suggested by Gorgias's host, Callicles, that Socrates and Chaerephon continue the discussion at his residence (447b), but we are never told whether or when the proposed change of location actually occurs. It is noteworthy however that Callicles' outspoken comments concerning the natural rights of the stronger are less likely to have been made in a public setting. I will argue that Socrates does bring the argument home – to Callicles' soul – and subtly but unmistakably draws Gorgias's attention to the nihilistic consequences of his pseudo-art.

On the other hand, this dialogue's flagrant anachronisms and indefinite location are strikingly counterbalanced by the shocking symmetry that is displayed with regards to its interior proportions. Plato clearly seems to have constructed the terrain of the *Gorgias* with a keen awareness of the very geometrical equality that Socrates reproached Callicles for neglecting (508a). The text of the *Gorgias* consists of exactly 80 Stephanus pages: 447a to 527e. Although this convenient number is coincidental, it certainly makes the symmetrical divisions that follow very easy to observe. These eighty pages divide into four equal parts: 447a–466a (Socrates' interrogation of Gorgias concluding with his speech about what oratory really is), 466a–486d (Socrates' victory over Polus, culminating in Callicles' famous attack on Socrates), 486d – 506c (Socrates' spirited discussion with Callicles concluding with the latter's request that Socrates finish the conversation on his own), and finally 506c–527e (where Socrates elaborates his own *logos* about the underworld and Callicles' positive contributions to the discussion are minimal).

The number four plays a very important role in this work. We need only mention Socrates' lists of the four genuine and four spurious arts and also note his account of the four cosmic principles: gods, men, earth, and sky. The contrast between the subtle logographic necessity of the form of the dialogue with the disorder and indeterminacy of its spatial and temporal references strongly suggest something akin to the difference between the epochs of Kronos and Zeus that Socrates describes in the concluding myth of the dialogue. Its Delphic subtext, the numerous references to Hades, an upside-down world (481c) and the quotation from Euripides regarding the difficulty in distinguishing between death and life (492e), all draw the attentive reader's eye to some of the elaborate formal (as opposed to merely rhetorical or cosmetic) contrasts that pervade the *Gorgias*.

As is often the case with Plato, the potential for a skeptical reading of a dialogue is sandwiched between its edifying but banal surface and a subtler, deeper justification of Socrates' original teaching. The complexity and richness of these various formal elements give further support to my suggestion that the nihilistic interpretive possibilities present in the *Gorgias* merely represent timeless psychic temptations that must be overcome by both interlocutor and reader. That acute witness from the moral underworld of the Gulag, Alexander Solzhenitsyn, referred explicitly to Socrates when he famously observed that the line between good and evil runs through every heart.[18] My interpretation of the *Gorgia*s will suggest that this work is constructed with every intention of testing, educating, and unifying the intellectual capacities and the ethical character of its readers. As such, the line between good and evil runs through the middle of every dialogue. The temptation to dismiss such ethical phenomena as ontic pandering must be overcome before one comes to grips with the true esoteric core of a Platonic dialogue. However, going far beyond proclaiming that those deficient in moral geometry should not approach the Academy, this dialogue shows us the causes and effects of moral incorrigibility.

The second matter that is best addressed before plunging into the text is its historical background. While we have already taken into account the impossibility of giving the text of the *Gorgias* a dramatic date, it still remains for us to recover background information, popular opinion, concerning the famous sophist that would have been known by any intelligent schoolboy in fourth-century Athens.[19] This information is also of the greatest help in exposing the true logographic order of a dialogue; although we cannot recover all of the suggestive ironies emerging between the speeches of the various Socratic interlocutors and their deeds, the remaining historical and literary data help immeasurably to better appreciating the political passions still echoing through the depths of a dialogue. Far from succumbing to historicism, we are merely returning to the *Gorgias* what is rightly its own and allowing the text to be read as it would have been in its own time. Refusing to do so would be about as unreasonable as Glaucon's demand in *Republic II* that the life of a just man should be necessarily distinguished by isolation, misunderstanding, and misery. Flatfooted anti-historicism of this kind only delivers the text up – as a mute, bound and shorn offering – to be processed via *a priori* procedures by an infallible answerer of all questions.

Treating philosophers as a superior contemplative species, untroubled by human events and cares, only leads to flagrant abuse of the principle of logographic necessity. Unchecked by historical context, the oracular interpreter

---

18   See Solzhenitsyn, *The Gulag Archipelago* vol. 1 (Harper and Row, 1974) p. 168.
19   See Strauss, *Persecution and the Art of Writing* (Chicago, 1988) p. 30.

becomes sovereign arbiter over the text and is freed to introduce perverse doctrines stemming from a foreign ideological position that are often at profound variance with Plato's deepest convictions. The origins of the two axiomatic beliefs – that all philosophers are atheists and that ethics merely serves as an exoteric pretext for helping friends and harming enemies – may be traced back to medieval Islam[20]; such a pessimistic hermeneutic of suspicion is profoundly opposed to the Platonic erotic impulse towards spiritual enlightenment. Indeed the *Gorgias* indicates the boundary between cultures founded on faith in the logos and uncivilized cults that demand submission to jealously irrational power gods and their prophets.

However, all these matters can be safely deferred until later; we shall try to see them emerge out of this most seminal text itself. For the present our task must be to move towards the *Gorgias* and establish an objective framework by which its text may be interrogated with minimal risk of hermeneutic violence or speculative cloud-seeding. Even though it is tempting to fight the dragon of historicism and restrict our inquiries to the dialogue itself, such a procedure makes only a text far more susceptible to prejudiced assumptions and does little to help us see how it would have appeared in its own cultural milieu. After all, we cannot forget that the dialogues were not primarily addressed to wise men, philosophers, or other initiates.

Beginning with the less controversial evidence external to the text, let us first consider Plato's other dialogues that refer to Gorgias. The afore-mentioned respect that Socrates seems to show Gorgias is especially startling because virtually all other references to the Sicilian sophist in the Platonic corpus are hardly very complimentary. Most notably, we have Socrates' reference to Agathon's Gorgias-inspired rhetoric in the *Symposium*, where he ironically echoes the great fear of Odysseus in the House of Hades that the disembodied Gorgon head itself would appear at the end of the tragedian's speech and turn him to stone (198c). This prospect was sufficient to cause that intrepid adventurer to cut short his greatest exploit of all.[21] It is noteworthy that handsome Agathon's contribution to the *Symposium* is perhaps its least substantial speech – all style and no matter.[22] Socrates seems to be giving expression to an entirely natural repugnance or shame upon being exposed to so grotesque a juxtaposition of physical beauty and intellectual vacuity. Gorgias also figures prominently in the *Meno,* where Socrates noted that Gorgias trained the Thessalians

20 See Rémi Brague, "Hellenism and Hebraism Reconsidered: The Poetics of Cultural Influence and Exchange," in *Poetics Today*, (Vol. 19, No. 2, Summer, 1998), pp. 235–59.

21 *Odyssey* XI. 632–35.

22 For an extensive analysis of Agathon's rhetoric see Stanley Rosen's magisterial *Plato's Symposium* (Yale, 1987; St. Augustine's Press, 1999), pp. 159–96.

to feign expertise by boldly giving grand and noble answers to any question asked of them (70b–c). Socrates added that Gorgias himself was ready to, and did, answer any question asked of him – presumably by this emphasis on style without substance. Later, after dodging several inquiries concerning what Gorgias thought wisdom was, the curious but morally corrupt Meno reveals that he most admires Gorgias for never professing to be a teacher of virtue, and indeed ridiculing those who made this claim, but rather setting forth to train clever speakers (95c).

Next, in the *Greater Hippias*, Socrates tells us that when Gorgias came once to Athens on a diplomatic mission, he not only succeeded in persuading the Assembly but also took a great deal of money out of Athens through giving public displays and tutoring the young. Indeed Gorgias (along with Protagoras and Prodicus) were said to have made more money out of "wisdom" than any craftsman made from any other skill (282b–d). Then, in the *Phaedrus*, Socrates ironically compares the long-lived Gorgias to aged Nestor, that survivor of the Trojan War, a man who maintained his superiority over the younger men who actually did the fighting before Troy by making long-winded speeches about his prior exploits a generation ago (261c). Socrates then mentions Tisias and his student Gorgias as those who valued probability more than truth, could argue concisely or at infinite length on any theme, and had the power to make great things appear small, ancient matters seem modern and *vice versa* (267a). And lastly, in the *Philebus*, answering Socrates' claim that a science dealing with what truly and unchangingly is must be superior to all other kinds of knowledge, Protarchus claims to have heard Gorgias insist that persuasion is superior to all the other arts because it enslaves all of them by their own consent (58a).

The attentive reader will see that these other dialogues all echo statements explicitly made by the sophist himself in the *Gorgias*. This could either suggest that these works were written after the *Gorgias,* or lead one to infer that the various fragments concerning his thought were re-assembled for the sake of a direct confrontation with Gorgias himself. At any rate it is sufficiently clear that Plato is operating with a consistent set of ideas that are identified as originating from Gorgias. Since it is necessarily impossible to give the dialogue itself a dramatic date, it also follows that while the actual conversation between Socrates and Gorgias never took place, it nevertheless represents a clash at the level of ideas between their accurate representations of their respective positions. Since we also have additional information from extra-Platonic sources about the historical Gorgias, it is worth our while to see if these objective facts are consistent with the vivid intellectual portrait that Plato has drawn for us of a man he most probably never met or knew. Surely Plato himself does not value probability higher than truth? I shall try to show how the *Gorgias* indicates gives a logos or true account of rhetoric in a way that goes beyond a simply journalistic understanding of factual truth. It was in much the same spirit that Aristotle famously declared poetry to be higher, and more truthful, than history.[23]

At the level of abstract metaphysical thought, Gorgias does not say much. His position is expressed through a rather convoluted, and very sophistical, argument made against the Parmenidean or Eleatic assertion of the Truth and Unchanging Oneness of Being. Gorgias was said to claim (a) that nothing exists, (b) even if it did, it is unknowable, and (c) even if it could be known, it couldn't be indicated to others (DK 3).[24] This argument contradicts itself at every stage, and it seems to do so intentionally. Gorgias's point seems to be that in the absence, inaccessibility, or inexpressibility of Truth our reality is held together by a worldwide web of persuasive words. Quite apart from being consistent with Protarchus' report in the *Philebus*, this inference is also supported by another curious statement that Gorgias made about women. He was said to assert that a woman should be known to the many through her reputation rather than by her appearance (DK 22). Now Gorgias clearly regards reality in exactly the same way. Even though he says, "Being is unclear if it does not meet with belief and belief is weak if it does not meet with Being," closer reflection lead us to see that, since beliefs create the appearance of Being, he is only saying that new beliefs must be consistent with older beliefs. It follows also that the making and continual renewal of truth depends on one who, like Penelope, weaves prudently and secretly in the absence of any signified or desired truth.

Both Gorgias's fundamental views and techniques are revealed more clearly in his "Encomium of Helen," defending the Spartan queen against the charges of having committed adultery and thereby triggering the Trojan War. In this *epideixis,* constructed with the explicit aim of displaying his ability to speak persuasively on any side of any subject, "and for my amusement," Gorgias argues that Helen was powerless before the mighty influences brought to bear on her. Thucydides' style is known to have been influenced by Gorgias, and we see how, in this earlier war also, the irrational flood-force of *ananke* carried all temperance and forethought before it.

Listing the many possible powers that could have overwhelmed Helen, the randomly chosen beneficiary of his godlike clemency, Gorgias states: "human anticipation cannot restrain a god's intention." He goes on to anticipate Callicles, "by nature the stronger is not restrained by the weaker . . . the

---

23 Aristotle, *Poetics*, 1451b5.
24 All of these fragments are translated in *Early Greek Political Thought: From Homer to the Sophists*, ed. Gagarin and Woodruff (Cambridge, 1995), pp. 190–209.

stronger leads, the weaker follows." Another equally irresistible influence is not physical force but persuasive speech: " if *logos* persuaded and deluded her mind . . . it is not hard to defend her or free her name from blame: *logos* is a powerful master and achieves divine feats with the smallest and least material body. . . . It can stop fear, relieve pain, create joy and increase pity." Since a good deal of what is said in this context must be seen to be spoken in the style and idiom of Thucydides, it is worth noting that the somber accounts of irrepressible *ananke* in the Peloponnesian War are artfully framed by a brilliant poet with a distinctive intellectual agenda.

Gorgias attributes the uncanny power of speech to the fact that human beings have uncertain knowledge. "If all men on all subjects had memory of the past, understanding of the present and foresight into the future, speech would not be as powerful as it is with us now." In our present condition of fear and ignorance persuasion expels thought . . . persuasion has the same power but not the same form as *ananke*." Gorgias argues persuasively that "persuasion when added to speech molds the minds as it wishes." According to him "the power of the *logos* has the same effect on the soul as drugs have on the body . . . words cause pain, fear, joy and boldness. They can benumb and bewitch the soul." We understand what Gorgias is about when he compares this art to that of astronomers who "make invisible matters apparent in the eyes of opinion." This making of "invisible matters apparent" applies very much to beautiful images of invisible truth being used to shape democratic opinion regarding the power and destiny of a polity. Such a procedure, we may venture to comment, eventually turns the impotent observations of astronomy into the over-determined pseudo-science of astrology. Instead of the art of lens grinding, which brought about the Copernican Revolution, we see here the art of soul grinding or warping that inevitably leads deformed man to view himself as the measure of reality.

Nevertheless, we cannot forget that man in the state of nature is, as Gorgias would annoyingly alliterate it, a pathetic plaything of fickle fortune and niggardly necessity. The ingenious remedies provided by artful speech may well be necessary, since the mind is all too prone to be debilitated by the shock of events, "Some who have seen fearful things have lost their present purpose in the present moment. So fully does fear extinguish and expel thought: many fall into useless labors, terrible diseases and incurable madness, so fully does sight engrave on the mind images of things which are seen" (DK 11, #17). It would seem then that in times of war, persuasive speech is presented as the cure rather than the cause; removal of the deleterious impressions left by strife is possible since the very sights that traumatize the soul also weaken its ability to resist persuasive speech and hold fast to its memories. The Orator's artful speech can reinterpret these dimly remembered but painful traumas and generate more agreeable narrative accounts. It was in this vain but not ungenerous spirit that Agathon spoke in the *Symposium* of the good and pacifying effects wrought by his sophistical muse (197b–e). Gorgias's art also calls to mind Diodotus's words about the incorrigible power of hope to breed optimistic beliefs unsupported by reality.[25]

However, while we have been occupied with the task of recovering the conventional opinions that any well-informed Athenian would have had concerning Gorgias, he would be the first to remind us that we have not had direct acquaintance with him or his art. This is why, fittingly, the dialogue begins at the point where the great orator has just concluded a spectacular display (*epideixis*) of his art in some undisclosed public area. Since we are not in historical reality but entering a Socratic dialogue, a charmed space where almost nothing accidental occurs, we must assume that Plato has admitted us at the right moment: the point where the finely polished ideas of our two antagonists finally meet. But let us face this intricate hermeneutic challenge with Gorgias's own words ringing in our ears: "Our contest requires two *aretai*: boldness and wisdom: boldness to withstand danger and wisdom to understand the riddle. Like the herald at Olympia, [and it is worth noting that we shall soon hear much about a great tyrant who rules at Olympia] *logos* summons anyone who wishes (to compete) but crowns the one who is able" (DK 8).

---

25 Thucydides, *Peloponnesian War*, IV. 45.

Chapter I: Flattering the Oracle

Polemou, meaning "battle," is appropriately enough the first word of the *Gorgias*. Socrates has not come not to praise Gorgias, but to bury him. Yet this word is spoken by Callicles, who rather condescendingly tells Socrates that lateness is only recommended in the case of battles or wars (447a). It is often the case in Platonic dialogues that the first words and scenes are especially over-determined, and the *Gorgias* is certainly no exception. Even though the precise destiny of the conflict is unknown, as is the case with almost every martial occasion, the suggestion is already conveyed that our context is polemical and agonistic. Furthermore, we are also reminded of the purpose behind Gorgias's mission to Athens. According to Diodorus Siculus:

> The Leontines were attacked by the Syracusans. Being hard pressed in the war they dispatched ambassadors to Athens asking the Athenians to send them immediate aid and save their city from the perils threatening it. The leader of the embassy was Gorgias who in eloquence far surpassed all his contemporaries. He was the first man to devise rules of rhetoric and far excelled all other men in the instruction offered by the sophists. . . . When Gorgias had arrived in Athens and been introduced to the people in assembly, he discoursed to them upon the subject of the alliance, and by the novelty of his speech he filled the Athenians, who are by nature clever and fond of dialectic, with wonder . . . he won the Athenians over to an alliance with the Leontines, and after having been admired in Athens for his rhetorical skill he made his return to Leontini. For some time past the Athenians had been covetous of Sicily because of the fertility of its land, and so at the moment, gladly accepting the proposals of Gorgias, they voted to send an allied force to the Leontines, offering as their excuse the need and

request of their kinsmen, whereas in fact they were eager to get possession of the island.[1]

Viewing the matter with hindsight, Plato's audience would know that the result of Gorgias's words would be the invasion of Syracuse. The gods deluded the Athenians into exchanging much gold (and priceless blood) for a few brazen words of flattery.

For his part, Socrates smoothly counters Callicles' ridicule regarding his tardiness by inferring that he has actually missed a feast (*heortes*); this suggests that Gorgias has offered the audience a battle disguised as a banquet. Of course this description can be applied both to Gorgias's embassy and the dialogue named after him; the clash of these two Titans was plainly most entertaining to a people "clever and fond of dialectic." When Callicles agrees with this prescient account of what he had missed, Gorgias's display of "all manner of fine things," Socrates blames a convenient scapegoat – his sidekick Chaerephon – saying that he detained them in the Agora (447b).

Socrates clearly does not like to waste time. Neither does he have any great respect for cookery. It is most probably the case that he did not want to listen to an overly wrought *epideixis* constructed so as to shift attention from the subject matter to the virtuosity of the speaker. Then again, he may already have heard Gorgias's speech before the Assembly, urging the Leontinian alliance upon the Athenians. Both the logographic economy governing a dialogue and Socrates' preference to shift the tone of speeches made in his presence in a dialectical direction suggest that his tardiness was not accidental but suited to his purposes. It is noteworthy that it is *Chaerephon* who says: "this is why we're here," when Callicles asks whether Socrates actually wishes to hear Gorgias (447b). This suggests that Chaerephon is more anxious to meet with the famous sophist than Socrates. The philosopher's earlier excuse also raises the question of whether or not they have actually left the domain of commerce in meeting with Gorgias. The fact of Chaerephon, having been distracted by other novelties in the Agora, may also be indicative of the quality of his interest in Gorgias.

It seems that Socrates would have preferred not to have to meet with the sophist at all. a delayed arrival is better suited to his pedagogic and polemic duty; he intends to discuss matters that could never be covered in windy set-piece speeches but were better approached through one on one dialectical discussions.[2] Callicles' gratified surprise at finding that Socrates wanted to listen

---

1   Diodorus Siculus XII. 53–54.

2   Benardete observes that "Socrates came at the right time if he wanted to learn from Gorgias about the power of his art. Had he come earlier, Gorgias would have

to Gorgias serves as explicit evidence of the philosopher's well-known impatience with this manner of speech.[3] Yet, as was noted earlier, it is Chaerephon who testifies to Socrates' eagerness to hear the sophist. The silence of Socrates is quite suggestive; his presence does not seem to be deliberate or even voluntary. Perhaps Agathon's dreadful speech at the *Symposium* is sufficient to both remind us of Gorgias's accustomed manner of oratory and explain Socrates' aversion to content-less logorrhea; the great sophist's banquet of words could truly be said to both be and not be. We can understand why, deliberately appearing only after Gorgias has projected an empty feast of images on the wall of the School of Hellas, Socrates is anxious to free his friends and himself from the flowery chains of flattery and fantasy fabricated by the famous flimflammer.

This is why, when Callicles tells Socrates, rather presumptuously, that he could visit his house at any time and Gorgias would perform for him, Socrates expresses his strong preference for a conversation. "As for the other thing, the display (*epideixis*), let him postpone it for later" (447c). In effect, this is precisely what takes place in the dialogue. After his short question-and-answer session with Socrates, Gorgias is made a display of, through the results of his own teachings being exhibited to him. Speech and deed are brought into perfect harmony in this fashion. Socrates will not only refuse to let the master-orator dress himself up in his own puffery, he will also expose the "nakedness of the father" through his sons, showing how his sins are passed on to future generations. Gorgias's so-called art does not operate only through words that burst like so many bubbles after they have given rise to much harmless pleasure; rhetoric will be shown to produce highly deleterious buboes that must be displayed to their progenitor.

There is another reason why Chaerephon's appearance in this context is most suggestive indeed; while his interrogation of Polus is much the lengthier of his two interventions in Platonic dialogue, the other being a single impetuous question in the *Charmides (153b)*, this eccentric is best known for another very significant reported event. As many commentators have reminded us, the presence of Chaerephon here serves to remind us of his visit to Delphi.[4]

been displaying his power and it would not been as easy . . . to figure out the truth of his display" (p. 8).

3   There is an element of comedy in Socrates' desire to avoid exposure to Gorgias's flowery obfuscation. He seems to be parodying Odysseus's deadly fear of the Gorgon's deadly beauty. Benardete observes that while Socrates is interested in Gorgias's art. "He wants to find out, without experiencing the power, what power rhetoric has. He effectively arranges for this by putting off any display on Gorgias' part and having Polus display all the flourishes of rhetoric in a minor skirmish" (p. 10).

4   See for instance, Saxonhouse, p. 140, and T. K. Seung, p. 28.

Socrates himself told his jurors that Chaerephon, a man given to intense enthusiasms, dared to ask the Oracle whether any man was wiser than Socrates and elicited a negative reply (21a). The parallel is striking; Chaerephon, who brought Socrates to Gorgias, was also responsible for going to Delphi to put a question that should strictly speaking have been asked by Socrates himself. Here we will see that it is Gorgias himself who plays the role of the omniscient Oracle.[5]

On this occasion, Socrates prompts Chaerephon to question Polus, who assumes the role of the Oracle's mouthpiece, about Gorgias's art. Leo Strauss famously observed that the very act of asking the "what is" question about piety is itself impious.[6] It is in much the same spirit that Socrates will indirectly ask this tripod-sitting Sphinx to expose the origins of his wisdom. For this, he will soon be accused of professional rudeness. This shift in the terms of moral outrage is not foreign to our own times of political correctness. The public asking of fundamental questions is still frowned upon in *bien pensant* intellectual circles, not least because their heartfelt belief that youth should not be corrupted by the impossible demands of trans-instrumental reason.

The cryptic responses of the Oracle were usually quite consistent with the celebrated axioms provided by Solon and associated with Delphi: "know thyself" and "nothing in excess." These replies had the effect of forcing the questioner to fall back upon himself. He would thereby understand the limitations of self-knowledge that led him to seek the guidance of the Oracle.[7] The guilty conscience or prophetic soul of the supplicant will usually do the rest. We have reason to suspect that the art of Gorgias may lead in the opposite direction, away from self-knowledge and conscience. Indeed, since Gorgias can answer all questions, there is no longer any need for supplicants to go all the way to the Oracle. Why go to the mountain when it will obligingly move itself to come to you? By his feigned omniscience, Gorgias – an intellectual molehill – has made the oracles, and indeed the gods, redundant. Surely it would seem

---

5   As Saxonhouse puts it, Gorgias sits "Oracle-like, promising to answer any question put to him" (p. 141).

6   See Leo Strauss, "On the Euthyphron," in *The Rebirth of Classical Political Rationalism; Essays and Lectures by Leo Strauss*, ed. Thomas L. Pangle, (University of Chicago Press, 1989).

7   Gregory Vlastos seems to distinguish between an Epimethean Delphic Oracle and a Promethean Socrates when he suggests that the Oracle deliberately gave responses "meant to be true only in a sense their hearers are virtually certain to miss." This meant that "the god is making fools of those who earnestly seek his help." By contrast Socratic irony does not set out to deceive, "given moderate intelligence and good will . . . no one would have reason to think that what he means in each case is simply the literal sense of what he says." *Socrates: Ironist and Moral Philosopher* (Cornell, 1991), pp. 243–44.

doubly necessary – at least to Chaerephon – that Socrates, who was notorious for his reluctance to leave Athens, should hasten to make the acquaintance of this new phenomenon and ascertain his nature anew in the light of this Delphic revolution. In the present context, despite the impossible anachronisms involved in such a question, it is worth pondering whether Chaerephon visited the Oracle before or after Socrates met Gorgias. After meeting Gorgias, can Socrates believe himself to be the wisest and/or most ignorant of human beings? At least one thing is certain: Socrates is not responsible for bringing this strange new god or post-theological phenomenon into the Agora.

Now it is clearly the case that Gorgias has conducted himself with great *hubris*. His boast that he could answer any question (447c), along with the complacent claim that he has not been asked a single new question in many years (448a), prepare us to listen with eager anticipation for the just punishment that is being prepared for him by Socrates. This arrogance is compounded by the assertion of Polus, Gorgias's graduate-student, that he too could answer questions with equal competence. It seems that Gorgias is not merely omniscient, he also capable of transferring his wisdom to anyone. While these two claims clearly go against the Oracle's warnings against exceeding limits, they lead us to wonder how this capacity is consistent with Gorgias's previously noted three-fold denials of Being, its accessibility to humans, and its communicability. Then, after a while, we realize that Gorgias's mastery of the *logos* is founded on the convenient inaccessibility of truth-in-itself. Only this virtual nihilism accounts for the confidence of Polus, when asked how he could do better that Gorgias, that he could provide answers that would be equally *satisfying* as those given by his teacher (448a–b).

It is worth noting a curious echo of the basis for the Oracle's confidence that no man was *wiser* than Socrates: the fact of all men being equally ignorant would follow from the non-existence, incomprehensibility, and inexpressibility of Truth! A basis of the power to answer any question would doubtless be very similar to the insight that Socrates received from the Oracle. The fact that no man was wiser than Socrates simply meant that no human being possessed knowledge of matters above the sky or beneath the earth. As a result, Socrates felt divinely mandated to promote human virtue. Gorgias however would use a variant of this revelation, that there was nothing divine that men could know, to emancipate his students from all religious and moral bonds. Since most men seek some transcendent basis to guide their actions, the select few enlightened by Gorgias would be free to use a mixture of flattery and audacity to gain influence and power in their cities by manipulating fear and credulity. The aforementioned unspeakable character of truth also suggests that these initiates would practice flattery and pay homage to order – all the while corrupting it through their opportunistic but esoteric nihilism.

Polus's words, asking Chaerephon what difference it makes who responds to his query as long as the answer "is good enough for you" (448b), suggests also that for Gorgias the questioning process ends not with truth, or zetetic insight, but in the termination of the wonder that gave rise to the question and its replacement by the satisfaction or pleasure of the questioner. To this way of thinking democratic citizens were but a herd of auditory animals ruled by desire, ignorance, and passion. Here again we see how it is that Gorgias has not been asked any new questions in many years. Most questions important enough to justify an expensive interview with a sophist or the Oracle, ultimately pertain to common human desires/insecurities and require no more than their subjective satisfaction.[8] In any time of cultural relativism and moral confusion, where meaning and truth have very little to do with each other, it is small wonder that the purveyors of generic artificial meaning invariably emerge as the wealthiest and most powerful members of our species.

Through rhetoric, hope and order are created out of what otherwise appears to be a chaotic and flux-like reality. Since most human beings tend to prefer even cruel deities and tyrannical kings to aloof gods and a natural order indifferent to their existence, providers of the soothing flatteries that give both meaning and pleasure to otherwise empty lives gain great power over their auditors. Yet, as we shall see, Socrates will oppose this bid to draw nihilistic conclusions from what must be seen as conditions for the possibility of human freedom and excellence. The absence of direct monistic truth should not lead us to the other extreme position, that reality is meaningless and vortex is king. While Gorgias's art promises morally vulnerable souls and polities the power to deny guilt and shirk responsibility by declaring moral bankruptcy, we shall see how this virtual immunity is gained at a pyrrhic cost.

Rhetoric is a knack (*empeiria*) that is the very opposite of self-knowledge: it is solely concerned with the answer that pleases its tired, insecure, and impatient questioners. The "customer is always right" only because the salesperson's interest in him is entirely instrumental, exploitative, and wrong. What is unique about him, his soul, is ignored. These "one size fits all" responses reduce many different persons into a single generic, ignorant, and speech/logo(s)-less *anthropos*. Here, arithmetic, the counting of identical units, replaces geometry, the art dealing with the ratios between naturally unequal entities. The implications of this approach are terrible: human beings are free to be bought, sold, and counted like money. It was in this mordant

---

8   Benardete points out that "the formulaic answers of rhetoric assume the absence of novelty in the questions, but Socratic questioning seems to be grounded in novelty. One comes to know what one does not know in a previously unknown way" (p. 10).

spirit that Aeschylus described Ares, the God of War, as a moneychanger in human bodies.[9]

Whatever the shortcomings of his intellectual training may be, Polus's *empeiria* leads him to swiftly size up Chaerephon and treat him as just another customer. Taken along with his general volatility, democratic sympathies (21a), and claim on the sophist's friendship, the fact of Chaerephon not being overly upset by Polus usurping Gorgias's role suggests that Socrates' companion had difficulty understanding his friend's self-knowledge and professions of ignorance.[10] This may have been what sent him off to Delphi. It also accounts for the inability of Chaerephon to ask the proper question about Gorgias. Clearly Polus and *his* master understood each other and their profession far better; we are reminded of the tag-team of brother sophists in the *Euthydemus*.

Conversely, since several of Aristophanes' plays attest to the weird and excitable qualities that Chaerephon was renowned for, and resound with the comedian's distaste for him,[11] we may also infer that he was significantly more "Pre-Socratic" than Socrates himself. This suggests that the *Clouds* itself may be a more accurate description of Chaerephon than of Socrates. If teachers are responsible for the character of their students and/or the quality of the company they keep, it is small wonder that Socrates could have been caricatured on account of his association with Chaerephon. Since it is also striking that Gorgias's radical skepticism is taken to be a Socratic position, it is worth our while to ponder why many of those who should know better are most comfortable viewing Socrates as either a batty scientist or a semi-nihilistic dialectician.

Socrates clearly suggests in his *Apology* that Chaerephon sought out the Oracle on his own initiative; the *Gorgias* offers us a parody of this mission: an encounter with a garrulous oracle, intoxicated by verbosity, whose preferences are clearly for excess and against self-knowledge. These tendencies are well illustrated by the ancient report that Gorgias actually visited Delphi and offered the Oracle a golden statue of himself![12] However, unlike the Delphic Oracle whose responses were typically enigmatic and short to the point of obscurity, the long-winded responses of Polus and Gorgias defy Socrates' best efforts to keep them brief and to the point.

9   Aeschylus, *Agamemnon* 437.
10   Here again, I disagree with Vlastos's view that Chaerephon was among the "initiated" to whom the meaning behind Socrates' "complex ironies" was readily apparent (p. 244). The paradoxes surrounding Socratic irony have far more to do with the fact that he was not a sophist who imparted information. Only the practice/incarnation of virtue makes what was self-evident to Socrates absurd to Polus and *vice versa*.
11   See Stauffer, p. 19.
12   See Dodds, *Gorgias* (Clarendon Press, 1959) p. 9.

Before Chaerephon began to question Polus, Socrates had told Callicles that he wished to engage in dialectical conversation with Gorgias and inquire about the power of his art and the content of his teachings (447c). Socrates' request, that *Chaerephon* ask Gorgias what manner of man he is, follows Callicles' report that the great sophist had offered to answer *any* question that was asked of him. In other words, since Gorgias had bragged, in so many words, that he was wiser than the Oracle, Socrates has the once or future suppliant of Delphi reverse the "And who is it who asks?" question implicit in all the enigmatic answers given by Apollo's Oracle to a hubristic inquiry. This Delphic approach is also clearly opposed to that taken by Gorgias, since the sophist bases his claims to omniscience on his power to reduce human diversity to a generic uniformity of need and desire through flattery and obfuscation. Even without venom, the great jaws of a python can adjust themselves to any question and accommodate any questioner.

This indirect procedure of questioning seems to mimic that followed at Delphi; here too conversation between the Oracle and the questioner occurred through two priests representing them. Furthermore, just as the Oracle has three Pythian spokespersons, so that they could relieve each other when the burden of omniscience proved too exhausting, this dialogue sees a wearied Gorgias replaced first by Polus and then by Callicles. This indirection also has the effect of delaying a direct encounter, allowing the principals to assess indirectly the capacities of both their allies and enemies before fully committing themselves to battle each other. We may also note a kind of separation, or geometrical inequality, between the views of the principal protagonists and their respective surrogates, as well as the varying responsibilities granted to the respective representatives of Socrates and Gorgias: Chaerephon and Polus. It is also noteworthy that while Socrates only trusts Chaerephon to ask questions, Gorgias does not deter Polus from answering them. This separation between sidekick and hero also illustrates the gap between knowledge and speech that must be bridged by both philosopher and sophist – albeit in very different ways.

First, Socrates briefly (and quite unsuccessfully) tutors his henchman in how he is to question Gorgias by using a familiar example: a maker of shoes would admit to being a shoemaker. However Chaerephon moves away from the Socratic model of making, which would have led him to ask what Gorgias made. Instead he proceeds by using the analogy of the skills practiced by Gorgias's brother, Herodicus the physician, and the brothers Aristophon and Polygnotus – who were both painters. Regardless of whether this is the intention of Chaerephon or Plato, there is also an implicit distinction made here between the objective, body-based, art of medicine and the more subjective satisfaction provided by a painter. Polus evades this distinction by suggesting that many arts arise empirically; both medicine and art would seem to fall under this "realistic" category; both artists and physicians had to first acquire their skills through trial and error, and then make their reputation through rhetoric. Experience and speech allow us to overcome chance and live out our span of life by art; here we cannot forget that Gorgias was reputed to have lived for over a century! Then, finally, Polus tells Chaerephon that the best men participate in the best arts (448c). Gorgias is one of them, and he practices the finest of all arts. Polus implies that he too is also one of these best men practicing the best art. It may well be the case that he would like to supplant his teacher; he surely believes himself to be Gorgias's equal in knowledge and his superior in energy – and he has learned that the latter is worth far more than the former

The opening of the *Gorgias* illustrates that problem of rhetoric has much to do with disciples and imitators. Chaerephon and Callicles both involuntarily misrepresent and voluntarily misuse what they've "learned" from others. Although, as we noted earlier, rhetoric is especially likely to give rise to this illusion of easily communicable wisdom, Chaerephon's words show that philosophy is not invulnerable to bad imitation and misrepresentation by enthusiasts. Ill-effects are all too prone to outlive the original intention that caused them. Those winged words of Shakespeare's Mark Antony over the bloody body of the soon-to-be-divinized Julius Caesar, "The evil that men do lives after them. The good is oft interred with their bones,"[13] are profoundly relevant here.

At this point, before returning to the dialogue, we should also note that Chaerephon's fascination with technique, and brothers, has prevented from asking the direct question about Gorgias's art that would have been harder for Polus to answer. While this theme of brotherhood (*adelphos*) is also a sly reference to Delphi, which literally meant navel or womb (*delphus*), we must also ask if Polus would have replied to this query by saying that Gorgias was a maker of human success or successful human beings. It may well have been the case that, when Polus became Gorgias's student, neither Sicilian had any need for a direct conversation concerning the content of their art along the lines of Socrates' famous interrogation of Protagoras on behalf of Hippocrates; the connection between the *logos*, the unspeakable, desire, and shame is one that we shall examine at considerable length later. Let alone Socrates' request that he find out what Gorgias makes, Chaerephon has made it possible for Polus to even evade the necessity of naming the art he shares with his teacher. It is striking that Socrates was never known to have claimed that Chaerephon was his student. We cannot but wonder what Plato's opinion of this batty hanger-on was. It is fairly well proven that he did not have a very high opinion of most of Socrates' other associates.[14]

13   William Shakespeare, *Julius Caesar*, III ii 72–73.
14   See Ranasinghe, *The Soul of Socrates* (Cornell University Press, 2000), Chapter 3.

Yet Chaerephon's interrogative ineptness is inconspicuous in comparison to Polus' embarrassing verbosity. This proxy battle has highlighted one of the main themes of the *Gorgias*: a pragmatic, result-based method of assessing the achievements of public figures. His student's empirical criteria suggest that Gorgias has not done a good job with Polus, and now the itinerant teacher has been forced, in a kind of inverted primal scene, to contemplate his flawed creation. Socrates may have missed the sophist's *epideixis* – his display of himself to others, but he *has* seen Gorgias see himself in this bad imitation of his own methods – for which experience he must surely take some responsibility. Even an itinerant will sometimes happen to see the fruit of his own actions and techniques, usually through some tragic accident that causes the effect to be turned back upon its cause. Even though Gorgias chooses to believe that his students would employ his art with the best intentions of the polity in mind, he would also strongly prefer not to verify this assumption.

The disappointing performances put on by their respective allies forces the principals, Socrates and Gorgias, to take the field in their own persons. Proceeding with ironic politeness, Socrates points out to Gorgias that Polus, despite his splendid equipment/preparation (*pareskeuasthai*) for speech (or battle!), has not really kept his promise to Chaerephon (448d). In other words, he has not really used his power (*dunamis*) well; the deeper significance of this statement will be explored later in the dialogue when Polus and Socrates cross words again. When Gorgias suggests that Socrates put the question directly to Polus, he is told that it would be better to interrogate the teacher rather than the student. Socrates goes on to state that Polus seems to have devoted himself far more to rhetoric than to conversation (dialectic). Asked by Polus to clarify his meaning, Socrates says that instead of naming Gorgias's art, Chaerephon received a defensive eulogy.[15] Strikingly *Socrates* is the first to name the art that the orators practice without naming.[16]

His discernment of this pattern, a flurry of flowery praise aimed at concealing a lack of substance, lies at the heart of the Socratic critique of Gorgias. Instead of providing a truthful account of the matter at hand, the rhetorician sets out to defensively over-compensate for his original reckless and hubristic denial of truth. This literally an-archaic foundation frees him to create democratic truth, by saying whatever he believes his audience needs and wishes to hear, in

15 Benardete notes that Socrates implies that "rhetoric can regularize the randomness of life only after the event and rectify in retrospect its irrationality. Rhetoric makes up stories that put the sheen of reason on what was experienced at the time as senseless." This Epimethean knack "must always react and never initiate. It can get one off but never start one off" (p. 12).

16 Arieti comments that Gorgias's sort of rhetoric can "bedazzle the multitudes but it cannot answer even the simplest question in a straightforward way" (p. 82).

order to defend himself. This approach even extends to the special case of providing an account of the sophistical art itself! It is noteworthy that the primary purpose of this art turns out to be defensive, deceptive and self-concealing by setting out to provide pleasure instead of substance; Plato surely means us to be struck by Socrates' diametrical deviation from this strategy as he set about speaking his own celebrated Apology, or defense speech. Yet Polus is so blinded by rhetoric that he imagines it to be a sufficient explanation of this art to state that it is the finest. This anticipates, or even creates, the last interlocutor in this dialogue, Callicles, whose name means "called fine or *kalos*."

Yet Socrates is typically unimpressed by reputation. He turns to Gorgias and after reminding him of the difference between praise and substance, asks the self-proclaimed omniscient to name his own art, thereby identifying himself. Gorgias's reply is the model of terseness: "Rhetoric, Socrates." He goes on to say that he may be called a good rhetorician – perhaps in comparison to Polus and certainly in relation to his art. His words are suggestive: "You may call me what, in Homer's words, I boast myself to be" (449a). Now that the cat is out of the bag, he not only names his profession but boasts of it. Somewhat mischievously comparing this statement to Descartes' famous *cogito ergo sum*, we could say that Gorgias "boasts therefore he is." Not unlike the Homeric heroes who boasted to their adversaries about their divine and supernatural lineage before giving battle, Gorgias's vainglorious proclamation is a consciously performative utterance. It remains to be seen how he, or his position, may be defended in a dialectical duel. Socrates then proceeds to ask Gorgias whether he has the power of making others like himself, certainly a power that Socrates himself never claimed to possess, as we can plainly see from his marked lack of success with Chaerephon. Yet his adversary again professes the ability do so, not only in Athens but elsewhere too (449b).

Now, further defining the terms of their duel, Socrates requests that Gorgias keep his promise to make his answers short and to the point (449b). This is strange because Gorgias has made no such offer so far in this dialogue; however, we have seen such a statement attributed to him in the *Phaedrus*. Perhaps Socrates is well acquainted with his rival's standard sales-patter; for his own part, Gorgias does not remember not speaking these words before Socrates, so set is he in his standard routine. Still Gorgias, after qualifying his statement by saying that some answers need lengthy accounts, explicitly claims that no one could say the same things more concisely than himself. This is in striking contrast to Protagoras's blunt refusal to play by Socrates' rules in the dialogue bearing his name (325a). This suggests that while Protagoras is self-servingly prudent, and cares more about winning than showing off, Gorgias is so much in love with his cleverness that he displays the naked truth of his art – in the hope of gaining greater acclaim.

The two dialogues may be compared in this manner: while the *Gorgias* is about the soul and forensic/apologetic speech, the *Protagoras,* concerned with public political oratory. Furthermore where the *Protagoras* is outward directed, the *Gorgias* is introverted and personal. Also, while the *Protagoras* describes the impact of sophistry on its first users and goes on to show Socrates in direct opposition to it, the *Gorgias* discusses the discoverer of nihilism and his first disciples; it then skips over the first listeners to expose the plight of Callicles: a representative of the second generation exposed to rhetoric, nihilism, and war. The *Gorgias* is about the effects of sophistry and nihilism on souls; unlike the *Protagoras,* it does not feature the public *epideixis* of a sophist. The *Gorgias* also offers a longer treatment of the dilemma that Protagoras was confronted with by Socrates; this had to do with the delicate position of a Sophist who, while posing as a friend of the polis, and bringer of enlightenment and culture, teaches the potentially subversive doctrine of nihilism. While Protagoras avoided directly answering this question by relying on his great myth, Gorgias is dragged into the dialectical current and made to see the long-term effects of his words.

Returning to our dialogue, we see Socrates then asks Gorgias about the subject matter of rhetoric; this was the second question that Polus, thanks to the ineptitude of Chaerephon, never had to answer. The philosopher offers two more familiar examples: weaving is concerned with making clothes, and music makes tunes. Socrates points out that Gorgias's response, that rhetoric has to do with speech, the *logos,* isn't specific enough. He now turns back to the physician's art for examples and points out that rhetoric does not show how sick people could live to become healthy. Once Gorgias concedes that rhetoric isn't concerned with all kinds of speech. Socrates then asks him whether rhetoric makes men good at speaking and when Gorgias agrees, pointedly tells him that he presumes "that it makes them good at thinking about the subjects that they speak about" (449e). Here he is making an important distinction between the things spoken of and the speeches themselves. A rhetorician may well understand his speech while being quite ignorant of that of which he speaks. In other words, he may know his words and audience far better than the true subject matter of his discourse; his audience may have far more knowledge about his topic despite being much less adept at framing it. Artisans without the power to give a *logos* of what they do silently are yet far more skilled than rhetoricians whose florid words are without issue. Socrates compares this rhetoric to medicine and gymnastics to suggest that true expertise in genuine arts makes their practitioners able to speak well and thoughtfully about health and illness.

If the "greatest and best of human matters" isn't persuasion and cannot be created by it, then the best life has an objective status and cannot be experienced as a body or even as an Athenian but only as a soul; such a life cannot be lived by a world-wearied solipsist. It follows then that the soul must be viewed as the command post of an active and erotic human life spent in the world. Yet the rhetorician only learns from experience to speak eloquently on these very subjects *through the experience of speaking frequently on them*, rather than through knowledge of what health and illness are. The danger is that this procedure could lead to the obscuring or permanent loss of the little objective (and truly empirical) knowledge one had to begin with. In other words, following a variant of Gresham's Law with regard to language, we may see how unjust speech drives out just speech: the more things are spoken of frivolously, the less intelligible they become to the speaker.

A good example of this effect would be the case of a war veteran with a familiar repertoire of stories concerning his exploits. It is often the case that when the raconteur recollects some famous feat of arms, *he remembers the last time he told the story* rather than the original experience itself. Also, the more expert he becomes at telling the story, and giving his admiring audience what they paid for, the more he will become alienated from the ugly and inchoate original experiences they seek. Many of those who were present at famous battles remember little of what went on beyond the smoke, carnage, fear, and confusion. Much later, they understand the agreed-upon significance of what they went through by reading a reconstruction of the battle undertaken by someone half their age, a person was not present at the event. This becomes the basis for the stories they tell their adoring children's children about the day when their grandfather stood up to a million Persians at Marathon. Nestor, the very person Socrates compared Gorgias to, practices this very skill in Homer's *Iliad* and *Odyssey*.

All these matters must be held in mind when Gorgias claims that, unlike these practical arts, rhetoric operates purely through speech. The adequacy of this definition is also challenged by Socrates, who reminds him of other theoretical pursuits that are largely or entirely transacted through words rather than actions. Socrates points out that these other arts possess a definite subject matter and asks Gorgias to name what his art is concerned with. His answer, "the greatest and best of human concerns" (451d), almost represents a return to Polus's (and Nestor's) level of discourse, but not quite; Gorgias is capable of thinking about what he does, as well as employing his reason instrumentally. Socrates points out that many other arts – those of the physician, the trainer and the businessman – could make similar claims to deal with the greatest human good through health, beauty, and wealth respectively. Even though there is a real distinction between what is truly good for man and the objects of the various desires, it is still the case that for Gorgias the art of rhetoric is not embedded in or related to nature, but rather represents the power of the eloquent will to create a realm of meaning that is independent of elusive or hos-

tile nature. Of course an itinerant, who does not have to live with the consequences of his words, will inevitably experience and portray reality as thoroughly fickle and changeable. Such a man will certainly be glib or self-
deceived enough to blame his students for not living up to his belief in their
virtue and not properly bridging the gap between the *logos* of speech and the
hule of nature.

We should always bear in mind that a rhetorician is concerned with speaking about the best and greatest human concerns – rather than with achieving
them directly. He does so through a pseudo-scientific power that seems to
order or conquer nature or reality. The practitioner of rhetoric expects to
achieve everything that is best and great through speech; he would gain these
triumphs within the realm of human words. A master of rhetoric will define
and persuade his fellow-citizens as to what the "best and greatest of human
concerns" are. As noted earlier, his power is more than empty flattery; used
skillfully, rhetorical claims become self-fulfilling performative utterances, but
ultimately everything depends on the lion's heart, speed, and power. These are
not qualities that become redundant by the mellifluous voice of his trainer.
Though Achilles played the lyre while sulking in his tent,[17] he isn't remembered for his delicate voice or beautiful hands.

Socrates has now prompted the Sophist sufficiently for Gorgias to recollect the subject of his *logos*. Before further explaining that it works through
employing the art of persuasion in any kind of political gathering – whether it
be a court of law, council meeting, or the Assembly itself – Gorgias claims that
his art is truly the greatest good *"because it gives the possessor not only freedom for human beings but also the power to rule in one's own city."* (452d).
We must see that this description is a significantly edited line from Thucydides
describing the natural but vain desires of human beings acting together to form
an exaggerated impression of their own capacities.[18] The original words were
spoken by the Athenian Diodotus, who described himself as an orator, during
the course of his famous debate with the demagogue Cleon over the fate of the
Mytileneans, an event that took place around the time of Gorgias's visit to
Athens. But Diodotus merely spoke of the illusion of "freedom and rule over
others." Since this dialogue was written well after Thucydides' death, Plato
seems have amended this line to imply that Gorgias is sincere in promising
"freedom for human beings and rule *in one's own city*" as the benefit of his art.
However, as Socrates soon points out, Gorgias and his students do not see that
rule of the temperate man over himself, as opposed to the power to rule over
others – even if this is limited to the populace of one's own city – is the greatest human action.

18   Thucydides, *Peloponnesian War*, IV. 45.

This amendment suggests that Gorgias, like Chaerephon, is a democrat and not a demagogue. He does not believe that his art supports imperial orders or ventures; these are reliant on silent barbaric violence rather than on *peitho* (persuasion): a word that Gorgias uses nineteen times but, like the dog that didn't bark in the night, is utilized by neither Polus nor Callicles.[19] Persuasive speech is used to secure one's ascendancy *within* the polis. Even though speeches are higher than deeds, the most important deeds are speech acts and those who follow the direction of speech-actors are no better than demotic artisans; the fact remains that *for Gorgias* natural limits are imposed upon the free sway of speech and deeds by the integrity of the polis. Otherwise put, speeches and deeds, even when they extend beyond the confines of Attica – as was the case during the Persian Wars – must be in service of the polis. Gorgias probably would not dispute Aristotle's famous definition of man as a political animal;[20] the polis does not go beyond the integrity of human nature – it realizes it. Even his famous mission to Athens was undertaken in support of the interests of his own city-state. He is probably quite a decent man – when not practicing his art.[21]

However, as his student Agathon's speech in Plato's *Symposium* suggests, Gorgias does expect to gain freedom, both for the rhetorician directly and for humanity indirectly, from an oppressive notion of unchanging and fatal truth.[22] This is why he must delight in the never-ending clamorous speech of democracy. Even though it involves him in various logical inconsistencies, his denial that anything exists could amount to the equivalent of the Epicurean position regarding the gods: even if there is some unchanging Truth, it is irrelevant to human affairs. This frees humanity to find happiness through artificial truths continually established and negotiated through human persuasion. In Gorgias's way of thinking, there is definitely a connection between epistemological liberation from false belief in the accessible presence of monolithic imperial Truth and the flourishing of a democratic regime that celebrates political freedom and virtuosity through artful speech and local temporary truths. What is deceptive in promising "freedom and rule" is the suggestion of a permanent conquest over flux or necessity. As his defense of Helen shows, Gorgias knows full well that these elements of Fortune will always have the last word. This is why he tries not to exceed the natural limits of the polis – and inevitably fails in this effort.

19 Benardete, p. 6.
20 Aristotle, *Politics* 1. 1253a1.
21 Weiss says that "Gorgias is not like his successors in the argument . . . he disapproves of injustice . . . it would appear that he aspires neither to political office, nor to committing atrocities against others, nor to the unlimited indulgence of appetite. And he is not an unjust man" (p. 70).
22 See Ranasinghe, *The Soul of Socrates*, pp. 136–43.

Even though Gorgias strives to respect the limits of the polis, the art of rhetoric does seem to give its possessor power over nurture; rule over others seems to be sufficient condition for bringing about freedom for oneself – at least from the consequences of one's actions. Here of course, as Socrates will point out, the danger is that this could include alienating freedom from oneself! A freedom that is created by speech alone tends to threaten to supplement and annihilate the *ethos* that gives it meaning. This counter-tendency was indicated when Gorgias, as noted earlier, elaborates that his art of persuasion will make it possible for a practitioner of oratory to sway juries, councils, assemblies, and all other civic gatherings. He claims that the other professionals mentioned earlier as candidates to be givers of the greatest good would be the "slaves" (*doulon*) of the man who can persuade both the professionals and the masses to follow his will (452e).

Strikingly, the persuasion occurs before the sophistical argument is made. This means that the pleasing personality of the rhetorician matters more than the quality or content of his argument.[23] Gorgias is seeking to overcome a situation similar to that existing among the Olympian Gods. Any dispute between them, for instance over who was the most beautiful, could only be settled by power. Accordingly, Aphrodite "proved" that she was the more beautiful than Hera or Athena by making the most attractive offer to Paris – even though the "proof" clearly follows, with its tongue hanging out, well after the persuasion. Gorgias's point seems to be that since persuasion is more attractive than raw power, it reflects the superiority of democracy over autocratic *force majeure*.[24]

Socrates now seeks clarification from Gorgias that this art of oratory operates entirely through the creation of persuasion or conviction. When this is confirmed, Socrates states that he believes himself to be, *for so he persuades himself,* one who is second to none in making it his purpose to know exactly what the subject of discussion is.[25] He also says that he believes Gorgias to be another such man (453b). It follows that they have both persuaded themselves of their firm grasp of those matters; Socrates set out to discover objective truth through dialectic while Gorgias preferred to exercise persuasive or creative authority over the flux by rhetoric. Even though he does not immediately see

---

23 Benardete sees Plato implying that "Gorgianic rhetoric is powerless, and whatever effect it appears to achieve is due to the effect already having being achieved. The rhetorician comes after the feast" (p. 9).

24 Giving much-needed content to Gorgias-tutored Agathon's effusive eulogy to himself and his art in Plato's *Symposium*, Benardete observes that rhetoric "brings freedom and slavery; it is the craftsman of willing slavery or unforced tyranny. Rhetoric dissolves the need for the use of force within a city. The speaker who persuades effects in the auditor who is persuaded a state of obedience" (p. 17).

25 See Benardete, pp. 17–18.

the significance of Socrates' remarks, Gorgias will eventually be made to see that the persuasion of others inevitably involves a great deal of self-persuasion, willy-nilly.[26] This comment also draws the attentive reader's attention to the subtle difference between rule over oneself and self-persuasion, a topic that Socrates will explore throughout the dialogue. Even though self-persuasion is attractive to one with a soft understanding of truth, and a natural suspicion of Stoic restraint, one cannot forget that the contrary danger of self-delusion always looms behind the heady rhetoric of freedom. The risk is that awareness of the objective results of his self-deception is involuntarily hidden from the unwitting perpetrator by the very delusory act of persuading himself that he is engaged in self-creation. The end result of this lie is nihilism.

Socrates, suggesting that he has not yet been persuaded, now confesses that he still does not have a sufficiently clear idea of what Gorgias means by persuasion, or of what it is about. Even though he admits to having a suspicion (*hupopteuon*) of what Gorgias means, Socrates still asks him about what he believes to be the nature and subject of that conviction. He will not voice his own view, not out of respect for Gorgias, but because raising the question will lead their discussion to reveal its subject matter as adequately as they can see it. The Greek is very awkward precisely because Socrates is trying to preserve the integrity of both persuasion and dialectic in this formulation. While Socrates is bringing out the genuinely reciprocal dimension of persuasion, and expressing his faith in a common world that is the precondition of human discourse, Gorgias does not seem to apprehend either of these ordinary marvels adequately, and prefers to treat human conviction as a feat of technical virtuosity – as something he has created rather than discovered. This attitude also makes *his* place in this *logopolis* quite incongruous. The sophist sees human beings as so many frogs living around a Mediterranean Sea of words but, unlike Polus and Callicles, he does not seek to be the Frog-King's speechwriter or a predatory Water Moccasin.[27]

The matter could be stated more forcefully by asking how sophists can genuinely interact with each other. As Socrates once pointed out to Thrasymachus, even thieves need honor. We noted earlier how Polus sought to speak in place of Gorgias, and we shall see how Socrates' three interlocutors in the dialogue engage in conversation with him and not with each other. It is striking that the three spokespersons for sophistry cannot persuade or converse with each other. We are reminded of the three Gorgons: they had but a single eye and tooth between them and passed these items around when one of them

26   "Gorgias . . . looks into the mirror of his own rhetoric and believes it to be true" (Benardete, p. 24).

27   Friedlander says that Gorgias "combines the power of the new art with a traditional morality" (p. 250).

wished to speak or see! The seeming exception to this rule occurs at the end of the dialogue when Gorgias tells Callicles not to give up his argument with Socrates; but on closer observation we see that Gorgias does not persuade (or dissuade) Callicles, he *orders* him to continue. This fact is well consistent with Gorgias's itinerant lifestyle. For all his love of persuasion, he cannot be around others like himself or exist self-consistently in reality.[28] Genuine interaction between avowed relativists and flatterers is impossible. As much as we admire the tacit understanding of the brother sophists of the *Euthydemus* or the *unspoken* synchronized motions of the sophistical cadre in the *Protagoras*, it must be recognized that this power is based on fear or greed rather than love. This is also why the Gorgons cannot speak with their own kind for fear of turning them, or being turned by them, into stone! It is also consistent with our earlier observations about the impossibly anachronistic dramatic time of the *Gorgias*.

Socrates only suggests this problem indirectly, as he draws Gorgias's attention to the problem of multiple practitioners of the same art. His explicit point is more basic. Zeuxis cannot be described as "the one who paints living beings" because there are many others who perform the same activity. Alternatively, we could even say that the sophistical art cannot address or depict genuine human beings in their psychic diversity. Still, rhetoric is not the only art that produces persuasion; all the other arts do so too. Gorgias is now persuaded by Socrates' dialectical art to say that rhetoric is about a specific kind of persuasion: that which is practiced in "law courts and other undisciplined crowds or mobs" and deals with the just and the unjust (454b). Gorgias's democratic preferences suddenly appear in a decidedly unflattering light! So this is what "ruling over one's fellow citizens" means! We also see why users of this art cannot share honest speech together.

After this damaging admission, Socrates drives the point home by drawing a distinction between knowledge (*mathesis*) and belief (*pistis*) (454d). Despite Gorgias's celebrated denial of our access to it, it seems that the very nature of dialectical discussion compels him to acknowledge the sufficient presence of truth. It should be noted here that there is a realm between eternally certain sun-lit knowledge, of the sort that Parmenides affirmed, and the murky regions of Syracuse where sophistry persuaded ignorant armies to clash in the night. The denial of our unmediated access to Being does not necessarily hurl us to the depths of non-being. Socrates' celebrated knowledge of his

28 Benardete suggestively observes that while the word *rhetor* literally means "speaker" and could be used to define man as a speaking animal, Socrates' preferred word *dialegesthai* is "the ordinary word for the speaking of one human being with another" (pp. 10–11). The choice is between solipsism and conversation.

ignorance does not make him into a sophist or nihilist; prudentially mediated human truth is available in the *metaxy* or the in-between realm, where we "participate" in reality without having creative mastery over it. Gorgias however seems to want to have it both ways; while denying that anything truly exists, he professes that it is his art that creates human truth and meaning *ex nihilo*.

Returning to the *Gorgias*, we now see the orator admit that rhetoric pertains to the non-didactic craft of creating belief without knowledge concerning justice and injustice. It is only by this manner of persuasion that he can sway the opinions of large mobs on great matters in a short time (455a). In other words he can fashion shadows of any shape or size in any cave. These shadows, or the permanent conditions for their possibility, replace formal structures in Gorgias's truth-less reality; they may also be seen to resemble the Clouds of Aristophanes' eponymous play. Yet it must be seen that the power of shadows or clouds does not prove the non-existence of formal, transcendental truth – if anything, the relationship is ultimately parasitic and better resembles the homage that illusion pays to reality. This power also reflects the great walls and building projects that the popular leaders of democratic Athens persuaded the people to build and glory in. Indeed it could be said that these leaders, like Gorgons, turned a virtuous polity into stone and marble.

Socrates now explicitly raises the relationship between rhetoric and popular democracy, asking Gorgias where it is appropriate for a rhetorician to offer advice to the city. Surely he would not do so in the presence of those genuinely knowledgeable in arts such as medicine, architecture, military strategy, or shipbuilding? He baits Gorgias by pointing out that quite a few of those present inside (*endon*) are desirous of learning his art. This could either mean that they are finally within the house of Callicles or that the desire of these potential students is secret and unspoken. Here the parallel with Glaucon's condition in the *Republic* is evident. Acting as a kind of go-between or pander between supply and demand, Socrates asks Gorgias, on behalf of both the great orator and his potential students, what they would gain by association with him. Will they simply learn about justice and injustice, or if they would also be able to advise the city about the other technical arts just mentioned by him (455b–d)? Socrates is clearly encouraging Gorgias to reveal himself and his art more fully but the orator is strangely blind to the unfriendly and/or medicinal purpose underlying the philosopher's flattering words. Perhaps, as Socrates will imply, Gorgias has persuaded himself, along with his customers, that oratory is all that he says it is. Indeed Socrates seduces him into overplaying his hand. While this procedure may be unfair on Socrates' part, it also demonstrates how flattery tends to generate hubristic vanity in its object.

After thanking Socrates for having prepared the way for him so beautifully, Gorgias agrees to reveal clearly the whole power of rhetoric. He points out that the famous long walls, dockyards, and strategic port of the Athenians were built on the advice of politicians like Themistocles and Pericles, rather than by following the counsel of the craftsmen (*demiourges*); it is rhetoric that gives advice and victoriously carries the assembly with it (455e–456a). Unlike Socrates, the midwife who merely helped people to regurgitate what they already knew, Gorgias takes credit – along with these other orators – for deeds performed by an entire civic populace. We recall Aeschylus' instructions that his epitaph should refer only to the fact that he fought at Marathon: a more different understanding of the relationship between speech and deed could scarcely be imagined. When Socrates now artlessly professes wonderment at the supernatural (*daimonic*) force of rhetoric and asks what its power (*dunamis*) could consist of, Gorgias throws caution to the winds and gives a hubristic account of the amazing power of his art over human beings. At this moment he is all sails and no anchor. If, as we suggested, the orator's soul overflows with excusable pride from his recent success in convincing the Athenians to sail to Sicily, it would surely be natural for Gorgias to give voice to his hubris. Socrates has persuaded the wordsmith to come out from behind his defensive stonewalling and expose himself to Laconic warfare.

Claiming that rhetoric has power over and gathers together almost every kind of human activity, Gorgias gives as an example his ability to be more persuasive than his brother, Herodicus the physician, in medical matters. According to him, patients who refused to take their medicine or submit to surgical procedures changed their mind after exposure to his rhetoric. Gorgias goes on to boast that in any polity a rhetorician would defeat a physician, even in an election to a medical position (456a–c). The same pattern would repeat itself in any contest between a professional and an orator that would be judged by a public audience. There is even the suggestion that many professionals could be made ignorant by their collective coming together as a *polloi*. It certainly is the case that professionals banding together for financial reasons often betray their vocation.

Gorgias claims that even though it can carry all before it, the power of rhetoric should not be used indiscriminately or against one's friends. If a student makes bad use of a skill like boxing or the use of weapons, "and he then strikes his father or mother," it does not mean that his teachers should be "detested and banished . . . for they passed on the skill intending that they should be put to a good use, against enemies and wrong-doers, defensively and not aggressively" (456d–457a). Likewise, in the case of rhetoric, the fact that an orator can deprive good men of their reputations does not mean that they are justified in doing so. Gorgias claims that rhetoric "like any other competitive skill" should be used rightly. If a student abuses his power "it is right to hate and banish and kill" him, "but not his teacher" (457c). It is noteworthy that Gorgias is defending the behavior of Aristophanes' caricature of Socrates in the *Clouds*. However, the Socrates of the *Gorgias* will reject this excuse when he criticizes the celebrated Athenian leaders of the past.

It is striking that Gorgias, who earlier portrayed himself as a perfect teacher who could answer any question satisfactorily, now refuses to take any responsibility for bad students. Is he now belatedly acknowledging natural and temporal limits to his rhetorical powers? Furthermore, where he originally stated that the orator tells large groups of people about what is just and unjust, he now separates the very art of rhetoric both from the power to use this power justly or unjustly and the true knowledge of justice and injustice. Is the standard of excellence in this art success in convincing others of what is just and unjust, or is it being successfully ruled by the intention to use this power to serve just ends – whatever they may be? Using a familiar image from the *Clouds*, Gorgias can give no guarantee either that just speech will triumph over unjust speech, or that his students will not perform outrages against their parents. His interests are technical and his main concerns are with efficient causality – even though he does hope that the means he provides will be directed towards the right ends. The problem is that his art functions through influencing the judgment of the many concerning what is just and unjust. He cannot have it both ways; he cannot claim to be a master of moral persuasion and confess that he cannot successfully direct the moral character of his students. Similar examples of upside-down asymmetry will recur frequently over the body of the *Gorgias*. There is something inherently defective about an art that can only reach the many but not the few; it is stranger yet when these very processes are seen to bring even less positive benefit to their practitioner – and indeed condemn him to be an itinerant.

Socrates' own response to these words, easily Gorgias's longest speech in the dialogue, seems to be polite and circumspect, even though its implications will turn out to be far-reaching and breathtaking in their implications. As always, he prefers long-term advantage to immediate gratification. Socrates once again states certain conversational ground rules that he believes himself, or to be precise, constantly tries to persuade himself that he believes himself to subscribe to, and offers Gorgias the opportunity to associate or disassociate himself from them. It seems that he still has difficulty in understanding the position that is being maintained by Gorgias on account of various inconsistencies of the kind that we have already noted. Before he brings these up, however, Socrates claims to be quite anxious that Gorgias appreciate that his goal in their discussion is not victory but truth. He goes on further to state that he tries to believe that he is one who "takes being refuted with pleasure if what he says is not true, and takes slightly less pleasure in refuting the statements of another that are untrue" (458a). He finds greater pleasure in being refuted than in refuting. "To the extent that it is a greater good to be released oneself from the greatest evil than to release another" (458a). He prefers taking medicine to administering it.

The problem with taking pride in one's ability to defend oneself convincingly and victoriously in debate is that after a while the desire to be victorious over all others replaces the far more natural apologetic desire to defend one's good intentions and heartfelt opinions. Even religious elements of a community could easily be seduced, through first being convinced that they were instruments of divine retribution and then bearers of manifest destiny, into implicitly seeing themselves as rulers over reality and truth through the sheer force of their wills. This progression from the subjective authenticity of saying *dokei moi*, so it appears to me, to the unrestrained ego's insidious tendency to seek hegemony and then sovereignty, first over the object and then above objective reality/truth, can only be checked by the intervention of error and correction. In other words, *dokei moi* should properly serve as the origin of a dialectical process by which opinion follows its natural *telos* and progresses towards truth. The seemingly self-confirming opinion of a collective group, such as the *ekklesia* of the Athenians, is all the more in need of an authoritative voice to restrain collective hysteria while empowering individual thought and judgment. The extent to which Pericles performed this role over the course of his long hegemony over the Athenians is a matter about which Socrates holds critical and distinctive opinions.

However we must bear in mind here that while being refuted, if one is such as Socrates, is sufficient for learning and improvement to take place, many persons tend to respond angrily and egotistically to such necessary experiences, thus growing in *thumos* rather than *eros,* especially if the *daimon* opposing their false opinions does so in a way that is humiliating and unpleasant. Socrates himself will have great difficulty in making Callicles take his just medicine.[29] Still, Socrates' avowal of his very singular source of the greatest pleasure is consistent with his claim that "the greatest evil for a human being is to have false opinions about the subjects that are presently being discussed" (458b). This is clearly a situation where Socrates would claim that the truth cannot destroy him – it only makes him stronger! Conversely, it would also follow from his position that the effects of the acceptance of non-truth would be deleterious over the long run. While this presupposes that reality has an underlying order that cannot successfully be evaded, Socrates said as much

28   Benardete suggestively observes that while the word *rhetor* literally means "speaker" and could be used to define man as a speaking animal, Socrates' preferred word *dialegesthai* is "the ordinary word for the speaking of one human being with another" (pp. 10–11). The choice is between solipsism and conversation.

when claiming famously in his *Apology* that injustice would ultimately turn out to be harder to escape from than death. The *Apology* is certainly consistent with the statement we have just discussed: while Socrates is proud of his ignorance of cosmology, this ignorance does not extend to the region of moral truth or self-knowledge.

After having made these two remarkably suggestive statements, which will duly be examined in conjunction with some even stranger claims regarding punishment later on, Socrates again offers to let Gorgias escape and kill the conversation if he is not of the same mind concerning the importance of the issues at stake – both intrinsically and in comparison to petty egotistical concerns. Even though Gorgias tries to avoid this trap, claiming that while he is of the same type as Socrates, the rest of the company might be too tired to listen to the continuation of the argument (588b–c), the master of rhetoric does not seem to have persuaded anyone. The father of the *logos* can no longer control his audience's unlimited appetite for words; once set in motion, mass phenomena turn out to have a voice of their own that cannot be silenced – even by their creator.

Both Chaerephon and Callicles insist that the discussion continue. That excitable democrat Chaerephon calls their attention to the uproar (*thorubos*) made by those present in their desire to hear more. The same word will also describe the equally raucous but negative response to some of the more provocative claims in Socrates' defense speech. Echoing Socrates' earlier words regarding the significance of the matters at stake, Chaerephon hopes that he may never be without sufficient leisure to listen to so important an argument. By contrast Callicles swears by the gods that no discussion has ever brought him as much *pleasure*; speaking in conditions quite unlike those prevailing decisively in the *Apology*, he claims that Socrates and Gorgias would be doing him a favor if they kept on talking all day (458d). Of course Callicles changes his tune later; most ironically as Socrates' final interlocutor, he tries desperately to conclude the discussion only to be overruled by Gorgias himself! For the present, though, it is Gorgias who gives in to the persuasion of the audience, admitting that it would be shameful for him not to continue the discussion after having offered to answer any question at all (458e). Since "it seems good to these men," the self-proclaimed master of persuading the many invites Socrates to ask any question he wishes to raise.

Having prepared the ground for his attack, Socrates asks Gorgias again whether he could make a rhetorician of anyone who listened to him. The orator answers in the affirmative, and assents again when Socrates then asks if this means making such a person able to convince a crowd in all matters, not by teaching but by persuasion. Gorgias is then prompted to state that in matters pertaining to health, the orator will be more persuasive than a physician to a crowd (*oxlos*). Socrates then gains his assent to the statement that by the crowd he means the ignorant, those who do not know (*mey eidosin*), since those who know (*eidosin*) will find the physician to be more persuasive (458e–459a). We may also note that the present company is exempted from this criticism since they did not follow Gorgias's preference! It also follows from the earlier statement that he who is without knowledge will be more persuasive to the ignorant. While this deduction applies rather damningly to Gorgias, it also holds true in the case of all the other arts. For an orator: there is no need to know the truth; one merely needs to have discovered a certain device or mechanism (*mechanein*) of persuasion to appear to know more than those who know, in the eyes of those who don't know (459c). Rather than being an art or specialized expertise, rhetorical skill serves as a kind of *deus ex machina* here; his very ignorance provides all the more proof of the sophist's uncanny power in an upside-down world without truth. In his new capacity as a wide-jawed replacement Pythia, Gorgias – the master of unjust speech – clearly seems to see himself as being more like a god than merely a technically proficient man.

However Gorgias's reply to the question is more pathetic than persuasive, indicating the extent to which Socrates has humiliated and unwittingly exposed him before those not blinded by ambition and love of victory: "Isn't it much easier that one doesn't need to know any other art but only this to be a match for all the other professionals?" Seemingly similar to, but ultimately strikingly unlike, the basis for Socratic wisdom, this involuntary self-revelation of the sort of private thought that a man can barely share with himself indicates the true potential for mendacity in the sophistical enterprise. It is clear that one subscribing to such a view is either a fool or a knave; the consequences of having "out-smarted" the experts reside at the level of reality rather than speech. Indeed the very images of things created by rhetoric turn out to be grotesque simulacra due to being fashioned with a view to stimulating desire; conversely, accurate representations of entities would convey the idea or look of the signified in such a way as to make it intelligible to the mind.

Using rhetoric as a *pharmakon* or "truth supplement" – as the least suspicious interpretation of Gorgias's motives would suggest – involves many grave risks. Even when rhetoric is used by politicians, with the best of intentions, to gain the support of a constituency opposed to the policy being sold, this approach necessarily involves the grave danger of misguiding and/or corrupting the very political community the orator is supposed to be strengthening and guiding. In the first place, as Gorgias would have been the first to admit, human affairs are ruled by probability rather than certainty; we don't merely know whether event y is fated to happen, we don't even know that action x is certain to lead to result y. In the second place, we often don't know whether event y will be a good thing for the polis or not; power corrupts at least as much as powerlessness and a political regime is often not strong enough to make good and prudent use of the glittering prizes that fortune places before it. And thirdly, the very means utilized to sell an undertaking must use methods and techniques that are corrosive of the political process. Projects such as the Sicilian Expedition are made popular by talk of great booty and cheap glory; a practitioner of Gorgias's art will not tell his people that he has nothing to offer but blood, toil, tears and sweat. He cannot say that he values the moral integrity of a polity more than the rampant passions for acquisition or revenge that often overwhelm its collective self-knowledge.

It is interesting that while the results of rhetorically advocated enterprises are far from certain, since the course of future events thankfully isn't pre-determined or self-evident, orators ignore the only aspects of an action that possess limited self-evidence: those ethical elements that are judged by the individual soul. This ostracism of the conscience is done out of a desire to achieve certainty with regard to the selling of the project. Paradoxically, the likelihood of a victory in persuasiveness is almost in inverse proportion to the chances of the predicted triumph coming to pass in reality; it is readily apparent that the more glowingly Alcibiades depicted the benefits accruing to Athens from the expedition to Sicily, the less prepared he left his audience for the great political vicissitudes that lay in store for it. Demagoguery of this kind is most harmful because it causes speeches, deeds, and moral integrity to be all at variance with each other.

While technique may supersede deliberative freedom in the case of bodily necessity, it can't lead to happiness, the true goal of all human actions, which can only be experienced by an individual soul and not by anything greater or smaller. Additionally, since most of the goals promised by the rhetoric of pleasure, envy, and glory are infinite and unlimited, they cannot yield happiness, which Aristotle wisely defined as a state that cannot be added to,[30] but seem to consist in contemplating the goodness of the world. While Socrates' understanding of the contemplated cosmos, as we shall see disclosed in the *Gorgias*, has erotic and daimonic elements absent from Aristotle's more intellectual vision, their views of *eudaimonia* is identical as far as our present purposes are concerned. They would also agree that statecraft consists in keeping a polity honest rather than seducing it towards impossible goals. In sum, the politics of virtue cannot, by definition, be waged by rhetoric, since it relies on bodily and external incentives that cannot reside in the soul.

Since Gorgias clearly admits that the experts have knowledge, his pride in the ability to defeat them in speech suggests that the effects of his power are more destructive than supplementary. Even if Gorgias's intervention leads a

---

30   Aristotle, *Nicomachean Ethics*, I. 1097b17.

sick man to follow the course of action endorsed by the physician, the expert's authority is undermined. This will tend to produce malefic results for his former patient, even if the true culprit can avoid responsibility for the long-term consequences of his intervention. Indeed, to the extent that reality-based knowledge makes deeper demands of us (such as a healthy regimen) that hedonistic rhetoric rejects, the two outlooks would tend to be opposed more often than not. Furthermore, even though verbal pandering is able to take us from the realm of idle words to that of deadly deeds with frightening alacrity, the return journey is infinitely more difficult to undertake. This relationship is quite non-commutative. All the king's horses and men cannot reassemble that proud master of words, Humpty Dumpty, after his great fall into the hardboiled realm of history. If anything, this artificial equality of the artisans and orators in the assembly (*ekklesia*) only indicates the fearful extent to which the divine gift of speech itself can become corrupted by the democratic art of counting lengthening noses. Furthermore, the martial art of being victorious by the easiest means cannot replace what it has destroyed. While any legionary, the less intelligent the better, can kill Archimedes, the power to reduce genius to a chunk of bleeding flesh does not prove Rome's superiority over Greece.

Socrates defers the question of whether the orator is indeed the equal of the professionals and points out that the orator does not know what is truly just, noble, good, healthy, or their opposites in any of the various arts he professes expertise in, but has merely devised a way of persuading the ignorant public that he appears to be knowledgeable (459d–e). This being the case, he asks Gorgias whether it is necessary that his students know these matters before they come to him, or if it is only his business to teach them to appear to know that which they are ignorant of, or if it is impossible to teach rhetoric to one unless he is already knows the truth about matters he will now also be persuasive about. Swearing by Zeus, Socrates asks Gorgias to tear aside the veil and reveal the true power of rhetoric (459e–460a). For ourselves, we must note that Socratic dialectic has quite the opposite effect, namely that of making persons aware of their ignorance concerning matters that they were previously confidently acquainted with. It could even be said that such an awareness of ignorance is the precondition for the very activity of engaging in dialectical speech.

At this point Gorgias is completely discombobulated. He lamely promises that if his student does not know these matters he will teach these to him also (460a). Now this is plainly dishonest. Gorgias has claimed to teach a method that could be used to dominate any or all of the various arts, the rhetorical equivalent of the master science that so attracted Charmides in the dialogue named after him. Surely he is not able to teach what is true and false, good and bad, about all of the various areas of human expertise? Wouldn't this knowledge be far more valuable than the ability to appear wise before the ignorant many? Why has he saved the best wine for last? This is also plainly inconsistent with the earlier mentioned report of Meno that Gorgias ridiculed those who professed the ability to teach excellence (*arête*). Is it possible to save Gorgias from his own boastful words here? The only remedy seems to be quoting Gorgias's own words denying Being and drawing from it the conclusion that truth, justice, and all the other terms are merely changeable and conventional. It follows then that the man who knows these matters are illusory would be wiser than all others inasmuch as he knows that there is no such thing as wisdom.

Cast in this light, Gorgias appears as a Socrates made slick, urbane, and cynical – a greedy *doppelganger*. No longer one who makes others wise, he would appear as one who takes away the possibility of genuine knowledge regarding a few things and substitutes deceptive and destructive nihilism in its stead. However, if we were to proceed more charitably, and in accordance with the downward trajectory of the dialectic, it would seem that Gorgias is more like Frankenstein than Einstein: he is an originally well-intentioned but irresponsible scientist who proves quite unable to educate the power of his own monstrous creation. As we suggested earlier, it is sufficient and profitable for Gorgias to display his art for fame and profit; this means that he does not need to engage in immoral behavior himself.[31] However, those who have learned rhetoric from him enjoy neither the gratification of a discoverer nor the profit of a wholesale merchant; they must gain fame and money from other, more explicitly vicious and adversarial, activities.[32]

Socrates now pursues a subtle line of questioning that conceals as much as it reveals to the inattentive reader; we must remember that neither Socrates nor Plato claimed be able to teach anybody – leave aside everyone – through dialectic or dialogue. Proceeding by analogy with other trades, Socrates persuades Gorgias that just as learning the building trade makes one a builder, and training in music or medicine turns a man into a musician or physician, similarly learning about justice makes a man just. Regardless of whether Gorgias is being taught a lesson about justice here, we can see that the analogy does not hold. Perhaps it is easiest to say that while the arts have to do with the intellect, eyes, and hands, knowledge of such matters of justice and morality pertain to a person's soul and/or character.[33] Alternatively we could say that the

---

31 Stauffer recognizes that while Gorgias values his knowledge of persuasion as an end in itself, this knowledge is also a means towards other ends – and can only be imparted to others as such (pp. 24–25).

32 Weiss notes that since Gorgias "does nothing to shape his student's character or even to alert them to the moral pitfalls that come with power, he is not guiltless when he produces a Polus or a Callicles" (p. 75).

very activity of *speaking* about justice for profit turns a man into a sophist.[34]

Certainly Gorgias's inability to understand this distinction does not reveal him in a very favorable light. Indeed, Socrates is helpful enough to point out to Gorgias that a just man must wish to do what is just and will never choose to act unjustly (460c). However, since the great sophist has already said that he can teach justice to those not aware of it, above and beyond being merely able to speak eloquently about justice, it follows that his students will never do injustice – not merely that they will never appear to be unjust. This is clearly not consistent with Gorgias's wary earlier statement that a teacher should not be held responsible for the misdeeds of his students. As noted earlier, this contradiction is even more glaring because Gorgias previously defined rhetoric as the power to speak persuasively before large gatherings about justice and injustice. We must see how skillfully Socrates is maneuvering the sophist here: he has to choose between being exposed as a knave or as a fool. Either he must give voice to nihilistic views about justice that are incongruent with his hubristic boast about his art or he must admit that he spoke carelessly and inconsistently. The latter choice would be most unpalatable to a self-proclaimed master of the *logos*.

Gorgias is silenced. The sophist may not be as wise as he claims to be, but he is certainly too intelligent not to be aware of the fatal choice that Socrates has forced upon him. He sees that he must now employ his unrivaled mastery of the art of making the shortest speeches and remain eloquently silent on any question that Socrates asks of him. However, illustrating by his combination of brash ambition and intellectual obtuseness the failure of Gorgias as a teacher, Polus bounds to his defense and attempts to shame Socrates into backing down. While this is clearly a rhetorical strategy, the surface reason for his outrage is that Socrates used leading questions to force Gorgias into an inconsistency. He asks Socrates "if any man would deny that he knows the good things and would teach them to others?" (461c). This is quite striking since, beneath his bluster, Polus is implicitly admitting what at least Gorgias, Socrates, and he know quite well: that Gorgias can neither deny nor affirm the extra-conventional existence

33   Benardete asks if it is possible for a single art to handle both "health of soul and the representation of its health." He says that "Socrates' question to Gorgias, whether in teaching rhetoric he also teaches justice (is) a variant of this question." Benardete suggests that while Plato discovers this art "for he represents the justice of philosophy while inducing in us philosophy," he does not "bring about in the individual the show and the reality of justice." This means that philosophy is a critical art. In Benardete's words "we try to emulate and not imitate Socrates" (p. 11).

34   Stauffer tersely notes that a Gorgian rhetorician senses "that justice is not a matter of the greatest significance." As a result he "will have no qualms about deception and manipulation" (p. 48).

of justice and injustice. His accusation also brings out something interesting about the *logos* itself; human speech itself requires or demands homage to these ideas. Any propositional statement contains an implicit promise that one is speaking the truth. This is the basis for such famous paradoxes as that involving the veracity of a Cretan who tells us that "All Cretans are liars." More pertinently, this paradox is also at the foundation of Gorgias's art. Even if there is no natural truth, human speech requires that artificial truths be created and maintained by those possessed of sufficient virtuosity to be the creators of the previously mentioned worldwide web of artificial meaning. Nobody truly desires chaos in either speech or reality. We are all good pragmatists at the end of history: even those enlightened enough to see its meaninglessness, earnestly feel that the "Great Conversation" must go on. This idea has been recognizably handed down from Gorgias to post-modernity.

While Socrates, having defeated Gorgias, gladly consents to being corrected by the much younger Polus, he only agrees to do so on the condition that the younger man abides by the same conditions of brevity that his teacher followed. Polus is not allowed to make long bombastic orations. Socrates will not allow him to intoxicate himself by the exuberance of his own verbosity! When Polus protests that Socrates is restricting his freedom of speech, Socrates suggests that Polus ask questions that he would answer, thus reversing the way of their previous *logos* and placing Socrates in the same allegedly unfair circumstance that Gorgias was left in. This would restore (retributive) justice, since Polus once again jumps at the opportunity to claim to know all the things that Gorgias knows (462a).

At this point in the discussion the concepts of political power and shame replace intellectual prowess and persuasion as the ruling categories of the dialogue. Not inappropriately, the tone of the conversation also becomes less urbane and more polemical. While Gorgias is obviously deeply attached to his art, he regards it with the love of a creator. As Socrates remarked to Cephalus in Book I of the *Republic*, persons who have made their own money have greater regard for it than those who inherit wealth (330c). Inheritors take a more instrumental interest in their assets, and Polus is certainly no exception to this rule as far as his Gorgian inheritance is concerned. Unlike Gorgias, who seems to take pleasure in his rhetorical virtuosity for its own sake – and is to that extent protected from the most morally corrosive effects of sophistry – Polus is more interested in using this wondrous art to gain power and honor. In this he may be said to resemble Cephalus's spirited son and impatient heir, Polemarchus; as noted earlier, Callicles will proceed to combine the crassness of Thrasymachus with the social position, and consequent frankness, of Glaucon and Adeimantus.

When Polus begins to question Socrates about rhetoric, the older man first sets out to contradict words that Polus himself has published on the topic: rhetoric is not an art but a certain experience. While this seems to restate Polus's own pompous earlier words about an art arising out of experience (448c), Socrates' point is that rhetoric is not an inductive discipline derived from experience, in contrast to unscientific revelations made by manic prophets and oracles, but the knack of producing a feeling of gratification (*caritos*) and pleasure in an audience. In other words, the experiences from which this so-called art is derived are subjective and ephemeral. When Polus naively asks whether it isn't a fine thing to produce such feelings in the people (*anthropois*), Socrates chides him for basing his assessment of something upon the impression it produces in people before first finding out what it is. This approach has even extended to his expecting Socrates to be impressed by his professed capacity to generate an overwhelming experience of pleasure that would override his knowledge of what it really is or even be amplified by the aforementioned asymmetrical proportion of substance to effect.

It should also be noted that while Gorgias appears to derive a great deal of intellectual pleasure from the subjective experience of his virtuosity – in both defeating experts and teaching it to others – Polus seems to prefer the admiration of others over the internal satisfaction found from the successful performance of a difficult task. This distances him further from the ranks of the genuine artisans while concomitantly increasing his dependence upon the opinions of others. In other words, while Gorgias is more content to masquerade as an expert, Polus would prefer to dance victoriously over the genuine arts and be seen as their powerful master and commander.[35]

While Gorgias's tendency towards nihilism does not go beyond the position that it is *as if* nothing existed, Polus is willing to explicitly affirm that all images of shame and morality are creations of power. In other words, while Gorgias does not dispute the validity of the sciences but believes that, since they lack the power to persuade the uneducated, artificial truths must invisibly hold communities of persuasion together within nature, Polus's view suggests that the inherent weakness of human nature makes it possible and necessary that rhetorical power should to rule openly over man, nature, and the arts. The sad words spoken by the twentieth century's only unrivaled hegemon come to mind: "Because I could." The Will to Power extorts a terrible ransom of *ananke* from those not prepared to wield it prudently.

Now that his challenger has further exposed himself, Socrates sets out to demonstrate why the production of gratification is not sufficient to call

---

35 Voegelin harshly characterizes Polus as "a representative of the great reservoir of common men who paralyze every effort at order and supply mass-connivance in the rise of the tyrant" (pp. 26–27).

something an art. He asks Polus to gratify him by asking what kind of art cookery is and answers his own question by describing it as no art but an experience that produces pleasure and gratification. Even though it is not the same as rhetoric, they are both parts of the same pursuit. Socrates feigns reluctance to name this pursuit before Gorgias for fear of seeming to make satirical mockery (*diacomodein*) of it (here we are reminded of Aristophanes' comic mockery in the *Clouds* of what he supposed to be Socrates' art), but he does posit that it is not one of the nobler (*kalon*) things. It is only after Gorgias demands that Socrates speak without concern for *his* feelings – demonstrating a laudable preference for truth above appearance, which Polus might not share – that we hear what the Athenian is talking of. Rhetoric turns out to be a pursuit that is not artful but belongs to one who is shrewd, daring, and naturally suited for dealing cleverly with mankind. The chief point of it is flattery; cookery, rhetoric, cosmetics, and sophistry are its parts, each devoted to a different type of business.

As Socrates gives an account of what rhetoric is, it should be seen that he also sets out to educate Polus (and indirectly Gorgias) in how "what is" questions should properly be asked and ordered. His chiding words thus constitute therapeutic punishment, administered by a genuine practitioner of *diaresis*, for the imprecise way in which both rhetoricians set about describing their so-called art. He now suggests that Polus ask him what kind of flattery before they get around to discussing whether it is a fine (*kalon*) or shameful/perverse (*aiskron*) thing. In other words, moral judgments cannot be based on something's appearance or our desire; they should instead come out of an understanding of its nature. Gratification or gratuitous charity (*caritos*) should not overthrow the sovereignty of objective truth.

Socrates further tells Polus that rhetoric is a counterfeit or simulacrum (*eidolon*) of politics. When Polus again asks whether it is fine or base, Socrates answers that it is base because he "calls all that is bad (*kakon*) base," but reproves Polus for jumping the gun again and looking for an expression of admiration or disgust before ascertaining what rhetoric was. This is but another version, enacted horizontally rather than vertically, of the famous question from the *Euthyphro*: is something holy because the gods love it or do the gods love it because it is holy? Surely to Socrates' disgust, Polus is clearly on Euthyphro's side of the question in preferring envy to knowledge. It is Gorgias who must intervene and ask the crucial question of Socrates: "What do you mean when you call rhetoric a semblance of a branch of the art of politics?" (463e). There is indeed a striking difference between Gorgias's intellectual curiosity, which saves him from the worst moral consequences of his art by leading him to voluntarily take his medicine, and Polus's single-minded interest in power and glory – qualities that would only deepen his alienation from himself were he not involuntarily subjected to Socratic punishment. The really difficult case of Callicles' invincible ignorance awaits us further along the road. The difference between the respective soul types or conditions of the three Socratic interlocutors in this dialogue is such that while Gorgias can be refuted privately, Polus's defeat must be publicly demonstrated to him for it to be educative, and Callicles can only be used to display before others the monstrous effects of psychic incorrigibility. In other words, while Gorgias resigns when his imminent defeat is clear to him, the less acute Polus must be checkmated, and Callicles refuses to play by the laws of Chess.

The introduction of the soul as a standard for assessing human conduct is justified within the *Gorgias* when, in expounding on the connection between rhetoric and politics, Socrates' statement that his reply is based upon the existence of body and soul is readily accepted by the sophist. He then gains Gorgias's further agreement that both of these have a state of health and that the body can also have an unreal appearance of health – that which only a doctor or trainer can see through (464a). Socrates now posits that there is also a state of soul that gives the false appearance of health without the signified reality. When Gorgias again agrees, Socrates launches into a lengthy speech that concludes the first quarter of the dialogue. This division seems to be appropriate because the next part of the dialogue, which ends with Callicles' incredulous intrusion into the conversation between Socrates and Polus, sees no further interventions by Gorgias. After Socrates has rendered a fully detailed account of what rhetoric is to Gorgias and Polus, the latter – who has little to no interest in this question – takes Socrates on with regard to the effects accruing from rhetoric. As we suggested earlier, he takes a pragmatic and instrumental view of his chosen profession. His transparent concern is not with the activity of rhetorical virtuosity, but with the power and glory that it brings to the one who wields this invincible tool.

Concluding his theoretical account of rhetoric for Gorgias's sake, Socrates proceeds to provide a comprehensive classification of the true and false arts of the body and soul in sickness and in health. According to him while politics primarily pertains to the soul, the many arts pertaining to the welfare of the human body do not have a single name – though they fall under the two basic categories of gymnastics/training and medicine. The political or psychic equivalents of these two bodily arts are legislation and justice. These too relate to the maintenance of good health and the overcoming of disease in the human soul by the body politic. Socrates states that these four arts: gymnastics/training, medicine, legislation, and justice are concerned with the "highest welfare of body and soul" (465c). It is worth noting a fundamental assumption smuggled in here by Socrates that seems to fly in the face of a literal reading of the *Republic*: the assumption that the polis exists for the sake of the soul and not vice versa. The importance of the role played by the soul will become increasingly evident as the dramatic action of the *Gorgias* unfolds.

The view that the apparent is the real, the equivalent of Rousseau's distinction between *amour de soi* and *amour propre*,[36] is the essence of rhetoric and sophistry. This is why four counterfeit arts develop to shadow the genuine arts pertaining to body and soul just listed. Possibly thinking of the *empeiria* referred to earlier, Socrates tellingly comments: "the pseudo-arts are instinctively aware of the division of function without any accurate knowledge" (464c). They function through mimetic cunning, rather than by rational thought, and divide into four pseudo arts. Each pretends to be the art it impersonates; each addresses genuine human needs that it seduces, and gives no care for what is best but concerns itself with catching fools and hunting after pleasure and immediate gratification. These false arts are cookery, cosmetics, sophistry, and rhetoric.

Socrates states that each of these four flatteries pretends to know what is best on the basis of gratification rather than a reasoned account or *logos* of the things it deals with. He calls them shameful and disgraceful pursuits because "they guess at the pleasant without concern or regard for what is best" (465a). Consequently, the flatteries can neither understand nor give a reasoned account of its activities but gain success and popularity through manipulation of base emotions. This is why he refuses to call any of these pursuits an art. Socrates also strikingly describes how the cosmetic perversion will undermine the gymnastic art, ignobly deceiving by shapes, colors, texture, and dress to create an appearance of beauty that ignores and discredits the natural beauty stemming from disciplined training. This means that a pastry cook will defeat a doctor over contests about medicine in an infantilized community where everyone: whether doctor, cook, or customer will die of disease and/or neglect. Even though Callicles will soon complain that Socrates has described an upside down world, it is very necessary that we recognize the truly absurd priorities created when appearance is set above reason and reality. Indeed, to the extent that reputation must be valued above appearance (*doksa*), as Gorgias's own words recommended, it is possible to see how even phantasms created with the most benevolent of intentions supplant natural phenomena and blind us to reality.

Socrates himself tellingly uses geometrical terms to describe the perverse ratios that the false knacks bear to the true arts. We are reminded of the divided line in the *Republic* where the crucial distinction was made between reasoning back to causes or towards the production of effects. The one way led out of the cave, while the other generated shadows on the wall that imprisoned both the prisoner and the deluded virtuoso creating his opera of phantasms.

36   Rousseau, *Discourse on Inequality*, footnote 'O.'

While recognizing the difference between the pseudo-arts of the orator and sophist, concerned with judicial defense and legislative projects respectively (although the demagogic techniques were very similar), Socrates observed that they could barely tell each other apart; both activities were different fields for the same predatory goal of profit from lies and ignorance. He draws a helpful analogy between cookery and medicine: their two skills would be hopelessly confused with each other if the soul were separated from the body, or dissolved into it and forced to judge health by the criterion of anticipated immediate pleasure in a Hades-like state. Given this condition, a sort of Anaxagorean chaos would exist; all things would be in each other without rhyme, reason, or order (465d). Eventually even the distinction between body and soul would be lost. The conclusion drawn from this reductive absurdity is that *Nous* cannot be known by efficient causality and cynical casuistry.

In the case of these four flatteries, who can tell the dancer from the dunce, or the knave from the fool? Socrates is clearly suggesting that the four counterfeit knacks are parasitic privations rather than genuine arts, but it is striking that they dupe both the practitioner and the victim – albeit in different ways. Although the *Gorgias* is not the *Sophist* or *Statesman*, this dialogue will be incomplete without at least an implicit account of the permanent propensities in body and soul to be susceptible to these vices – either as predator or victim. The absence of clear and definite knowledge, especially with regard to nature and the gods, is partly responsible for the prevalence and proliferation of flattery, but this being the case, how can we account for one man becoming a Socrates and another a Gorgias? Both men were both acutely aware of the absence of definite epistemic knowledge concerning the most important matters; however their responses could not have been more diametrically different. All these questions point us towards the soul and the foundational moral experiences constituting it. These matters will loom ever larger before us as the psychic drama of the *Gorgias* unfolds. Furthermore, historical matters and references will play an increasingly more prominent role in the remaining three-quarters of the dialogue as the social and moral consequences of the Peloponnesian War and the Sicilian Invasion combine with the intellectual corruption caused by rhetoric with disastrous effect. The all-important question of whether the human soul possesses adequate internal moral resilience to deal with cataclysmic external events must necessarily be confronted directly.

Chapter II: The Tyrant's Invitation

The second quarter of the *Gorgias* begins with Polus indignantly asking Socrates whether he thinks that rhetoric is but flattery. The older man's reply is critical of Polus's poor memory, "I said that it was a *part* of flattery; do you not remember at your age? What will you do later?" (466a). This suggests to us that Polus, who lacks Gorgias's ability to reflect on his mistakes, is about to receive a lesson that will be strikingly memorable and unflattering. His poor memory and impatience could also be related to the ambition and instrumental thinking that drive his career in rhetoric.[1] These qualities are of course clearly less important in a profession that is essentially opportunistic and itinerant. Nevertheless, even though Polus has significantly less interiority than Gorgias, he is clearly irked by the fact that Socrates evidently holds rhetoric in such contempt.

This is why Polus, undeterred, continues to press Socrates: "So good orators are regarded as base flatterers in the polis?" Socrates' response, asking him whether he has asked a question or begun a speech, point to the philosopher's own impatience with an interlocutor who asks questions that amount to little more than slogans or ejaculations. It seems that Polus, by sheer force of habit, continually seeks to short-circuit genuine propositions and turn them into self-evident tautologies. When Polus claims that he did ask a question, Socrates' quite dismissive reply: "it seems to me that they aren't thought of at all" (466b), also translatable as "they don't count for anything," both anticipates the idea that the sophist takes residence in non-being, and also suggests that rhetoric is inherently incapable of gaining the kind of recognition it seeks – the very acknowledgement that Polus wants of Socrates.

The whole purpose of rhetoric is to make the unlikely seem obvious and probable; paradoxically, just as was the case with Gorgias being able to defeat

---

1   In Stauffer's words, "Polus assumes as many do, that it is not hard to discern what is good." (p. 53).

experts, this means that a rhetorician can receive accolades for his originality and cleverness only by undoing his dazzling illusions and revealing the deceptions that he performed.[2] Likewise, a brilliant criminal defense lawyer gains *kudos* for an acquittal only when it is known that his client was actually guilty. We may well reflect on the storied career and artful stratagems of Themistocles at this point: were it not for the great deceptions that he performed at different times on the Athenians, Spartans, and Persians alike, the Persian Wars would have followed a very different course. Nevertheless, the fact remains that the hero of Salamis did not receive the prize for valor awarded by the allies, was ostracized and denounced as traitor and bribe-taker by the Athenians, and ended his life committing suicide while under the protection of his erstwhile enemy, the Great King of Persia.[3]

Socrates rejects Polus's view that rhetoricians have great power in the polis by means of a curious argument. He says that if by power Polus means something that is good for its possessor, then the orators have no power at all; indeed they turn out to be the least powerful in the polis (466b). It should always be noted that the word translated power, *dunamis*, means "potential" and is not considered something desirable in itself.[4] As any student of Aristotle knows, raw potential needs to be realized and actualized as *energeia*; otherwise happiness (*eudaimonia*) will not result. Polus is locked in a mindset that is quite curiously modern; the demagogic orator values power for its own sake because he cares more for his *amour propre*, his reputation in the eyes of others envying or fearing him, than for his own inner experience of joy at being at home in the world.

Polus now sets out, like Glaucon in the *Republic*, to proclaim the power that successful orators possess: like tyrants, they can kill whomever they want, confiscate property, and exile anyone they see fit (466b–c). Unlike Gorgias, who found satisfaction from his own ingenuity in exonerating Helen of Troy, Polus craves power in the real world; he would surely despise language games and imagined literary encounters such as the dialogue we are presently studying. Indeed, rhetoric itself would hold little attraction for Polus if it was purged of its pandering aspects and transformed into a philological pursuit devoid of political power.[5] It is clear that the only use for potentiality that Polus recognizes

2   Plutarch quotes Gorgias as discussing dramatic deceptions "in which the deceiver is more justly esteemed than the non-deceiver and the deceived is wiser than the undeceived." *The Older Sophists*, p. 65.
3   See Plutarch's life of Themistocles in his *Parallel Lives*.
4   Saxonhouse points out in a footnote that the word *dunamis* (used in the sense of power) is co-joined with rhetoric countless times over the first half of the *Gorgias*. p. 145.
5   Benardete observes that Polus "seems quite willing to sacrifice the rationality of

culminates in the gaining of unlimited power. Yet Socrates refuses to be impressed by the many powers listed by Polus. Swearing by the hybrid dog of the Egyptians (the patron of lost souls who seems to be invoked when a contradictory or aborted thought is exposed by him), Socrates likewise claims to be of two minds: wondering whether Polus is stating his own opinion on these matters or asking him (466c). The seeming self-evidence of rhetoric turns out to be completely dependent upon its audience; were Polus truly self-assured on these matters, he would not be so obsessed with impressing Socrates. Lacking self-sufficient happiness or fulfillment, even actualized power urgently craves recognition – either in the form of fear or envy. Polus's envy of the infinite craving of raw power is absurd; neediness and insecurity lead his soul to grotesquely invert and distort its natural desire for actual happiness.

Socrates points out that Polus is saying two things at once (466c). He is both rhetorically asking whether orators can exert tyrannical power to kill, despoil, and exile, and also asserting that persons in such positions have the greatest power. Socrates affirms the first question (which is but tautological) and denies the second proposition. He claims that tyrannical acts of this kind defeat the purposes inherent in human action itself: to desire and do what is best. "They do nothing . . . of what they intend (*boulontai*) although they certainly do what seems to be best" (466e). The word stem *boule* normally translated "wish" has overtones of deliberation that has nothing to do with fairy tales or coins in fountains. His meaning is best understood by reflecting on Jesus' words on the Cross: "Father, forgive them, they know not what they do."[6] When Polus stupidly asks or maybe asserts whether this ability (to do whatever seems best) is having great power, Socrates claims that Polus himself would not say so, pointing out that he himself earlier accepted that having great power is good for its owner. He makes Polus admit what Polemarchus learned at the Piraeus: that it is not a good thing, or great power, if one who lacks intelligence does what seems best to him (466e). If a capacity does not benefit its possessor, then it cannot be power because all power is for the good.[7] This is a *Modus Tollens* argument. We should note the strong sense of *telos* that comes into play at this stage in the *Gorgias*.

Socrates' wordplay seems to be employed to suggest that Polus's rhetorical ploy of making falsely self-evident statements ends up subverting itself by

rhetoric if he can retain its power. He knows that flatterers are despised and live from hand to mouth" (p. 33).

6　Luke 23:34.

7　In Benardete's words, "Socrates has Polus agree that power is something good for whoever has it, and it cannot be good if one senselessly does what one wills" (p. 39). Looking towards the end of the *Gorgias*, he suggestively points out that it makes no sense to perform tyrannical atrocities "for the hell of it" (p. 40).

going against the very grain of speech. By disguising a propositional statement as a tautology, and insisting that potentiality is actuality, he only destroys the very deliberative capacity essential to making something turn out for the best. Likewise, just as we suggested earlier that human speech contains within itself an implicit assurance that one is speaking the truth to another, Socrates is trying to show Polus that speech, the *logos*, also reflects this rational striving towards what is best. Anticipating the end (and *telos*) of the *Gorgias*, his point is that the power of speech isn't just an exploitable tool for rhetoric; rather, it is the ether binding both the human being[8] and the cosmos together.

This pedagogic and teleological trajectory becomes increasingly explicit as Socrates now reveals to an incredulous Polus that orators do not do what they wish (467b). When he is accused by Polus of making statements that are "shocking and monstrous" (467b), Socrates resumes the role of questioner and sets out to teach the younger man the meaning of truly purposeful human actions. Polus must be made to see the "shocking and monstrous" nature of the raw power he wishes to wield. While Polus has already admitted that persons lacking intelligence lack power or cannot use it well, he cannot extend this recognition to see that an orator's speech acts may also be ultimately driven by mimetic desire rather than deliberative rationality; the mere ability to deceive the ignorant cannot be equated with freedom or the knowledge of what is truly good. Polus tends to equate positivistic instrumental reason with rationality itself. While Socrates believes that the human good is more objective and accessible than could be allowed by Gorgias, who denied any meaningful connection between the sublunary web of words and hyper-uranian transcendent being – it remains to be seen how Polus can be made to share this awareness.

When Socrates, resuming the role of questioner, seeks his views on purposeful behavior, Polus readily agrees that many actions are undertaken for the sake of ends that are higher than the act itself. Socrates now divides everything into three classes: good, bad, and neither good nor bad.[9] Polus admits that wisdom, health, and wealth are good and their opposites bad (467e). (Socrates probably includes wealth among the good things to hasten Polus along the way; if pressed, he could use his earlier argument about power and claim that one lacking the ability to use it well is not wealthy.) Polus then agrees that

---

8   Benardete reminds us that Socrates' four-fold division does not include a power that unifies the psychic and physical aspects of man. "The absence of a name for a comprehensive art of soul and body puts in doubt the apparent theme of the *Republic*, that a true city, in which the arts are geared to satisfy the needs of the body can be put together seamlessly with the city in which the philosopher is king" (pp. 33–34).

9   He exactly follows Glaucon's tripartite classification of human actions in Book II of the *Republic*.

things neither good nor bad in themselves may participate or share (*metaxei*) in the good or bad and at other times share in neither. He also grants that these in-between things, whether actions or objects, are sought for the sake of the good things (468b).

As a result of these admissions, Polus is led to see that the various actions he previously admired – killing, exiling and confiscation – fall in this in-between category of deeds that should only be performed when they are beneficial and not when they are harmful. He also concedes that one who does these deeds mistakenly, wrongly thinking that they will bring him benefit, does not do what he wishes or intends. It also follows according to the previous argument that such a person who performs these deeds does not have great power in a polis. This bears out the truth of Socrates' earlier hotly contested claim that it is possible for a human being (*anthropos*) who does in the polis what seems good to him, to not possess great power or to do what he wishes. The power to command oneself is a necessary condition for the successful use of power over others. As we noted earlier with Gorgias, power should not be purchased at the cost of self-knowledge; the seductive dream of being anything I want to be also involves the risk of losing my own soul.

But there is another serious practical issue that Socrates does not seem to have dealt with here. The philosopher has described an ideal situation where reasoned deliberation rules over the passions. In such a world, philosophers would rule and orators could only be animal trainers. In the real world, with humans as they are, things couldn't be more different. Here, while the most violent claims made by the senses are as self-evident as tautologies, rigorous proofs of the sort that Socrates has just made are highly unreliable and viewed as impractical assertions or drooling ejaculations by men of sound practical sense. It is against this background that Polus, who is clearly describing his own moral state, asks Socrates not to talk as if *he* would not welcome the opportunity of doing good in the polis or not experience envy when he saw others killing or imprisoning their enemies, and confiscating property as it pleased them (468e). Indeed, we might even note that it could even be said to follow from Socrates' own argument that if wealth was a good thing in itself that it should be acquired, especially through ridding the polis of bad people. The best way to reach the rational state Socrates has described would be by killing, punishing, or enslaving those who would disrupt its order and tranquility. Cutting to the chase, Polus finds it self-evident that Socrates would deliberately choose to be of the Guardian class in the *Republic*.

Socrates' response is to ask Polus whether these acts were performed justly or unjustly. When told that it did not matter either way, he urges Polus to be quiet and tells him that one should not envy the unenviable or the wretched but only pity them (469a). When Polus incredulously asks him how on earth someone could be wretched and pitiable when he was free to kill justly whenever it seemed good to them, Socrates replies "No, not me, but I wouldn't call him enviable" (469a). He explains that while one who kills wrongfully is both pitiable and miserable, even one who kills rightly should not be envied (469b). When Polus sarcastically interjects to suggest that surely one who is wrongfully put to death is pitiable and miserable, Socrates makes the further claim that such a person would be less miserable than either the man who kills him or the man who is justly put to death. This is because "doing injustice is the greatest evil" (469b).

This Socratic axiom, which would later become a basic tenet of Christian morality, is again met with incredulity by Polus: "Surely it is worse to suffer evil?" but Socrates replies that while he would prefer to avoid both fates, if forced to choose he would rather suffer evil than perform evil actions (469b). The two men are clearly on very different wavelengths because Polus's next question "Then you wouldn't want to be a tyrant?"[10] is every bit as absurd to Socrates as it is self-evident to Polus – who obligingly provides us with a definition of this value-laden term. A tyrant according to him is "one who can do anything he wants in the state, killing, exiling and getting his own way in all matters" (469c). Polus provides us with a stronger definition of this term than was customary, since the term "tyrant" was commonly taken to simply mean "non-hereditary ruler" and thus may not necessarily come with all the violent connotations given it by Polus and repeated in more modern contexts. Polus is obviously thinking about someone set on using all of the power vested in a tyrant to support all of his needs, desires, and appetites.[11]

Here Socrates again tries to rescue Polus from his dangerous fantasies by offering the example of a man with a dagger up his sleeve who, walking into a crowded market square and taking pride in his power, could kill anyone or do damage to their clothing (469c–d). But surely such a person is not equivalent to a tyrant? Perhaps Socrates' deeper point is that purely destructive power is hardly very attractive or useful – especially when regarded from the standpoint of his earlier articulated view that power should be sought for things good in themselves. Polus, however, simply points out that the man with the dagger is not comparable to a tyrant because he is likely to be punished after performing his bad deed. Socrates is content to introduce the theme of punishment here and asks Polus whether being punished is an evil, suggesting perhaps too easily, though with deeper dialectical intent, that bad acts are punished and consequently not beneficial. He then asks Polus to articulate the

---

10   Cf. Thucydides, *Peloponnesian War*, I. 5.
11   Friedlander points out that while Socrates speaks of a demagogic orator, Polus has a real tyrant in mind. This suggests to him that Plato "wants us to see the unmistakable connection between the two types" (p. 255).

criterion, or draw the line, between when it is and is not better to perform actions of the kind mentioned earlier: killing, banishing, and dispossessing. Despite Socrates' claim that deeds of this kind are better when they are right and worse when they are wrong, thus repeating his earlier standard of moral teleology, Polus responds that while Socrates is usually a hard man to argue with, in this instance even a child could prove him wrong (470c). Clearly Polus believes, along with Thrasymachus of the *Republic I*, that it is only a poor and petty kind of lawbreaker who bows down to the law or is broken by it; the truly successful wrongdoer will break the law with impunity and even frame legislation that will exclusively promote his personal interests.[12]

Polus's example of Archelaus the King of Macedon is a particularly striking contemporary example of a powerful and successful tyrant who ascended to the throne after performing acts of great brutality against his own flesh and blood and soul. Although the *Gorgias,* or more pertinently Polus, only mentions the most unattractive features of his fourteen-year reign, the full story of this remarkable man's life would have been well known at the time. Indeed, for political reasons these less-than-attractive qualities may well have been downplayed or ignored in Athens itself. Polus could also be suggesting that the friendship of Archelaus, perhaps the Athenians' most valuable ally in the later years of the Peloponnesian War, was sought by them purely on urgently utilitarian grounds utterly separated from moral considerations. The massive task of replacing the hundreds of ships lost after the disastrous expedition to Syracuse was only possible because Archelaus placed the vast Macedonian forests at the disposal of the Athenians. Were it not for Archelaus, the Spartans and Persians would have triumphed ten years sooner; this ironically resembles the benefit conferred by Socrates' alter-ego Diotima – who postponed the plague ten years. In recognition of his great assistance to them, Athens gratefully declared this former slave and multiple-murderer, along with his children, to be *Proxenos* and *Euergetes* of the people.

Yet the picture is even more complex, for Archelaus was a very successful ruler who instituted many internal reforms, building strongholds and roads while also improving the organization of the cavalry and hoplite infantry. He also reorganized the Olympia, a religious festival with musical and athletic competitions held in Macedon. The greatest athletes and artists of Greece came to this; perhaps Gorgias and Polus also attended. Archelaus was also a great cultural patron. In Pella, his new capital, he hosted poets, tragedians, including Agathon and Euripides (who wrote some of his greatest plays in Macedon), musicians,

---

12 Benardete suggests that while Polus boasts of the power of rhetoric to acquire power, he does not seem to have a *logos* to govern its proper use once gained. "Polus lost himself in the example of tyranny, but he cannot imagine tyranny except from the outside" (p. 39).

painters, including the most celebrated painter of his time, Zeuxis, and perhaps even Thucydides.[13] Only Socrates declined an invitation to visit or relocate to what Aristophanes wistfully called "The Fleshpots of Happy-Land."[14]

Exiled Thucydides credited Archelaus with doing more for his kingdom than all his predecessors together.[15] Archelaus seems to be the model of the kind of enlightened despotism that Polus finds so irresistible that he cannot believe Socrates' disavowals of ambition. Archelaus was killed in 399 by a beloved page – who had been promised one of his lover's daughters in marriage. When the King reneged, the enraged boy killed him while they were hunting. By this time Macedon was a much stronger power, well on the way to becoming the political juggernaut that would crush both Athenian democracy and Greek liberty itself just ten years after Plato's death. The fact that both Socrates and Archelaus were both killed in 399, albeit under very different circumstances, is a suggestive coincidence. Their lives and deaths stand strikingly juxtaposed; together the two seem to represent an unflattering contrast between a just and unjust human life. While Socrates didn't cultivate the muses, Archelaus spared no effort in this direction. Strikingly, another Archelaus (a natural scientist) was reputedly Socrates' first teacher[16] – literally his *arche*, or origin.

When Polus asks Socrates if he thought that Archelaus was happy or miserable (470d), the young orator is clearly making another of those supposedly tautological proclamations observed earlier. It is self-evident to Polus that Archelaus is supremely happy. Socrates' reply, "I don't know, for I have not been with the man" (470d), delicately reminds us of the declined invitation to Pella and also draws attention to the great mimetic attraction that Archelaus exerts on Polus. Indeed Polus's long catalog of Archelaus's sins only seems to highlight their incongruity in comparison to a state of almost divine bliss that our aforementioned Athenian schoolboy would have assumed and found unnecessary to list; we are not being asked to consider an uneasy Macbeth-like tyrant here! His only rival seems to be the Great King of Persia. We see another distorted representation of the idea of the philosopher-king here, the very idea that reputedly thrice led Plato to Syracuse. The intoxicating dream of setting up a just and beautiful regime can never be discounted.[17]

13 See Dodds, pp. 241–42.
14 Aristophanes, *Frogs*, 85. The felicitous phrase is quoted by Dodds.
15 Thucydides, *Peloponnesian War*, II. 100.
16 Diogenes Laertius, *Lives of the Philosophers*, II.23. Since this Archelaus was also Anaxagoras's student, Plato could be playfully suggesting a process evolving from the Anaxagorean chaos caused by Gorgias that was described earlier (465d). In other words, Archelaus is to Anaxagoras what Polus is to Gorgias.
17 This perennial temptation is exhaustively studied in Stanley Rosen's *Plato's Republic* (Yale, 2005).

To Polus's way of thinking, the interior (the intellect) is a calculating infra-structure that exists purely for the greater glories of one's image and passions. Likewise, private secret vices can claim to only exist for and/or are justified by the public benefit or virtue that they provide. So the murky murderous origins of Archelaus's life either do not matter or could even serve to highlight the benefit he brought upon Macedon. Even his scandalous death could be spun so as to suggest that he did the right thing by his children, even at the cost of his own life, and left behind a strong expansionist Macedonian monarchy. This outlook fits in well with the denial of any afterlife; all that remains is a glori-ous reputation. Indeed a quick death like Archelaus's is not inconsistent with his Achilles-like outlook. It protects him from a reflective old age – a Cephalus-like state in which his powers of thought and potential for fear would exceed his ability to enjoy pleasure.

It must also be seen that the well-known connection between poet and tyrant is both exemplified and explained upon consideration of the life of Archelaus. By hosting the great poets of Greece, including Euripides – who even wrote a play titled *Archelaus* about his Patron's namesake – and thereby corrupting the very persons who would tell the story, the tyrant did all he could to ensure that his legacy was spun to the best extent possible. Such a man then controls or corrupts the very sources of poetic inspiration – though the fact that posterity didn't preserve Euripides' *Archelaus* suggests that it was neither inspired nor good! Producing uninspired but effective poetry on call is clearly the very province of the practitioner of rhetoric who, like Machiavelli's Prince, trusts in his own arms and dependents and does not depend on providence, for-tune, or muse. This makes the court laureate or public orator very much like the tyrant whose praises he will sing. The bond will be long and fruitful because their interests will coincide and not enter into conflict. Speech and deed will follow parallel paths of glory, continually saying "after you" to each other.

Lacking certain knowledge persons prefer the mythic account of reality sustaining their given reality and gloriously justifying the life they have cho-sen, willy-nilly, to accept. Pusillanimous Stoics turn out to be good reliable slaves and excellent sycophantic orators. By this token, Virgil was a better Stoic than Epictetus, Seneca, or even Marcus Aurelius. It is quite possible, and even desirable, to have and create a Stoic philosophy of history while leading an Epicurean lifestyle. Man may be a rational animal but poets of this kind become rationalizing animals *par excellence* when they are bought and sold. For self-evident proof of this rough judgment we just need to visualize Polus, salivating at the prospect of being forced to serve as Archelaus's court orator.

Yet Socrates sticks to his guns and even seems surprised that Polus believes that his view, that unjust behavior is not beneficial, was refuted by the story of Archelaus. When Polus accuses him of stubbornness: "You do not want to [agree] since you see what I say" (471e), appealing to the "self-evidence" of conventional opinion regarding unjust Archelaus's irresistibly enviable power,[18] Socrates calmly replies that proofs of this kind fail to move him. Unimpressed by the demagogic rhetoric used in the Athenian law courts, where witnesses are lined up to refute and intimidate one who would speak truly, he readily admits that most Athenians will take Polus's side. Still he, "being one man," will not agree. "For you do not compel me by reasons. Instead, by providing many false witnesses against me, you are trying to expel me from my rightful substance, the truth" (472b). He refuses to be evicted from himself by an army of echoes and shadows.

This Archimedean Point of personal integrity represents an understated reference to what is surely *terra incognita* to Polus: the human soul. To anyone ruled by the dual exigencies of heteronomous opinion and physical survival, Socrates' conduct at various notable points in his career surely seems as inexplicable as it is foolish. However, the sheer brute fact of his individual power to stand up to seemingly irresistible mimetic and instinctual pressure exerted by both his body and the many suggests that he is ruled by forces other than those famous sinews and bones that would otherwise have fled readily from the sentence of death passed on it. The point is of no little importance, especially in our own troubled times. While many of those implicated in the atrocities of human history, ranging from the Peloponnesian War to the Holocaust, not insincerely claimed that they were unable to resist their evil rulers – who exercised imperatival power over their banal habits and unreflectively law-abiding behavior – the rulers themselves turned out to be no better than survivors in a kill-or-be-killed world. Socrates however seems to have found within himself the authority to silence, override, and resist this coercive force of *ananke* itself.[19] In other words, while Polus regards the soul egotistically as a power capable of triumphing in the shadow games played out on the wall of the cave, Socrates' soul exists in another dimension of reality – one where moral principles are not created by necessity but rather guide the actions of free men.

Back in our text, Socrates states that nothing worthwhile will have been accomplished unless one of them, either Polus or himself, gains the other's assent *qua* rational individual and bears witness to his truth, bidding those sycophants and demagogic procedures good riddance. He adds that the matters

18 Friedlander says, "Polus cannot see what difference right and wrong can possibly make and must regard with, astonishment, the radical Socratic rejection of 'the tyrannical ideal' as incredibly paradoxical" (p. 255).

19 For a penetrative account of this power, see Hannah Arendt's discussion of Socrates in *Responsibility and Judgment* (Schocken Books, 2003), pp. 82–97.

which the two of them disagree over are not unimportant but rather the things that are best to know and most shameful to ignore: it is the question of who is and isn't happy (472c). Here it is clear that the question of method has everything to do with the answer itself. Is the matter to be resolved by power of opinion and rhetoric, or by the actuality of reasons and dialectic? Which principle should rule the human person? In an important sense, Socrates is arguing that the integrity of the individual person can and must withstand the external pressures exerted by a multitude not composed of genuine "ones."[20] As we shall see, it will also follows that true happiness is not gained by fashioning one's own reputation and then sharing in the external evidence of popular opinion that one is happy. Rather, it comes from the pursuit of benevolent actions in the world that reveal its goodness and consolidate the doer's awareness of his integrity.

We must remember that both Polus and Socrates are marshalling self-evident states against each other. Polus is claiming that the splendid phenomenon of a life such as that led by Archelaus naturally and rightly evokes feelings of envy and/or sycophancy – thus leading to an immediate emotional self-evidence that reason can only pander to and serve in an instrumental capacity. Yet, Socrates is of the equally firm view, presumably from his own internalized experience of happiness, that *eudaimonia* has everything to do with the flourishing of one's personal integrity – a blessed state that renders its possessor immune to the slingers of envy and the archers of desire.

Socrates now proceeds to summarize the basis of his disagreement with Polus: the young orator believes that it is possible for a wicked wrongdoer to be in a state of *eudaimonia*, putting Archelaus forward as an example of such a life (472d). Socrates himself however believes that such a condition is impossible. As an even more anachronistic illustration of his view, *contra Archelaus*, we may use Dante's striking tale from the *Inferno*. Here, in the third ring of the ninth and lowest circle, the once ambitious poet learns of sins of betrayal so terrible that, upon their perpetration, the soul of the malefactor is sent straight to Hell, and an evil *demon* (the opposite of *eu-daimon*) takes over the damned man's body for the rest of his life.[21]

According to Polus, the doer of injustice will be happy if he does not meet with just punishment and retribution, since these will make him wretched. Socrates counters this with the claim that while one who does injustice and is unjust is wretched, "He will be more wretched if he fails to pay the just penalty or meet with retribution and less wretched if he pays the just penalty and

---

20   *Ibid.* p. 103. Also see my review essay of "Responsibility and Judgment" in *Society* vol. 42 (2) pp. 87–90.
21   Dante, *Divine Comedy*: Inferno. Canto 33.124–27.

meets with just judgment from gods and men" (472e). It is well worth noting that Socrates does not claim that unjust or excessive punishment is good; it would not be good for a minor offender to be delivered into the hands of sadistic and vicious judges. We may well contrast the strikingly different manners in which Jesus and Socrates were executed. It is also significant that Socrates viewed the relatively mild manner of his death as a sign of great divine favor.

When Polus claims that Socrates is trying to say strange (*atopos*, literally out of place) things (473a), implying that they go against the very nature of speech, as he understands it; Socrates promises that out of friendship he will try to make Polus himself say these very things to him, presumably after a maieutic process producing self-knowledge. When asked further if he can discredit or expose (*elegxo*) Socrates' position, Polus sarcastically claims that this will be even harder to overturn than the older man's previous outlandish or unrealistic statements – concerning evil and tyranny. However, Socrates serenely assures him that what is true can never be refuted (473b). From the philosopher's perspective it can be said that it is Polus who is *a-topos*; the young man is ruled by many irrational desires that take him out of himself and invert the true order of his soul. We should note that while Polus granted the existence of the soul, he sees it as the locus of his *amour propre*. This view, of soul as a shame-center, will be dialectically refined and interiorized by Socrates. Contrariwise, Callicles will be seen to view the soul as a pleasure-center.

What is self-evident to a rightly ordered soul could not be expected to coincide with what is seen from the standpoint of a psychic regime twisted and contorted by ignorance and passion. This is why Polus once again summons up all of his rhetorical power to depict a man caught plotting unjustly to set himself up as tyrant. He is tortured, castrated, blinded, mutilated, compelled to witness the sufferings of his family, and then finally painfully executed. He asks Socrates how on earth it could be said that this man would not be happier if he succeeded in setting up a tyranny and spent his life doing whatever he wished – envied by citizens and aliens alike for his happiness (473b–d). Before proceeding, we should note that Polus does not bring up the case of one trying to set up a *just* tyranny – understood in the customary value-neutral sense. Although Polus could not be said to believe in an objectively just autocratic regime, preferring instead to admire a tyranny like that of Archelaus which would bring material benefits to its subjects, it is significant that nothing along the draconian lines of the *Republic* is championed by Socrates here.

Instead, responding to the scenario that pitted successful and unsuccessful outcomes of unjust power-grabs, Socrates accuses Polus of trying to frighten him with a horror story this time, instead of appealing to a mob of false witnesses. He responds to this pair of contrasting visions, similar in its gruesome details to those drawn by Glaucon in *Republic II* of the perfectly just and unjust lives, by singling out the important way in which the victim of injustice described by Glaucon differs from the picture painted by Polus. It could be said that the lengthier work was necessary because Glaucon described a circumstance that was fundamentally unnatural: a good and just man without friends. Here, after getting Polus to confirm that he said that the man just pictured was *unjustly* trying to set up a tyranny, it is much easier for Socrates to claim that then surely neither one of them would be happy. However, he goes to state that one who succeeded in setting up a tyranny would actually be the unhappier of the two (473d).

Polus, who claims to find this claim laughable, in keeping with Gorgias's dictum that one should fight tragedy with comedy and vice versa,[22] then responds to Socrates' saying that laughter isn't refutation by telling him that he is making such outlandish claims that no man could assert. However, his appeal to the gathering present is cut short by Socrates' reversion to his earlier distinction between appealing to public sentiment and making a rational argument. Socrates confesses he does not know how to call for a vote from the many. He is pointedly referring to the notorious and illegal collective trial of the victorious Athenian commanders at Arginusae when furious demagoguery overrode both the law and the best interests of the Athenians to deprive them of their last crop of good generals. Then Socrates courageously but unsuccessfully tried to stop the proceedings when he was the officer presiding over the Athenian Council.[23]

Decisively squelching Polus's appeal to demotic common sense and laughter by providing this shocking example of the folly of the many, Socrates claims that the clear thought of one man is superior to thoughtless popular sentiment. His words are directed to one man: Polus; he cares not for what others think for he is not talking to them. This suggests that his proof is purely for Polus's soul and that other persons, at other places and times, must find their own proofs for themselves. Socrates now claims that even Polus and the rest of humanity share his belief that doing injustice is worse than suffering it, and that evading a just penalty is worse than accepting it (474b).

It requires little effort to see that this counter-conventional assertion appears to be patterned after Socrates' earlier claim that those who ignorantly seek to exile, pillage, and kill do not do what they truly wish. Once again, Socrates tries to set the true purpose of the *logos* itself, conversation and self-knowledge, against envy-ridden and superficial manipulative speech which corrupts both the speaker and his audience. He places punishment on the side

22   "An opposition's seriousness is to be demolished by laughter, and laughter by seriousness." See Aristotle *Rhetoric* III. 18, 1419b3
23   See Kagan, *The Peloponnesian War* (Viking, 2003), pp. 461–66.

of just speech, and shows how apologetic casuistry is in the opposite camp of unjust speech. While just speech is placed in the service of asking the hard questions that make genuine personal growth possible, unjust speech tries to conform reality to prefabricated answers that make one appear most worthy of envy to those who don't and could never know him. Unjust speech is addressed to everybody and no man. By rejecting the *ad hominem* character of just speech, rhetoric tempts the individual to hide from himself in non-being – a state made of false images and ephemeral pleasures.

Socrates is now told by Polus that nobody, not even Socrates himself would prefer suffering injustice to acting unjustly: "Not you, nor I nor anyone else" (474b). We may infer that the rhetorician prefers to believe that what today is called "the wisdom of the body" would and should override abstract ethical prohibitions – once faced with the self-evident prospect of bodily pain. Even though Socrates' acceptance of his death penalty was the ultimate proof of his ability to rule *his* body, the rest of humanity must somehow be brought over to the same side also. Socrates must at least get them to the point where they would concede that it is he who occupies the high ground in this matter, even if incontinence prevents them from following his example.

While Polus believes that it is worse to suffer injustice than to inflict it, he grants that it is more shameful or ugly (*aiskion*) to do injustice than to suffer it (474c). This allows Socrates to point out the curious fact that that Polus does not consider the fine and beneficial or the ugly and painful to be one, as one would normally expect. This split reveals much about Polus's character; despite his selfishness and "realism" he still recognizes the disjunction between conventional opinion and authoritative judgments about what is noble/fine (*kalon*) or ugly/shameful (*aiskion*). Somehow, this young man's sense of shame extends beyond easily manipulated popular opinion. This is why he finds the case of Archelaus to be evocative of both disgust and admiration. The King of Macedon was by some mysterious alchemy able to use shameful and ugly deeds to turn a backward and almost barbaric kingdom into a flourishing and powerful nation.

The line between good and evil that runs through everyone now generates dissonant responses from the two halves of Polus's soul. This is how Socrates now gains Polus's agreement to the proposition that things (bodies, colors, shapes, sounds, etc.) cannot be said to be noble/fine without some sufficient reason or standard that would either have to do with the benefit (*opheleo*) or the pleasure (*hedone*) that they bring. Next, with Polus's enthusiastic approval, "Your use of this principle is fine, Socrates," the same principle is applied to laws, observances, and the various *mathema* or sciences (475a). It also follows that what is ugly or shameful is so with reference to the opposite standard of pain/sorrow or evil (475c).

The attention of Polus is now directed to their earlier agreed-upon distinction between what was shameful and bad: while suffering wrong was bad, doing wrong was more shameful. It follows then that if doing wrong is more shameful than suffering it, this greater shamefulness must derive either from greater pain, evil, or a combination of the two. Since it is very clear that doing something shameful is not more painful, it can only be so because it is more evil (475c). This turns out to be the reason why doing injustice is worse than suffering it.

Polus is now urged to be manly and take his medicine as he would from a doctor; he must admit that doing injustice is worse than suffering it (475d–e). So far however this defeat of Polus has been purely at the level of words. He has been shamed, but the basis for this shame has not been explained at all. While we have seen that Polus is ruled by shame, and will not *admit* to doing what is shameful, this does not mean that the necessities of the body will not lead him to do what is shameful in secret. Coming into possession of something like the Ring of Gyges would diametrically change Polus's behavior; he would no longer be restrained from injustice by the fear of being shamed. So far all that Socrates has done is to make the weaker argument stronger in speech. Expertly using shame, he has forced Polus to testify against himself and denounce his desires, however this does not mean that the sophist will not emulate Leontes in the *Republic* and let his wretched desires rule his incontinent will and govern his deeds. This would make him both a miscreant and a hypocrite! Polus's very responses over the course of this argument: "So it appears," "It seems that way," maintain this invisible barrier between speech and deed (475d–e).[24] We have also seen that Gorgias privileges reputation over appearance. This means that mimetic corruption can and does overwhelm the innocence of contemplative awareness.

Accordingly, Socrates ought to somehow show Polus, and his desires, why they should not do what is shameful – even if there is no risk of their being shamed and exposed to public ridicule or dishonor. This inner self, that which has been moved by the just *logos* to denounce what is shameful, must be given reasons to speak out against the self-evidently unjust *logos* of his still shameless body. He must know why what is shameful and bad, is bad *for him*. But before this happens, the identity of this self that is willing to undemocratically testify against its hitherto sovereign desires must be gradually revealed.[25] All these questions must be answered before Socrates' *logos* can be existentially, as

---

24 Stauffer, p. 75.
25 Stauffer sees Socrates suggesting that "*nearly everyone* is of two minds about justice: if beneath ordinary justice there lurk grave doubts about whether it is always wise to be just, there also lurks, beneath these doubts, a deeper belief in the goodness of justice" (p. 66).

opposed to polemically, successful. We shall see how he prepares the way for these concerns by evoking the appropriate moral and psychic phenomena.

The next phase of the argument explores the question of punishment. This follows logically since Polus's body is happiest when it avoids punishment altogether, even though this brings it into conflict with the standard of what is *kalon*. Socrates secures Polus's agreement that all things that are just are fine (476b). Polus is still speaking, more on behalf of his ambitions than for himself, from the sublime vantage of the fine, even though this is in conflict with what is bad for him by virtue of its association with what is unjust. It was in this pseudo-transcendental spirit that Hegel claimed that what is tragic for man appears comic from the standpoint of the gods.[26] Likewise, from Polus's standpoint, the superior tyrant will regard the tragic human inability to know truth as comic because one like Archelaus is able to create truth, on the slaughter-bench of morality, out of all-too-human sufferings and vices. Socrates however tries to establish a geometrically symmetrical relationship between the macrocosm and the microcosm: ruler and ruled. This will bring the soul into greater prominence as the very principle bridging the gap between the respective interests of the body and the cosmos. The seemingly tragic disjunctions between man and nature or the individual and the community are not upheld as the ultimate constants of reality.

Polus is now brought abruptly back into his body as Socrates discusses the case of beating. If something beats justly, then it follows that what is beaten is beaten justly (476e–477a). Of course the commutative symmetry of this claim is only truly verified when we find that the beating is just from the standpoint of what Aristotle called the ultimate particular[27] – the individual beaten; the goal of punishment should be the betterment of the criminal's soul. Sadistic punishments do not satisfy these rigorous criteria – which anticipate Kant in not allowing human beings to be used as means, but only as ends in themselves.[28] Otherwise abstractly imposed justice could turn out to be no more than revenge. Any punishment caused solely by a furious desire for vengeance is only likely to breed more spiritual disorder and long-term violence.

Recognizing this symmetry in the just imposition of punishment, Polus now agrees that he who pays the just penalty has something fine done to him and suffers good things (477a). This is consistent with Socrates' earlier classification of justice as what restores the unhealthy soul to its proper condition. It follows that one who is subjected to just punishment is released from badness of soul. This is described as the greatest evil by Socrates; he then goes on

26 See Hegel, *Phenomenology of Spirit*, #731.
27 Aristotle, *Nicomachean Ethics*, VI. 1142a8.
28 Kant, *Groundwork of the Metaphysics of Morals*, vol. IV, p. 428 of Akademie Edition.

to name the two other kinds of human evil: those pertaining to one's possessions and to one's body. While poverty exhausts the first kind of evil, having
to do with one's property or equipment; such things as debility, disease, and
ugliness pertain to bodily evils. Socrates then raises the question of what
makes the soul base. Here, he situates such matters as injustice, ignorance, and
cowardice (477b).

Socrates now suggests to Polus that of the three kinds of human baseness
the defects of the soul are the most shameful of all; poverty and disease do not
necessarily evoke responses of moral repugnance. When Polus agrees,
Socrates then claims that precisely because it is the most shameful, baseness
of the soul is the worst of all (477c). As we anticipated, this is the crucial transition from speech and opinion to deed and reality concerning ethical matters
that must take root in Polus's soul for anything more than hypocrisy and incontinence to result from this conversation. Otherwise put, the action of this part
of the *Gorgias* depicts Polus being punished in the personalized manner that
he had just been led to see as being fine. Through this punishment he will be
rehabilitated, in the sense of being properly situated within his soul; it is only
from this microcosmic perspective that the reality and psychic effects of evil
can be fully revealed to him.

One of the deepest insights provided by the *Gorgias* is its psychic account
of evil. Most accounts of the problem of evil ignore the connection to the soul
and thus tend to generate despair and nihilism. Indeed, selfish Epicurean
behavior results from the very attitude that readily grants the existence of cosmic evil while denying that it has anything to do with oneself, or even using
this fact to justify one's apathy. This view ultimately follows from Gorgias's
bracketing of truth and its accessibility to humans; this cosmic pessimism
frees us to be parochial hedonists, waging war against anything that stands
between imagined pleasures and our ravenous appetites. The plague of war
itself is a shameless assault on reality spawned by lying words and nihilistic
thoughts.

Further explaining his claim that what is shameful is worst of all for the
human being, Socrates now tells Polus that what is shameful can only be so,
by virtue of their earlier agreement, through being painful or harmful. Since
injustice of the soul has been agreed to be the most shameful, it follows that
this condition must be the cause of great pain, harm, or a combination of the
two. Since the various defects of the soul – injustice, intemperance, cowardice,
and ignorance – are certainly not more painful than material poverty and bodily sickness, it must follow then that they far surpass them in harm and thus
are the greatest evils of all (477c–e).

Next, in a move that perhaps could account for his earlier categorization
of money as something good in itself, Socrates points out to Polus that the art

of earning money is the remedy for being poor and the art of medicine cures physical disease. He then asks Polus for the name of the corresponding art that cures baseness and injustice. When Polus has difficulty with this question Socrates asks him where the sick are taken to be cured, and is told that they go to a physician. When asked then where the unjust and intemperate are taken, Polus replies that they go to the judges and courts of law, further agreeing that this is where they will pay a just penalty and be punished correctly using some kind of justice. It is the art of justice that must provide the cure for intemperate and diseased souls (477e–478a).

Here, it is noteworthy that Socrates does not praise or criticize the Athenian legal system, but merely contents himself with indicating the purpose of justice. Recall that his statement about persons who benefited from being punished covered only those who were *justly* punished; he does not say that *any* punishment is good for *any* wrongdoer. The various shortcomings of the legal system, either then or now, merely remind us that they do not surpass the ways human beings make money or cure disease; all three arts are powers that are very far from being perfected. This position is also quite consistent with Socrates' denial that any man was wise and Polus's hesitation in naming the art of justice, which in its current state has a greater resemblance to his own shadow art of rhetoric; the status of the legislative art (charged with maintaining the health of a soul) is even more problematic as we shall see. The genuine art of justice needs to be discovered and practiced before it will be beneficial for men to seek punishment for themselves and those they care about. We may also bear in mind Gorgias's great skepticism concerning truth and its availability, probably derived in no small part from his awareness, through Herodicus his brother, of the highly unscientific state of Greek medicine. This is clearly why Gorgias's winning bedside manner turned out to be more valuable than the physician's knowledge. Thucydides' comments about the popular discrediting of both medicine and religion in the wake of the plague, which occurred just before Gorgias's visit in 427, are most relevant here.[29]

The genuine and spurious arts are related as Prometheus was to Epimetheus. While not as glibly articulate, rational forethought is manifestly superior to rationalizing afterthought. Socrates showed Polus that neither life nor pleasure could be viewed as an end in itself – however self-evident this seemed to the uncultivated *anthropos*. We also see why Polus's rejection of arguments that could "refuted by a child" had to do with false anthropocentric measures that, although attractive to the infantilized demos, are far from self-evident to a cultivated soul or *aner*. Just as the cravings of unhealthy body and the mimetic passions of the many are unreliable measures of goodness, the

---

29 Thucydides, *Peloponnesian War*, II. 53.

ability to pander to these passions cannot be called a genuine art. Still, a morality based on superstition is easily replaced by engineered necessity in the moral chaos that follows disasters on the scale of those the Peloponnesian War brought to Athens. *Ananke* replaces fate.

Back in the *Gorgias*, Socrates now elicits the admission that justice is nobler and finer than either wealth or medicine (478b); this also means that it produces the greatest pleasure or benefit according to the principle earlier agreed upon. When Polus is then asked whether it is pleasant to be medically treated, he replies that it is not, even though he admits that being healed is clearly beneficial to the patient. Even though this disease corrupts its victims' consciousnesses so much that they resist its treatment, we must have sufficient foresight to know that the great benefit of being restored to health justifies the very painful procedures and coercive means employed. But, in a manner that anticipates the distinction between getting better and being well that will play a prominent role in his looming clash with Callicles, Socrates points out that while one who is cured is glad, the fullest physical well-being is enjoyed by one who is not sick at all (478c). Happiness in matters of the body consists in the relatively tranquil state of health, rather than in the intense pleasure in being released from illness or by extension, other physical excesses.

Perhaps we could extend this thought further and suggest that true justice helps us to attain liberation from false and dangerous ideas concerning bodily well-being? Polus's earlier mimetic model of envy-based happiness would be one of the false arts pandering to such an unhealthy and deleterious conception of health. The true arts would then be powers that connect the self to reality, rather than knack-like methods for excessive material accumulation or *thumotic* display without any moderating form or limiting principle. It would also follow from the many paradoxes unveiled here that one who is undergoing the painful process of being healed, whether monetary, medical, and spiritual, is actually "happier" than one who remains diseased and isn't aware of it on account of the "false consciousness" that is not the least dangerous symptom of his condition.

These lead us back to Archelaus, and Socrates suggests to Polus that one like Archelaus, who "Does the greatest injustice and, through great injustice, contrives not to be either reproved or punished" (478e–479a), must be one of those who lives the worst life of all, "along with other tyrants, orators, and oligarchs." Socrates tells Polus that for these men to fear justice, the cure for their disease, is as absurd as it is for someone gravely ill to childishly refuse medical attention because it is painful. There is definitely something very peculiar about a disease that disguises its own symptoms so much that it goes about in deadly fear of being cured.[30] The paradox deepens when we see that this

---

30   Sophocles' *Philoctetes* subtly illustrates this complaint.

malaise afflicts the seat of awareness itself, the soul, and destroys its sense of reality. Their fear of being cured is why these men do everything in their considerable power to force reality to fit the confines of their fantasy, "preparing for themselves wealth and friends" and ensuring "that they themselves should be as persuasive as possible when speaking" (479c).

In the case of Archelaus it seems that he spoke through the mouths of a chorus of well-paid sycophants. Socrates' account of the dis-ease afflicting the unjust further explains the natural alliance between the tyrant and the poets that was mentioned earlier. This joint enterprise sets out to makes the tyrant's version of truth believable; these efforts sometimes succeed so well that they believe their own lies. The Christian Platonist Simone Weil well describes this fearful state of her affairs in her brilliant essay *The Iliad, A Poem of Force*. She saw that "The only people who can give the impression of having risen to a higher plane, people who seem superior to ordinary human misery, are the people who resort to the aids of illusion, exaltation, fanaticism to conceal the harshness of destiny from their own eyes. The man who does not wear the armor of the lie cannot experience force without being touched by it to his very soul."[31]

Socrates now draws out further implications of this terminal condition of injustice. Doing injustice has been shown to be worse than suffering it, but refusing the cure for injustice is worst of all: it makes the evildoer suffer the consequences of his own diseased state more completely than any accidental victim of his passion ever possibly could. This is because the successful virtuoso of injustice becomes trapped in his own paranoid fabric of lies, deceptions, and betrayals. Socrates' account of the tyrant in *Republic IX* vividly portrays a melancholy monster of erotic desire languishing loveless in a black hole like soul from which nothing can escape.

Even if we avert our attention from these fortunately exceptional circumstances, however, it should be seen that the important distinction between becoming virtuous and being virtuous from the *Protagoras* (339b–346e) certainly applies to the *Gorgias* also. Here Socrates separates the arts of legislation (*nomothetiken*) and justice according to the criterion of health, making the former apply to the soul when healthy and the latter in disease; it seems clear that legislation has to do with the art of being virtuous or flourishing in virtue, an art that could also be called happiness. The corresponding physical virtue of gymnastics, which genuinely produces the health that cosmetics falsely suggest but accurately represent, clearly both maintains and celebrates bodily well-being. Both legislation and justice are said to be concerned with the soul;

---

31   *The Iliad: a Poem of Force* in *Simone Weil: An Anthology* (Weidenfeld and Nicolson, 1986), p. 194.

this is important because the soul rather than the city is identified as the unit of consequence with regard to virtue. However, while justice applies to punishment of the individual wrongdoer, legislation necessarily occurs in a political context. In other words, human flourishing or happiness occurs in a setting requiring the individual soul to interact with others in the world through speeches and deeds. As we have seen, this is precisely what an unjust life cannot allow since it seeks to make itself the center or *omphalos* of being. Accordingly it sets out to warp everything, including the perception of other humans, around its singular and diseased perspective on reality. This image helps us better understand the absurdity and inadequacy of shallow and centerless Gorgias supplanting of the proper occupant of the center of the world, the Delphic Oracle.

An obsession with justifying his lies and misdeeds to others but most especially to himself, often through the false invocation of necessity, traps even (or especially) the most successful evildoer in a solipsistic cave or virtual reality of non-being where genuine virtue and happiness cannot be experienced. We could even go so far as to surmise that this very apologetic obsession is itself a mark of the true power of the *logos*, which will not allow someone to admit to himself that he is a murderer and predator without insanity following. In the Platonic cosmos the power of rationality is shot through with the categories of moral reflexivity; as Socrates demonstrated to Polus, all actions aim towards what is good. Polus inadvertently gave further support to this notion when he admitted that the categories of speech somehow had sufficient authority to make the inflicting of injustice appear more shameful than suffering it, despite recognizing his self-evidently strong bodily "truth" or preference for the contrary position. Gorgias could be said to have inadequately anticipated and opposed this position in his claim that nothing true could be said, thus expressing a disjunction between existence and speech.

It may now be seen that the political arts of legislation and justice, which turn out to be concerned with the health and happiness of the soul, are essentially and necessarily conducted through *logos*. Even though Gorgias correctly saw that persuasion played a very important role in this activity, and claimed that his art gave persuasion "on the greatest and best of human matters," he failed to recognize the significance of intra-personal speech in attaining happiness. The chronic democratic temptation to pursue "freedom for oneself and hegemony over others" ignores the crucial Archimedean point of self-rule. Socrates earlier drew Polus's attention to this internal activity of giving the law to oneself, when he made reference to his knowing how to call a vote from *one* person only – himself or his interlocutor – but the full significance of this procedure was not immediately apparent. However the situation he describes, where a soul seeking justice is able to cry out "*J'Accuse*" to itself, dramatically brings out the bracing spirit of rigorous self-examination and exuberant honesty that pervade every Socratic conversation and Platonic dialogue.

This is why when Socrates stated that he would rather be refuted and relieved of ignorance than perform the same service to another (458a), he was quite serious. But does this mean that he was equally serious when he proclaimed his even stranger preference to denounce himself, along with his family and loved ones, so that crimes be brought out of concealment (in the soul) into the light of day (480b–c)? Only in this way could appropriate punishment take place and the soul's health be restored. As it is childish and irresponsible for us to fear hard work and medicine, surely it is equally absurd to flee justice.

On the other hand, is it not absurd *not* to flee from injustice – especially when it masquerades as justice? Is it possible for a morally weak person to receive just and rehabilitative punishment when the legal system itself is corrupt? Exposure to incarceration, then or now, can all too often lead to a kind of graduate education in crime: petty incontinent youths become hardened and cynical recidivists. There are far too many situations in our world where absolute powerlessness in the hands of sadistic and venal authority corrupts almost as much as absolute power; the oligarchic axiom that one should "always help one's friends and harm one's enemies" all too often creates conditions where we protect wealth and lose commonwealth. We cannot afford to end up spoiling our friends and multiplying our enemies. All of this means that while we certainly cannot ignore or discount the extent to which Socrates brilliantly conducted his own trial in such a way that the desired results were produced, we cannot forget that this triumph was achieved by a extraordinarily just man, one who provided his fellow citizens with a rare and striking example of virtue. The *Apology* certainly does not vindicate the Athenian judicial system.

However, since neither opportunities for adequately compensated hard work to overcome poverty nor affordable access to medical procedures to fight illness are available to the vast majority of humanity, we may surely wonder whether the moral resources available for the art of psychic rehabilitation to overcome moral disease are in any better shape? Put differently, just as theft and/or economic exploitation seem to overcome monetary neediness today while fast food and/or plastic surgery lead the postmodern body to believe itself to be happy, it may well be the case that our current models of punitive retribution and "incentivized" hedonism are equally inadequate substitutes for those genuine (and limited) arts of justice and legislation that could be derived from an understanding of the defining limits of the human soul.

What then does Socrates mean when he says that *if rhetoric has any legitimate use at all*, it has to do with publicly denouncing the errors of one's friends and family while condoning and fostering every misdeed performed by one's enemies (480e–481b)? This claim, which has had much to do with the opprobrium that the *Gorgias* has attracted, must surely be explained.[32] Even though Socrates does conduct many interrogations of friends and persons well known to him, it cannot be forgotten that these are all *private* interventions in speech that do not involve any punishment beyond psychic humiliation and the loss of false knowledge.[33] Just as all gain when some become rehabilitated by effective punishment, there is no gain or profit for anyone when men become more wicked. Socrates does not believe that we can help our friends and harm our enemies by the same actions. Rather, while we improve our friends by helping our enemies and thereby enriching their world, we only hurt our friends and impoverish their world, by corrupting our enemies.

The alternative to the rhetorical corruption of enemies and the public punishment of friends is the private punishment of individuals through the dialectic. In every dialogue, Socrates uses the maieutic magic of *reductio-ad–absurdum* argumentation to draw out the fullest implications of a tempting but dangerous idea in order that it may be aborted at its source – instead of either being actualized or continuing to tantalize and corrupt the imagination. Since Socrates never makes explicit the contrary of the position that he subjects to the *reductio*, he thereby preserves the essentially private and non-rhetorical nature of his interventions. The argument-disguised-as-action of the *Republic* is best understood in these terms also. In this longer work Socrates allowed Glaucon to see what will happen as the perfectly unjust life, disguised as the perfectly just life, creates a monstrous anti-cosmos.[34] In such a regime, everything is subject to the will of its tyrannical rulers. The spiritual descent from books VII to IX show how the veneer of justice is gradually stripped away until the deeply pathetic condition of the tyrant is exposed. Though this revelation occurs over time, Socrates' point is that the bad end of the seemingly just city is contained in its flawed origins. We shall see how the *Gorgias* follows a similar course.

The anachronistic dramatic setting of the *Gorgias* also helps us to see that Socrates means that the description of rhetoric as self-indictment should be

---

32 For instance Arieti doubts Socrates' seriousness, asking if he would really want to allow criminals to go free. This leads him to reject philosophy if it would lead to these absurd actions. Unfortunately his indignation leads him to regard Callicles as being representative of the practical man (p. 84–85).

33 Friedlander reminds us that despite the seeming claim that "we should accuse ourselves and relatives or friends, to uncover their offences . . . the author of the *Euthyphro* condemned the charge brought before a son against his father when this actually happened before a court in Athens" (p. 238).

34 See Ranasinghe, *The Soul of Socrates*, pp. 1–27.

understood in a very negative light indeed. The reference to the infamous trial of the Athenian leaders at Arginusae points to perhaps the most gruesome example of how overcharged demagogic rhetoric led the furious democracy to tear itself apart and lose every advantage just gained from their miraculous victory. As Socrates was the only person present who opposed this travesty of justice, we cannot expect him as a supporter of the rhetoric of suicidal self-denunciation – procedures that have little to do with the political art that he claimed to possess. While Socrates did find it necessary to explode some of the false myths and delusions of competence that were so widely disseminated during the heady days of late empire and the desperate times of war, he did so as a private citizen in one-on-one discussions that would be most likely to reach the soul of his interlocutor. We may turn to the *Apology* itself for confirmation of Socrates' self-understanding of this activity. He says that he "always minded your business, by visiting each of you in private, like a father or elder brother, to persuade you to care about virtue" (31b). And again, "I went to each of you privately and tried to perform what I claim is the most beneficial deed. . . . I tried to persuade each of you to care first not about any possessions but about himself and how he'll become as good and wise as possible, nor to care for anything which belongs to the polis before caring for the polis itself" (36c).

It must also be seen that Socrates is again actively opposing the *thumos*-driven belief, illustrated in the *Republic*, that one best helps friends and harms enemies by covering up the misdeeds of the former and obsessing over every appearance of wrong-doing by the latter. In more familiar religious terms, he urges us to clear our own eyes (take out the log) before furiously denouncing the sins of others.[35] We do not preserve our souls, leave aside purify them, by zealously punishing the apparent sins of our enemies. Yet Socrates says nothing that leads us to believe that there is a special providence in the fall of a sparrow. Furthermore, despite the murderous events of the times following the end of the Peloponnesian War, there is nothing apocalyptic about the tone of the Platonic dialogues; Socrates does not believe that the form of the world is passing away.

Reflecting on the civic chaos that prevailed at the end of the Peloponnesian War, we note that the dramatic trajectory of the *Gorgias* strongly suggests that the seeds of this disaster were sown by practitioners of demagogic rhetoric a generation or two earlier. Because rhetoric is always victorious at the level of words, where words mean exactly what we want them to mean, it is used to inflate the morale of a state. Pericles knew that Athens was invulnerable as long as she stayed within her walls and avoided substantial over-commitments on land.[36] Unfortunately too little contact with reality leads

35   Matthew 7:5.
36   Thucydides, *Peloponnesian War*, III. 62.

people to blur the difference between words and reality. Ambitious parties, those of Lincoln's "family of the lion or the tribe of the eagle"[37] desirous of power and glory, used cheap rhetoric to paint the rosiest pictures of future prospects for victory and plunder to the ignorant and credulous demos. The problem with being wholly surrounded by self-binding illusions is that state-sponsored solipsism does not guarantee invulnerability to reality. Perched high up on a rostrum, the demagogic orator is as isolated from nature as a self-enclosed egg. Consequently, just like Humpty Dumpty, the Athenians encountered far harsher conditions once they were seduced, by their own lying rhetoric and vain desires, to leave the long walls and fall down upon the hard ground. Defeats and humiliations, inevitably experienced when optimistic plans are roughed up by reality, naturally generate much anger and suspicion. Once an angry populace (used to cheap victories gained by boldness and bluster) demands accountability, it is easiest for a demagogic orator to blame enemies within and accuse them of sabotage. Filled with fury, and deliberately nurtured without the power to see the truest causes of their discomfiture or learn from it, the desire-enflamed many now tear each other to shreds in paroxysms of paranoia.

I have argued that Socrates' real purpose has been to show Polus that rhetoric, a pseudo-art that is only impressive to an ignorant many, is useless in any circumstances under which genuine moral rehabilitation should occur. The last words he speaks to Polus bear this out literally: "To ensure that result Polus [to sustain one's enemies indefinitely in their crimes] I allow oratory may be of use, since it seems to me to be of little use to one who is not going to do wrong. That is, assuming it to have any use at all, which our earlier discussion has shown it not to have" (481b). Further, we have already noted that in both the least fanciful part of the *Republic*, Book I, as well as in the *Apology* itself, Socrates makes it clear that by indulging or corrupting others, whether friends or enemies, we only harm ourselves by poisoning the cultural and physical environment that we hold in common with them. Only those like Archelaus, who are spoiled enough to believe that they can create an imaginary world for themselves, could fall prey to such folly.

This is why when reading of persons cheerfully delivering themselves up for punishment, and/or maliciously corrupting their enemies, we must heed the distinction between just and unjust punishment that Socrates emphasized to Polus. While just punishment is a political necessity, excessive zealotry in the punishment of vice is not virtue; this warning must be seen to cover both sadism towards our enemies and masochism towards ourselves. We must not

37   Abraham Lincoln, "Lyceum Speech," 1838 in *Lincoln: Speeches and Writings 1832–1858* (Library of America, 1989), p. 34.

conflate the trials of Jesus and Socrates. Socratic *Eudaimonism* is as far removed from perverse forms of post-Christian masochism as it is from Communist show trials; both extremes are ideological and ultimately nihilistic views in their contemptuous impatience with common reality. Socrates was not an antinomian; he was, we recall, quite critical in the *Republic* of democratic regimes where convicted felons go unpunished and live like heroes (558a). Neither is he promoting a draconian moral scenario where children denounce their parents to the state, and conscientious Kantians prepare to betray the whereabouts of hidden Jews to the S.S. While these draconian measures could be derived from a literal reading of the *Republic*, and provides strong grounds for suspecting that this text should not be read literally, it should at least be evident that the art of justice can hardly be made into a totalitarian political science as long as we do not even know what political justice is. Indeed this very ignorance explains why it is so much easier for a rhetorician to focus the energies of the many on waging foreign wars against injustice.[38]

Our ignorance about what is positively just is unavoidable as long as the state, rather than the soul, is viewed as the origin of virtue. The individual soul's awareness of good and evil, however indistinct, cannot be replaced by a collective *thumotic* experience of injustice.[39] This is why a so-called science of justice cannot, and never should, supplant the duty of each soul to pursue virtue freely and purposefully. A true regime of virtue can only be founded in the soul; it can never be imposed on any larger unit. Friendship is higher than justice. It is neither built on shared enmity nor fostered by complicity in predatory revenge. While friendship and virtue are positive moral categories, political justice – a privation – is seen only in its absence and commercial justice is no more than backward-looking bookkeeping. The *Republic* saw that this view of virtue reflected the psychic economy of the aged Cephalus and his desire to be posthumously called just by gods and men. Living men become hucksters and debt-collectors when this "value" rules the agora.

Understanding the paradoxical category of justice helps us to better understand the impossibility of making men just through political rhetoric. Socrates' words and deeds indicate that moral improvement occurs through debunking the many false desires and beliefs that lead human beings astray. This procedure of removing false wisdom must be seen to benefit both friend and foe alike. This is the best and more efficient way of fighting injustice. It

38 In Benardete's words, "the *Gorgias* is the positive print of an etiolated negative. It captures forever the ghost of justice" (p. 7).
39 Benardete reformulates the quarrel between the philosopher and the city as follows: Socrates "can make room for philosophy only if he dissolves the apparent well-being of morality" (p. 58).

follows from this premise that we ought to be very critical of the way by which imperial Athens became rich and powerful. The practice of taxing allies in order to wage profitable wars against their common enemies falsely and seductively suggested to the gullible demos that fighting injustice is more profitable than practicing justice in one's own life; this was the dangerously false belief that Polemarchus had to be relieved of in Book I of the *Republic*. Violence is not an instrument of state; it is far more like a plague that infects all who come into contact with its Ares-like two-faced necessity. Socrates seems to suggesting that the soul is freed to practice positive virtue when the illusory quality of doubly negative punitive justice is exposed. This also means that reality cannot be regarded in zero-sum terms; anything that makes a man's enemies worse will probably have a bad effect on his own life and polity. Since increased wickedness makes its victims violent and predatory, one's efforts to practice positive virtue will be interrupted by the tempting need to curb and punish his enemy's vice. A polity is corrupted when its citizens renounce the difficult pursuit of private virtue and choose fighting evil as a profitable way of becoming just.

Let us now return to the *Gorgias* and apply these insights to our text. It is apparent that in Polus's worldview, which is both a cause and effect of war, appearances are violently imposed on the recalcitrant and chaotic prime matter (*proto hule*) of reality. Although the victories are necessarily short-lived, the real recompense gained is in the inflated currency of *kudos* or glory. This martial context seems to necessitate that allies be praised and their sins be concealed by rhetoric. The same self-fulfilling code of loyalty requires that the reputations of enemies be blackened. Socrates teaches Polus, a professional rhetorician, to see the limitations of this outlook by helping him to understand that speech and truth, rather than being derivative from manipulated appearances, were founded on the moral quality of the soul and the reality of the world. In other words, Polus is shown the intentional structure immanent in speech itself; he also sees how this order reflected the self-evident teleology of the human desire for what was truly noble and good. Rhetoric is less than useless here since this pseudo-art of happiness operates through cloyingly deceiving the ignorant many; its purposes are diametrically opposed to the rough purgative medicine that should be brought to bear on the only unit of capable of maintaining genuine happiness: the soul.

Rhetoric works through breaking down the unity of the human soul into a great many unruly and needy desires. Since it also fuses individual citizens into a mob or undifferentiated many – with a short attention span and hubristic desires – it may be said to both turn the one into a many and many into a one. Conversely, Socrates' art sets out to restoratively recollect the integrity of the individual and the genuine plurality of the citizenry. By these *metanoic* turnings he also restores the self-knowledge of the soul and the self-evidence of the *kalon*; these are essential to resisting the many unwholesome tautologies deployed by the pseudo-arts to seduce souls and misrule cities. Rhetoric seduces those who use it to live outside their diseased souls and view themselves according to its false self-image.[40] There is a pattern of removal: the rhetorician first knows himself as mind or tool of calculation like Gorgias, next as image or reputation like Polus, and finally the student-victim of rhetoric self-deconstructs into a heap of insatiable irrational desires.

We see this last stage of decadence exemplified when Callicles bursts into the conversation with a vehemence that is both more sincere and quite as violent as that displayed by Thrasymachus in the *Republic*.[41] It is worth noting here that the designed impossibility of assigning the *Gorgias* a dramatic date suggests strongly that it should be read not before or after the *Republic* but beside it. Callicles first asks Chaerephon whether or not Socrates is serious (*spoudazei*) or just kidding (*paizei*) and then asks the question directly. Callicles goes on to claim that if Socrates is serious, and what he says is true, human life has been turned upside down and people are doing exactly the opposite of what they ought to be doing (481c). Before going on to consider Socrates' rather provocative reply to this question, we should first consider the possibility of dramatic irony in Callicles' very words. Could it be that Callicles' own response itself is just as diametrically opposed to what it should be? Should we beware of being sidetracked from the deeper issues that have been raised in Socrates' very substantial conversation with Polus?

This would be the case only if Callicles were to veer off the tracks even more than Polus did originally,[42] and if he does so we must wonder whether Socrates substantially contributes to his seduction by taunting him about his love life. Yet this itself indicates some important differences between the respective characters of Gorgias, Polus, and Callicles. While Gorgias is blindly enthralled by the technique of his art and Polus is fascinated by the possibilities rhetoric offers for power, Callicles is far more of a hedonist and nihilist. Because of this, he is far harder to educate than either of the other two men. If Gorgias represents the intellect corrupted by non-being, then Polus (whose

40 Benardete points out that "the actual opacity of wickedness is replaced by the moral certainty of the experience of injustice, it can work backwards from its affect to what kind of wickedness initiated its experience." He adds that "self-denunciation . . . is the punitive bringing into the open of one's opinions . . . [it] checks the will from denouncing others and guessing at their wickedness" (pp. 58–59).

41 Voegelin says that at this point "the battle has now reached the real enemy, the public representative of the corrupt order" (p. 28).

42 See Benardete, p. 2.

very name means young horse) represents anti-intellectual spiritedness. Callicles, as we shall see, is the spokesperson for the blinded and speechless desires. Otherwise put, Gorgias stands for the solipsistic intellect enthralled by its own cleverness, Polus lives for the view that ends justify means, and Callicles embodies the view that the means justify the end – whatever it is.

Socrates responds to Callicles by both pointing to a commonality of experiences that is the basis for the possibility of meaningful speech (or rhetoric) between men, and also accounting for the curious phenomenon of humans doing the very opposite of what they should.[43] Also implicitly replying to the third of Gorgias's denials, that the unknowable could be expressed to another, he states that human beings would not be able to understand one other if each had experiences in a way unique to himself. However since both Callicles and he are lovers, each in love with two things, he suggests that his fellow Athenian would be able to understand him better. Socrates publicly confesses, on behalf of both of them, that while he loves both Philosophy and Alcibiades, the son of Cleinias, Callias is in love with the Athenian people and the son of Pyrilampes. In other words, they are both in love with a human being and something other than a person (481c–d).

This dyadic structure of their affections could obviously help to account for contradictory behavior traits that would be otherwise inexplicable. Furthermore, since the son of Pyrilampes bore the name of Demos, Socrates is suggesting that Callicles is torn between his love for two different kinds of Demos, both of which turn him into a many: his aristocratic beloved and the Athenian mob. According to what we are told about Demos (the man) by Aristophanes, he was beautiful;[44] Eupolis however calls him stupid.[45] Indeed Callicles himself, whose name means "reputed beautiful," may well represent Athens: the polis famously dedicated to the pursuit of the beautiful and yet led astray by its vain pursuit of hedonistic beauty and popular reputation.

Callicles' acute agitation at the discussion Socrates has just had with Polus could thus also be explained by the fact that Socrates has alleged that his

---

43 Voegelin states that while "in their exposure to pathos all men are equal . . . they differ widely in the manner in which they come to grips with it and build the experience into their lives . . . the *pathema* experienced by all may result in a *mathema* different for each man" (p. 29). He adds that "Behind the hardened, intellectually supported attitudes which separate men, lie the *pathemata* which binds them together. However false and grotesque the intellectual position may be, the pathos at the core has the truth of an immediate experience. If one can penetrate to this core and reawaken in a man the awareness of his *conditio humana*, communication in an existential sense becomes possible" (p. 30).

44 Aristophanes, *Wasps*, 98.

45 See Dodds, p. 261.

eponymous activity of seeking after a beautiful reputation is both fundamentally misdirected and basely founded. His love of what is *kalon* (beautiful) becomes detached from the *agathon* (good) of the dyad *kalos-agathos* – an expression customarily used to described the "best and brightest" of Athens – by his reckless pursuit of reputation. Another possible interpretation of Callicles' name also supports the theory that he represents Athens in some way: Callicles could be seen as a composite of names of Pericles and Callias (the sometime wealthiest man in Athens; bankrupted by his lavish expenditure on sophists, this worthy also married Pericles' castoff wife when Aspasia gained the affections of the famous statesman). Of course, all of this speculation regarding Callicles derives from the fact that we have no data from outside the *Gorgias* concerning this outspoken young man – either from within the Platonic corpus or from all of the historical records available to us.

Socrates also tells Callicles that despite being terribly clever, he is quite unable to contradict any opinion of his lovers and so has to terribly contort himself, literally turning himself around up and down, on all matters. This means that in the Assembly he has to continually change his positions to agree with the opinions of the many. Likewise with Demos, son of Pyrilampes (Plato's step-brother), Callicles suffers other embarrassments because of his incapacity to oppose the beautiful young man in any way. This is why Callicles, despite his reputed intelligence, says so many strange things (481d–482a), presumably on account of the stupidity of both his beloveds. Socrates is suggesting that Callicles contorts himself and lives upside down, contradicting his own intelligence, because of the many concessions continually made to his beloveds. This obviously counters Callicles' earlier claim that it is *Socrates* who expects people to live upside down – as though they were bats in his cave. This question, about the proper direction of the best life, runs right through the *Gorgias*. As we have suggested, it may reflect the line between good and evil.

Callicles is then warned that he should not be surprised to hear strange sayings emanate from Socrates because his beloved, Philosophy, makes him speak this way. He will stop speaking in this inspired daimonic idiom only when philosophy is silenced. Socrates goes on to state that philosophy is always constant and much less capricious than his other beloved, Alcibiades, who is given to saying different things at different times. Because philosophy will always make him say the same amazing things that he says now, Socrates urges Callicles to refute his claim, by showing that doing injustice and not paying the just penalty when one does so are *not* the two worst evils. If he cannot do so, and here Socrates swears by the dog of the Egyptians for emphasis, Callicles will be dissonant with himself his whole life through. As we noted earlier, Socrates seems to swear by the beast-divinity – *Anubis* – only in a situation involving an existential contradiction. The warning that he gives Callicles against contradicting himself also serves the purpose of drawing our attention to Callicles' name and the attendant overtones already taken note of. Socrates' own opinion concerning the danger of self-contradiction seems to place it among the greatest evils: "It is *kreitton* (superior, nobler) that my lyre be out of tune with the musicians, and my song be dissonant with the chorus, or that I be opposed and contradicted by most human beings, than that I, being one man, should be discordant with myself and say contradictory things" (482b–c). In this context, it is well worth noting that Socrates' own name means "enduring-power."

Before turning to Callicles' notorious response to this plea that he should defend injustice, we should observe that Socrates' words echo many similar themes in the *Greater Hippias*. In this much shorter comic dialogue, which deals with many themes addressed in the earlier parts of the *Gorgias*, Socrates harasses the eponymous sophist and polymath by the unusual device of inventing an unnamed acquaintance, one who would be likely to raise all manner of objections to Hippias's many fine statements regarding what is fine. It is only towards the end of the dialogue that we discover that this person is the son of Sophroniscus (298b), and a close relative of Socrates, who lives in the same house as he (304d). The alien Elian does not know that Socrates is speaking as his father's only son, and this is comic; however, the serious point that emerges from this encounter with Hippias "the Fine and Wise" is that fine answers are insufficient if they rely on flashy surfaces but don't have any connection with wisdom. By virtue of his entanglements with both forms of Demos, clever Callicles is also in danger of losing his personal integrity and become a mere mimetic echo of whatever his stupid but beautiful beloveds happen to say. Thus Callicles has become like Demos: anarchic, called-beautiful but stupid. In contrast Socrates, thanks to his father's son, stays true to himself. Socrates' adroit use of this device also suggests that even a poor man stuck with friends as intellectually astute as Chaerephon and Crito still possesses internal resources sufficient to stay true to himself, as long as he does not chase false opinions and vain images of what is called fine.

Callicles' response evidently has something to do with his anger at what he regards as a personal attack. Though he eschews references to either of his two reputed lovers, Callicles' exaltation of both the natural right of strength and the joy of hedonism suggest that neither of his loves has any power over his speech – at least on this occasion. Throwing back the charge made against him, he accuses Socrates of practicing demagogic speech. Socrates has used a crafty debater's trick that he will now expose. Polus was trapped by Socrates' use of the very device (shame) that he originally accused Socrates of using against Gorgias. When Gorgias, who evidently does not believe in the objective status of justice, was asked whether he would teach justice to one who did not know it, he agreed because he was afraid of the anger of the human beings (*anthropoon*). This led him into contradiction with his earlier attitude that the art of rhetoric spoke about the highest matters from above them. Then Polus was also led to contradict himself by shamefully conceding that suffering injustice was less shameful than doing injustice. Since Polus too was ashamed to publicly say what he truly thought, he "got his feet entangled and his mouth gagged" (482d–e).

It seems that only Callicles is able to say that nothing exists. Gorgias and Polus respectively found these words to be unspeakable and unknowable. This, we recall, was the third step of Gorgias's self-contradictory argument denying Being. We have already seen how Gorgias overcame the unspeakable nature of truth (by political rhetoric making beautiful and flattering lies) and Polus hoped to transcend its being unknowable by man (by tyrannical creativity making truth out of chaos). Callicles now proposes to boldly live where no man had been before: in Non-Being. To this absurd man nothing exists beyond the addled confines of his own fragmented polymorphous consciousness – objective reality for him is no more than a simulation or game.[46]

According to Callicles, Socratic demagoguery is founded on his exploitation, while pretending to seek the truth, of those tiresome things that are fine by convention (*nomos*) rather than nature (*phusis*). Here, Callicles boldly states that nature and convention are in most cases opposed to each other. As a consequence of this opposition, persons are ashamed of what is truly fine by nature; daring not to speak their mind, they make contradictory utterances. Understanding this, Socrates wickedly or unfairly (*kakourgeis*) sets verbal traps for them. If someone speaks of what is natural, he counters with conventional standards and *vice versa*. As an example Callicles cites Polus's refutation when he spoke of what is naturally worse, suffering injustice, only to be tripped up by Socrates' mischievous appeal to convention.

At this point, it is not unworthy of interest to ask why Callicles does not cite an instance of the opposite case, of Socrates refuting what was conventionally worse by looking to nature. Is such an example unspeakable? Can it be that he fears that such appeal to natural right would be seen to speak to conscience rather than power? As we have tried to suggest, there is something about the very nature of human speech itself, the *logos*, which leads its users to naturally remind each other of what is good and noble and elevate these things above the merely egotistical and selfish. This applies both to what is good, noble, and

---

46 "Callicles likes to look at the lion from the outside and measure what it needs to live by what he needs. He knows nothing of the nature of the lion; all he sees is how much it gobbles up" (Benardete, p. 71).

true in the cosmos, as it does to "the better angels of our nature" in the soul. It is self-evidently unnatural and shameful to speak to each other in any other way. Even Gorgias conceded that rhetoric is concerned with "the greatest of human affairs and the best" (451d). The experiences that Socrates (and Plato) keeps appealing to, in opposition to the sophistic axiom that speech is artificial, suggest that there is a mysterious and beautiful proportion between speech and reality, thought and being. Language is no more or less of our making than a lusty teenager is the creator of a new life. In other words, there is something about the *logos* that exceeds and eludes the often-blind strivings of efficient causality towards images of it. While the unschooled will and desires override the mind's preference for beauty over pleasure, the empty and ephemeral character of pleasure – which semi-deliberately targets the silencing of the mind as its end – involuntarily points beyond itself.

Yet Callicles persists in his proudly shameless effort to describe a state of nature quite opposed to pusillanimous convention. He does so by claiming that he can account for the *genesis* of *nomos*. But first the brash Athenian prepares the ground by stating that suffering injustice is a fate appropriate not to a real man (*aner*) but to a slave for whom death is better than life, as he lies trodden over by necessity and helpless to help either himself or those he cares for. Callicles claims that these weaklings, who cannot live according to nature, devise human laws and norms. They proceed to set down the laws to their advantage, praising their weaknesses and condemning their fears. In doing so, they set out to exclude and marginalize those who are naturally powerful so as to cause artificial circumstances where all will be equal. They say that taking more is shameful, and declare unlawful the activity of seeking to have more than others (482e–483c).

Now even though they are reflective of his corrupt psychic regime, Callicles' words are clearly and deeply anti-democratic. They cut far deeper than the Socratic criticisms of rhetoric, which merely condemned the methods by which public opinion was flattered, un-individuated, and collectively corrupted against its objective best interests – Socrates is not opposed to governance for the good of the people. However, Callicles sweepingly rejects all notions of equality and justice. According to him, nature itself reveals that it is just for the better and stronger to have more than the worse and the weaker. As examples of this natural right he cites two of the actions of the great kings of Persia, claiming that he is choosing two of a countless number available to him (483d–e). Yet, as many scholars have pointed out, his examples are badly chosen. Xerxes' invasion of Greece and Darius's invasion of Scythia were both markedly unsuccessful. The invasions undertook by these men, whose offspring were admiringly mentioned by Polus as examples of self-evident happiness, caused the deaths of countless numbers of their warriors.

It is hard to imagine how Callicles could have chosen two worse, or more "politically incorrect," examples to support his case; this suggests that his wisdom has been unreflectively received from a pro-Persian source. Perhaps he means to suggest that a ruler like Archelaus or Alexander is indifferent to the inconveniences sustained by *hoi polloi* as they perform those actions that will win them all immortal glory; like Shakespeare's Henry V at Agincourt, he feels that his soldiers' lives only gain meaning through participation in his great enterprise. His rare example assumes a qualitative difference between the lives of rulers and ruled. Thousands of zeroes are not worth as much as one real man. The career of Cyrus matters more than the lives of his ten thousand mercenaries. It was in the same spirit that Achilles selfishly jeopardized the lives of his comrades, as he sulked and schemed to make Agamemnon acknowledge his god-given natural superiority.

Callicles claims that these actions were all performed in accordance with the "law of nature" and by this he means that the ideas of equality, nobility, and justice are but so many chains and shadows created to hold the best natures in an underground prison. While Callicles does not make this comparison to the cave of the *Republic*, the parallel is easily made. He does complain that the best and most forceful of the young are caught like young lions and tamed by myths and charms until they are slavishly uphold the ideal of human equality with all their spirit.[47] But Callicles believes that a man with a sufficiently powerful nature will shatter these chains of habit and taboo to get away and see things as they are. Such a man will destroy all the laws and conventions that oppose nature, and his superiority will shine forth in the light of natural justice (484a–b).

This hope, expressing Callicles' take on the philosopher-king, reveals a great deal about his soul. Callicles is an example of what could happen in the second generation of sophistic rhetoricians. He also illustrates the dangerous consequences likely to ensue when there is more than one sophist in the same locale. Polus, who treats the content of his education from Gorgias as a professional secret, wishes to be an advisor to a tyrant wielding power indirectly by showing his patron how to rule prudently and inconspicuously. However, Callicles wants to *be* a tyrant for the sake of the unlimited opportunities for pleasure that will come his way. He would be both master and natural slave.[48]

47 Also relevant is Aristophanes' view that while it is best not to rear a lion in the city, once he is grown it is best to defer to him. This advice was offered by the shade of Aeschylus re: Alcibiades (*Frogs* 1420 ff.).

48 Benardete notes that "Callicles' fusion of the perspectives of ruler and ruled is a necessary consequence of his feeling himself to be a part of an imperial people. One outbraves and outsmarts the enemy as Demos and enjoys one's triumph as little man" (p. 72).

Unlike Polus, who prefers to be one of the manipulators of shadows in the cave, Callicles desires to be powerful and shameless enough to charge into the cave like a rampaging lion and terrorize its hapless denizens. He believes that he has nothing to be ashamed of but shame itself. While Polus is a modern, who believes in using power to order and perfect reality, Callicles is unabashedly a postmodern; he revels in the incorrigibility of the flux. In his intellectual milieu, the precepts of sophistical nihilism are taken for granted as the axioms of the best and brightest. Hegel's earlier-noted comment about events that would be tragic to men but comic to gods is now reversed. To these young nihilists, developments that would seem tragic to Socrates, Gorgias, Polus, or even Nietzsche, appear in a comic light. It was in this spirit that the crowd in the marketplace urged Zarathustra, the anguished bearer of sad tidings of God's death, to bring on the Last Man.[49]

Callicles now goes on to reveal himself as a bad student and insensitive reader of poetry. He quotes a fragment from Pindar where Heracles, who was renowned in classical times almost as much for his brutish stupidity as for his great strength, is praised for rustling cattle on the grounds that the property of the weak is naturally at the disposal of the stronger man (484b–c). Callicles does not mention that Heracles performed this act as a slave; he was ordered to perform this act of theft by and for his master Eurystheus – to whose bondage he had been delivered on the orders of the Delphic Oracle for killing his wife and children in a fit of madness. A nearer approximation to Plato's own opinions on this claim are revealed in the *Laws* III where his Athenian Stranger says that claims of this kind pertain better to the animal kingdom. According to this man, *pace* "clever Pindar," this so called "decree of nature" must be replaced by "the rule of law." In human affairs it is far preferable that the wise should rule with the consent of the governed instead of imposing law on them by force (690b). It seems that even though Callicles has inherited enough to be able to host an expensive sophist or two, he has acquired little more than a few sound-bytes of cynicism to support and justify a hedonistic way of life. It is quite interesting that his speech has little in common with the character described earlier by Socrates; we note how swiftly Callicles has changed from a rather pathetic and incontinent man torn between two lovers to an openly intemperate nihilist and would-be tyrant. At least in speech, he has swiftly traversed the final stages of decadence described in the *Republic*'s last books.

It is in this new identity that Callicles administers his "dressing down" of Socrates and simultaneously exposes his own naked intemperance. Speaking with all the boundless enthusiasm of a convert, albeit to a nihilistic creed,

49   Nietzsche, *Thus Spoke Zarathustra*, Prologue.

Callicles tells Socrates that he will make much progress once he puts philosophy aside and moves to greater things; in Callicles' upside down world, which inverts the hierarchy of the *Republic*, philosophy is the earliest and lowest stage on the intellectual ladder that culminates in tyranny. Callicles generously concedes that philosophy is a graceful thing, a whimsical pursuit to be moderately indulged in by the young, but he warns against the corruption that ensues if it is not outgrown. Even the very best natures are corrupted (*diaphthora*) by it – this not only harkens to the famous accusation in the *Apology* that Socrates corrupted the young, it also inverts Socrates' own lament regarding the corruption of the best natures in *Republic* VI (503b–c). On the other hand, it may also be said that even those with lesser natures just as fully lose the ability to experience both their own souls and reality itself by vicariously participating in the fevered follies of imperial Athens.[50]

Callicles' further complaint is that one engaging in philosophy as an adult loses the capacity to gain experience in the things of the city, in the speeches one must make in private and public associations with fellow citizens, in the pleasures and desires, and all the character traits appropriate to a human being. Of course he himself, cannot imagine what the city looks like from inside, to its ruler, and instead is content with feasting his eyes on her reputation and participating vicariously in its glory[51] – albeit at the expense of his own capacity for virtue and happiness. It is from this blind vantage that he warns Socrates that philosophers are just as ridiculous in private or public affairs as non-philosophers are made to appear when they are trapped in the ridiculous activities and speeches of philosophy (485a–e). Although Socrates declines to share in this fine feast of words laid out by Gorgias and Callicles, it is for the latter a foregone conclusion that the siren song of philosophy that leads one into the dead end of non-being, false images, and empty reflections; it is a never-never land where even a person of great promise can lose his manliness and character. Socrates is thus held up for ridicule as a sort of aged Peter Pan. Though he himself is more fool than knave, he should still be publicly humiliated for the sake of the impressionable young who could yet be seduced by him into belief in truth, thought, or speech.

After having displayed his mastery of Pindar to his satisfaction, Callicles next turns to Euripides – the great tragedian who fled Athens in the last years of his life and joined the court of his patron and *deus ex machina,* the tyrant

---

50 "Within the city, the rhetoric of indulgence has prevailed without a word having been spoken about indulgence. That the imperial city does what it likes cannot but be experienced in each citizen as the right to do whatever he likes. Democratic equality is on the books but the strut of the tyrant is in everybody's heart" (Benardete, p. 74).

51 See Thucydides, *Peloponnesian War*, III. 43.

Archelaus. In following him here we are at no little logographic disadvantage; this is because Euripides' *Antiope*, the tragedy used (or misused) as Callicles' proof-text, is lost and only available to us in the form in fragments and through allusions made by other classical sources. Even though much Platonic irony is surely lost to use as a consequence, we already know enough about both Callicles' character and the basic plot of the *Antiope* to follow this aspect of his indictment of philosophy well enough to see that it is consistent with his main theme.[52] The *Antiope* was best known for a passionate debate between two brothers, Zethus and Amphion, concerning which way of life was better, the active or the contemplative? Callicles assumes the identity of Zethus, the proponent of the active life, in this *agon*. Here it is vital to remember that the origin of the legend of Antiope is to be found in the Homeric underworld.[53] As Zeus was the father of Antiope's sons, their quarrel reflects a chronic division in the human psyche between natural and transcendental attributes.

    Closely following his model of the opposed realms of philosophy and public affairs, Callicles quotes Euripides' observation that persons naturally devote the better part of their attention to whatever they happen to be best in, and praise them – thereby indirectly glorifying themselves. Conversely, they flee pursuits for which they have no aptitude and revile them (484e–485a). But even though Callicles claims that for his part he glorifies both philosophy and practical affairs, the only use he has for philosophy is towards a sort of dema-gogic education that has nothing to do with interior cultivation. He claims that while it is not shameful for a youth to philosophize, when practiced by an older man such behavior becomes ridiculous. It follows from this that while there is nothing wrong with Gorgias professing to speak of "the greatest and best of human concerns," and profiting handsomely from this activity, it would be inappropriate for him to actually strive to *live* according to the highest ideals. As Polus suggested, exteriors and appearances mattered far more than thought-ful interiority. This means that the soul's existence is denied or depreciated and artful hypocrisy, the tribute vice pays to virtue, must now be valorized as the very source of order.[54] It is in much the same cynically conservative spirit that

52   Here I have relied heavily on Andrea Nightingale's article, "Plato's Gorgias and Euripides' Antiope: a Study in Generic Transformation" in *Classical Antiquity* vol. 11 (1), pp. 121–41.

53   *Odyssey* XI. 260–65.

54   Stauffer seeks to avoid talking about the benefit virtue brings to the soul by say-ing that human nobility is inherently admirable and "resistant to explanation in terms of benefit or pleasure" (p. 72). The trouble with this attitude is that it treats the noble as what is envied by others – rather than an inner quality of soul that one should jealously guard. The crucial question has to do with how seriously one takes Socrates' understanding of the soul as the seat of moral agency.

atheistic shepherds champion religious fideism for *hoi polloi* they exploit and abuse.

The problem is that in times of famine, plague, and war, the master-narratives that give life meaning break down and the integrity of human nature itself is no longer believed in. The response of the sophist is simple and self-serving. Humans are separated into gods and slaves; the latter need meaning so much that they will sacrifice their freedom so that their gods would have unlimited license to create new truths through their divinely amoral pursuits. The examples set by Darius, Xerxes, and Archelaus must surely come to mind! Fools like Socrates – who believe in transcendent ideas and compare political reality to a cave – live in an underworld. Only unchained lions can live in the real world. Alternately, and just as pertinently to our times, philosophy turns into a language game that future leaders must learn to play so that they may lie fluently to the masses when it's time to go down to the cave and preside over the shadows. Speeches and deeds seem to be as necessarily opposed as nature and convention, according to Callicles' worldview.

Callicles claims that whenever he sees an older man engage in philosophy, he feels it to be as inappropriate as lisping and acting playfully is in an adult. Even though he takes pleasure in small children acting in this manner, because it seems appropriate for one who is free to be playful, and finds it slavish for a young boy to speak precisely, the reverse principle seems to apply in the case of adults. This is why he says that both the playful man who lisps and the man who philosophizes deserve beatings (485b–c). Perhaps Callicles has witnessed Socrates teach Meno's unschooled slave boy how to speak with geometric precision, and maybe he is making a veiled allusion to Socrates' lisping and frivolous beloved, Alcibiades. However, this still does not quite account for his animosity towards philosophy. In his anger, Callicles now repeats himself a third time, saying that although he admires philosophizing in the youthful as a mark of freedom, while one who does not do so betrays his illiberal nature and ignoble birth, he believes that older men not released from philosophy deserve a beating. According to him, even a man with a good nature becomes unmanly (*anandro*) when he shuns public spaces of a polis, where (in Homer's words) men grow distinguished,[55] and instead slinks around and squanders his life – whispering with three or four lads in corners and never saying anything free, important, or vigorous (485e).

We could also suppose that Callicles is so ill-disposed towards philosophy because reflection is inimical to the decisive and vigorous actions that he so admires. As we have already suggested, Callicles seems to have learned from

---

55 *Iliad* IX. 441. Socrates is implicitly likened to Achilles – sulking in his tent while his comrades do battle.

Gorgias that experience is held together by speeches – and does not enjoy any support from being or reality. This is why, to the extent that he and his name represent Athens and its love of its own glorious reputation, he must find that Socrates' attempts to make appearances conform to reality, and to give a rational account (a *logos*) of what is so unintelligible that it cannot be known or spoken of intelligibly, are deeply inimical to the shining illusions that hold the empire together. Put differently, he is deeply and fearfully anti-rational. Unlike Polus, who would use rational means to pursue trans-rational ends, the poorly schooled Callicles seems to believe that reason itself is the enemy. This is why rationality/philosophy is only to be encouraged in children whose liberality will lead them to see and exceed its limits.

According to Callicles' upside-down realism, men can only grow up when they become just as unjust, irrational, and power-driven as reality itself. Anticipating Nietzsche, he must hold that any belief in enlightenment by reason is a sign of childish optimism and deep decadence. In this regard, he is also clearly on the side of one of the most notorious demagogues of all, Cleon, who at this time, during his debate with Diodotus, excoriated the Athenians for their preference for intelligence over force and a concomitant tendency to indulge things most damaging to empire: pity, love of speeches and a sense of fairness.[56] According to this outlook, the making of unreasonable demands on reality clearly deserved a whipping or defeat at the hands of fortune itself; to this extent the punishment that Callicles yearned to give Socrates perfectly fit his crime. The idea of equality, which Callicles so roundly condemned earlier, is clearly also seen by him as yet another one of those impossible illusory goals that optimists try to impose upon harsh and uneven reality. He cannot see that noble ideals do not flatten souls; they only remind us of what we are capable of. Even though these ideas are derived by osmosis from Gorgias, and are certainly not Callicles' independent discoveries or creations, he is the first person shameless enough to articulate them openly in the marketplace. Over the swift but deadly course of this process towards true decadence, enigmatic winged aphorisms metamorphose into banal clichés.

As we suggested earlier, the course of decadence runs from Gorgias's "discovery" of Non-Being, a revelation so shattering that it could only be whispered to a few students in private, to the point where Callicles can publicly speak – in the name of that demotic common sense that Cleon appealed to earlier – and chastise believers in rationality for being childish, superstitious, and personally offensive. To Callicles, nothing exists beyond boldness and reputation. This is the true culmination of Gorgias's boasting himself to be. In striving to contain and defeat this baleful plague cast on language, Socrates

56   Thucydides, *Peloponnesian War*, III.40.

reveals hidden motives and worldviews animating the exoteric actions of the three sophistic orators as they follow the falsely self-evident logic of *ananke*. His "upside-down world" exposes the roots, as it scorns the unhealthy fruit, of rhetoric.

The ignorant hubris of Polus and Callicles leads to the breaking down of the city walls that served as natural limits to rule for Gorgias. Furthermore, Callicles' intemperate desire for glory in the eyes of the demotic many surely reflects the quickened pace of Athenian imperialism; this caused both excesses of speech, such as the Melian Debate, and hubristic deeds, such as the second great expedition to Syracuse, the end result of which was catastrophic disaster for Athens and the permanent loss of autonomy for Gorgias's own Leontini. But the most damaging result for Greece as a whole was a general loss of confidence in the human ability to use rationality and speech to dwell beautifully and meaningfully in the world. It was replaced by a deep pessimism in the many and a predatory hubris in the few who lived purely to satisfy these desires; these few were active nihilists who believed and/or proclaimed that their violently beautiful virtuosity held the world together.

This matter may be made clearer by drawing an ugly contemporary parallel. Every new generation of the twentieth century has had the disconcerting experience of finding in old age that the current technology is so incomprehensible that it might as well be magic. This means that well-educated persons are no longer defined by a combination of a desire and capacity to render or possess an account of how reality is held together. However, the twenty-first century is sharply different in that, with the triumph of postmodernity, it is a mark of the best-educated persons that they no longer desire or expect to gain access to something as discredited as a meta-narrative. As a recent seeker after a genuine education discovered to his chagrin, after having wasted most of his high-school years marketing himself and "networking" to get into Harvard, almost everyone at Harvard spent all of their time there "networking" their way into cushy jobs.[57] This crass "realism" trickles down all the way to the working-class cliché that it's not what you know but whom you know. Higher education today has little or nothing to do with understanding and appreciating the soul and the world; it all too often amounts to a certificate to an employer that the bearer has been both thoroughly vaccinated against all childishly idealistic desires and also reliably infected with all of the insatiable desires appropriate to adult workaholics. Furthermore, the best and the brightest, the "*kalos kagathos*" of our day, learn what they want to hear: that greed is good, and that private vices are the very public virtues that keep the economy strong and productive. Meanwhile, the natural order and the environment

---

57   See Ross Douthat, *Privilege* (Hyperion, 2005).

are inevitably ignored and exploited under such circumstances where spin and interpretation replace reality. It is a tragic irony that rightist libertarian economics and leftist literary theory have so much in common.[58]

This digression at the exact midpoint of the *Gorgias* has been undertaken with a view towards reiterating the contemporary significance of this dialogue. The second part of the *Gorgias* consists of both a response to Callicles' invincible ignorance and an attempted demonstration of how the highly contagious plague of demagogic rhetoric could be either contained or cured. The great popularity of Callicles' speech in our own times is testimony to the timelessness of Plato's insights into the human condition. Since it should at least be assumed that Socrates, rather than Callicles, is the spokesperson for the position Plato himself espoused, it is surely worth our effort to go deeper in the text to find out how Plato proposed to cure a disease so endemic to the human condition. What can our own desperately nihilistic times learn from the first person to accurately recognize and diagnose this malaise? It is often the case that many books resemble ineffectual physicians to the extent that while their diagnoses of the ailment are perfectly accurate, their proposed solutions fail to achieve the desired result.[59] Bearing in mind that Gorgias himself claimed that his art was superior to the physicians, to the extent that it could persuade the human will – albeit at the cost of the soul – we at least know that Plato was fully aware of the distinction between intellectual and volitional assent.[60] Even though Callicles himself is so corrupt that his soul seems to be incorrigibly corrupted, his punishment may very well prove to be exemplary to both his times and ours.

What remains of Callicles' long speech is less substantial and more rhetorical. Claiming to feel quite friendly towards Socrates, he concludes with a brotherly reproach to Socrates, using words that seem to throw back the older man's ironic comment regarding their shared condition of being torn between two lovers. Callicles quotes Zetheus's words to Amphion to tell Socrates that he has been careless of the things he should have taken care of and neglected nurture of his noble soul. Since he conspicuously fritters his time away in childish play, Amphion/Socrates cannot make meaningful interventions in

---

58   As the Sixties student leader Todd Gitlin put it, "The Left marched on the English Departments while the Right took over the White House," *Letters to a Young Activist* (Basic Books, 2003), p. 108.

59   This is the charge that Stauffer levels against Socrates (p. 80).

60   Peter Euben points out that even if we give intellectual assent to Socrates' arguments, he has failed if we do not do what agreement with Socrates should entail: living the examined life by devoting ourselves, as he did, to the search for the good life. See *Corrupting Youth: Political Education, Democratic Culture and Political Theory* (Princeton, 1997), p. 221.

public affairs on matters of justice or make persuasive speeches concerning what is probable in the Assembly. Speaking now in his own voice, Callicles goes on to reproach "his friend," first asking him not to be angry because he speaks with goodwill towards him, whether it isn't shameful to chase deeper and deeper (*elaunontas*) into philosophy. He tries to clinch his case by claiming that if someone were to unjustly accuse one like Socrates of a crime and seek to imprison him, he would surely feel dizzy and gape at his accuser, quite incapable of defending himself (465b–486b). Callicles goes on to declare that once in court, Socrates would prove to be equally helpless, especially if his accuser was unprincipled enough to demand the death penalty against him. This is but an *ad hominem* version of the tales told by Glaucon and Polus of a tortured and disgraced man who chooses the substance over the appearance of justice.

In conclusion, Callicles ridicules the kind of wisdom that can take a man of talent and spoil his gifts, leaving him unable to defend himself or anyone else from the greatest dangers but liable to be stripped of all his substance and left dishonored in his own polis. Callicles claims that such a man could be slapped in the face with absolute impunity. Callicles clearly feels that this self-evidence of this probability is surely enough to clinch his case. Quoting Zetheus's words again, Callicles urges Socrates to "abandon argument and follow the virtues of an active life that will give him the reputation of a prudent man." He is urged to leave the fruitless and negative pursuit of the art of refutation to others. These trivial and silly activities will only lead him to "live in a barren house." Socrates is told instead to emulate those men with substance, reputation, and all other good things (486c). It seems that Socrates could yet follow the example of Euripides and become the tame and spoiled lackey of a tyrant before time runs out; we recall that Euripides' controversial innovation, the *deus ex machina*, figured prominently in the *Antiope*. Aristotle says that when Archelaus invited Socrates to Macedon, he refused on the enigmatic grounds of hubris – explaining that "one is insulted by being unable to requite benefits as well as by being unable to requite injuries."[61] Even the Delphic Oracle could not have given the tyrant a better response.

---

61 Aristotle, *Rhetoric*, 1398a25.

Chapter III: A Soul Turned Upside-Down

Socrates receives Callicles' violent rebuke with his customary ironic aplomb. He compares Callicles to a touchstone by which he could test the quality of his soul and, saying little of the specific criticisms leveled at him, goes on to call his accuser a gift of the gods (*ermaio*), literally a gift from Hermes (486d–e). Here we recall that the original gift of the gods was given so that Odysseus could successfully resist Circe's power to turn men into beasts.[1] In this context it is Callicles himself who claims to have attained a state of shameless moral bestiality. This must be the real reason Socrates believes that if *Callicles* would agree with the ideas in his soul, then there would be no further need for him to make investigations regarding the proper way of life to be lived. His stated reason is that there are three qualities which should be possessed by one with whom he could conduct an examination of his views; these are knowledge, goodwill, and outspokenness (487a). Even though Gorgias and Polus had the first two qualities, they were too ruled by shame to be truly outspoken with him in public about the greatest things (487b). Socrates tactfully desists from making any reference to Chaerephon; since this excitable character is both well disposed towards Socrates and outspoken to a fault, his deficiency must be intellectual.

Socrates' evidence to support this glowing assessment of Callicles' virtues is slim indeed. Many (*polloi*) in Athens would declare him to be well educated, and his being well disposed towards Socrates is proven by indirect evidence that pointedly ignores Callicles' several recent explicit protestations to that effect. In response to a question that Callicles never asks, Socrates claims to have overheard him in philosophical discussions with three friends (all of who are independently known to be associated with money, oligarchic views, and sophistry) discussing how far one should cultivate wisdom, and coming to a

---

1   *Odyssey* X. 275–306.

general consensus that it should not be studied with too much precision for fear of being unwittingly ruined by over-education (487b–e). While Socrates does not mention this concern as further evidence of Callicles' intellectual (im)moderation, it may certainly be contrasted to those very huddled conversations with youths that Callicles ridiculed. These bouts of *thumotic* trash-talking take the place of honest conversations between sophists about their art that, for all the reasons we have discussed, could never place.

The Delphic wisdom of these young men is quite striking: nothing in excess – especially self-knowledge! This superficiality has already been revealed in Callicles' literary displays; the mindset displayed here is in conformity with his advice to Socrates that philosophy should be learned by children only – in other words, by those who lack the freedom and resources to put their ideas into practice. Furthermore, since reality and rationality are not consistent with each other, philosophy is learned so that it may be later used to expose the pathetic claims of idealists. It cannot be studied as an end in itself since solipsistic reason cannot conceive of or grasp the absurd flux of reality. The only positive knowledge that adults gain from philosophy is limited and Epicurean; truth is inaccessible and unthinkable, and any gods that exist are indifferent to human affairs. All meaning here on earth is created by the power of words. This frees the best men to pursue power and pleasure at the expense of those too weak to face the abyss.

Socrates claims to deduce that Callicles is well disposed towards him from the fact that the latter shared with him the same conclusions he arrived at with his friends. He also knows, both from Callicles' assurances on this matter and the outspoken character of the young man's words, that he will speak his mind without any inhibition. As noted earlier, this quality is at variance with Callicles' prior sycophancy towards both the Demos and his high-born beloved of the same name. Can we really know for sure that Callicles is speaking his own opinion this time, or is this yet another chameleon-like adaptation to the occasion? Perhaps the best proof of Callicles' sincerity on this occasion derives from the fact that this stance towards reality results from the failure of all of the others. Callicles' self-consciously limited learning and unschooled desires, along with his desire to enjoy tyrannical power and hedonistic pleasure, explains his pragmatic compliance with the mob at one time, and the wishes of his beautiful but dense lover at another. His failures – in both love and politics – mark him out as a perfect candidate for corruption by sophistry.

However, it should also be noted that, just as Polus has mixed feelings about his *beau ideal* Archelaus, Callicles has called beautiful something that represents the *telos* of his mindset but does not actually correspond to his actual psychic state. To infer what is happening here, we may think of Callicles' ardent apologist, Nietzsche, who used as his spokesman a projection of himself grown old and wise: Zarathustra. By ridiculing Callicles' divided erotic loyalties, Socrates seems to have forced him to describe the zenith of his upside-down hierarchy. There are good reasons to infer that Socrates has egged Callicles on to give premature birth to this monstrous image of evil both for Gorgias's sake and his own; the midwife's son is forcing the irresponsible itinerant to behold the culmination of the process of corruption he set in motion. This is how Callicles could say: "Gorgias is staying with me" (447b) and invite Socrates to visito Gorgias anytime. Like Prospero facing up to Caliban, Gorgias must accept "this thing of darkness" as his own.[2] Unlike Kronos, who sought to eat up his own children, Gorgias is forced to see his illegitimate intellectual grandchild cannibalize himself.

We should now observe that the obstacles that Socrates faces in his *agon* with Callicles are quite unlike those he encountered with Gorgias and Polus. Socrates' discussion with Gorgias was an abstract and cerebral discussion conducted on the chessboard of ideas. Despite the great deal of money that it brought him, it seems that Gorgias pursued rhetoric as an end in itself. He was defeated when Socrates pointed out a glaring shortcoming in the intellectual credentials of his so-called art. With Polus, the quality of the argument was different since it is conducted in the everyday world of ambitions and conflicting passions. As noted earlier, the younger rhetorician saw his technique as a means rather than as a pure art to be enjoyed for its own sake. Socrates refuted him at the level of human spiritedness by making it clear to Polus that his means would not enable him to achieve his ends. The orator was made to see that the *logos* pursued its own *telos*; this goal was not consistent with his stated personal pursuit of political power and glory. Neither could the envy of others lead to real happiness within oneself. Polus was defeated by his honest admission that shame was worse than physical pain. This contradicted his stated view that appearances could redeem reality – even though the interior of the soul was never really studied.

The case of Callicles is quite different because, as we briefly suggested, for him the means justify the ends since the means are the ends. Callicles' cultivated shallowness ensures that his pursuit of hedonism cannot be interrupted either by pure intellectual speculation or by practical reflections within himself concerning the compatibility between his methods and his long-term goals. Callicles is free to adapt himself to the hedonistic possibilities presented by any situation because he has convinced himself that he has no conscience to impede the drive or *conatus* of his hedonistic consciousness. "*Libido ergo sum*" is his intemperate motto. Unlike Polus, who seeks to use power to create order in the common world, Callicles aspires to be the

2   William Shakespeare, *The Tempest*, V ii 278–79.

strongest beast amid chaos.[3] In other words, in conspicuous contrast to the two sophists who discreetly disguise the nihilistic truths that let them exercise power behind the scenes (this is like Gyges' secret: only one man could see the Queen naked),[4] Callicles' shameless words, once acted on, will help to create the chaos in which he expects to thrive. This is why he dares Socrates to deploy the category of shame against him. His deliberately shameless attitude derives from a nihilism that makes him all but invulnerable to dialectical refutation; it will be a source of acute embarrassment to Gorgias.

Gorgias and Polus are ranged among the cowards who make the laws in the cave because they fear the naked violence of the state of nature. Though astute enough to suspect that these laws and conventions were not founded on anything ontologically substantial, they kept their teachings relatively esoteric. However, in the hubristic and fevered climate of wartime Athens, these crude doctrines mutated alarmingly. Having been exposed to the fearful spectacles of moral depravity so accurately depicted by Thucydides, Callicles and his kind were "born and bred in the briar patch" of nihilism.[5] The explicit revelation of Gorgias's skepticism merely gave an intellectual basis for an ethos of immorality that had been bred earlier in the century and came to fruition during the war. It cannot be forgotten that desperate and shameless men of this kind dominated the Thirty – the murderously brutal *junta* that briefly ruled Athens after the War; Socrates himself narrowly escaped execution by these worthies when he disobeyed their illegal orders. This is why Callicles' thrice-repeated threat to strike Socrates is not a rhetorical flourish.

We may now return to Socrates' response to Callicles – albeit with a better appreciation of the looming threat he represents. Callicles is told that, since Socrates has every reason to trust his wisdom, benevolence, and honesty, he should follow up on his admonition and help the older man to understand the truth. Echoing his words to Thrasymachus, Socrates assures Callicles that the course of life he presently follows is not voluntarily pursued but results from his ignorance. This is why Callicles must follow up on his chastisement, and indicate to Socrates what goals he should aim towards and how he should accomplish them. Socrates promises that if he were caught not living as he had been persuaded to, Callicles would be at liberty to write him off as a complete

---

3   Voegelin states that while Socrates interprets existence "in terms of the Eros towards the Agathon," Callicles sees the meaning of life as consisting in "the victorious assertion of the *physis*" (p. 32).

4   See Ranasinghe, *The Soul of Socrates*, pp. 10–11.

5   Saxonhouse (p. 141–42) points out that Callicles is from Acharnia. This territory was most exposed to the depredations of the Spartans. While Aristophanes named an early (425) anti-war play "The Archanians," it is just as likely that, by the end of the war, one from this deme would be bitter, bellicose and cynical.

failure and never bother to denounce him again, for he would be worth nothing (488a–b). It is noteworthy that these last words will be spoken again at the end of the *Gorgias* in a slightly less complimentary tone; they suggest that it is Callicles who will be urged to distance himself from his intemperate words. In the present context, however, they afford Callicles every opportunity to distinguish himself before both an international intellectual celebrity and some of the "best and brightest" Athenians. Socrates is following this strategy in order to force Callicles to justify his behavior in speech, rather than through violent and contemptuous deeds. Since Callicles, unlike Gorgias and Polus, explicitly prefers chaos to order, his rehabilitation or punishment can only occur after he enters the realm of speech and justification.

Callicles' reentry into the arena of the *logos* begins when Socrates asks to be told how Pindar (the professional praise-singer) and he would explain the just according to nature. Socrates sums them up as saying that the strong violently bear away the property of the weaker, the better rule the worse, and the superior have more than the inferior. After confirming that this is still his position, tacitly conceding that he is not pure flux, Callicles is then asked if he considers the same man to be both superior and stronger. Socrates confesses to not having understood what this meant. Relating this question to Callicles' earlier statement about the natural right of great powers to bully weaker states, the stance taken by the Athenians in the Melian debate,[6] he wonders if strength is identical to superiority (*beltion*) and whether being better or worse is just a matter of physical power. Asking Callicles to entertain the possibilities that one could be superior and yet physically weaker, or stronger and yet more vicious (*moktheroteron*), Socrates requests that he define whether the mightier, the superior, and the more powerful are all one or different (488b–d).

Once Callicles clearly iterates that all three are the same, Socrates asks him whether the demotic many are stronger than the one since, as Callicles himself said, they set down laws. Callicles asks how this could not be, only to be then asked whether since the many are stronger, their laws are therefore superior and fine (*kalon*) according to nature. He is then asked whether or not the many hold that equality and doing injustice is shameful. Here Socrates urges Callicles not to succumb to shame like the others did before him. He repeats the question and asks Callicles not to deny him an answer, especially now that he has finally found a man of discernment who could confirm his opinions. When Callicles reluctantly admits that the many customarily hold this view, Socrates ends this game of cat and mouse to point out that this means that the belief that pursuing equality is just and, holding that it is less shameful to suffer injustice than to inflict it, is not merely conventional but also true

6   Thucydides, *Peloponnesian War*, VI. 84–116.

by nature. This also suggests to him that Callicles had not spoken truthfully earlier when he claimed that since nature and convention were opposed, it was Socrates who worked evil in his arguments by demanding that they coincide (488d–489b).

In response to this devastating broadside, Callicles is forced to accuse Socrates of laying verbal traps that he then regards as "gifts from the gods." Now Callicles asserts that of course he means that only better or superior men are strong. This after all was the whole point of his earlier speech; how could Socrates suppose him to be saying that when a rabble of slaves and riff-raff, of use only for physical exertion, gets together and makes assertions – that then these amount to laws? Socrates smoothly replies that he suspected that his blustery interlocutor, whom he calls a *daimonic* man, had something of this sort in mind, and that he repeated his question because he craved to know exactly what Callicles meant. He is sure that Callicles at least does not regard mere numbers as any basis for superiority, and neither could he see his slaves as being superior just because they has more physical strength. So, he asks Callicles to start from the beginning and explain who these superior men were, since he evidently didn't equate this quality with physical might. Callicles tries vainly to escape by accusing Socrates of irony, only to have Socrates swear by Zethus, and remind Callicles that he used the analogy of Zethus and Amphion to make much ironic play at his expense (489b–e). It is worth bearing in mind that it is Amphion who has the last laugh in the *Antiope*; once again Callicles proves himself to be a half-baked scholar.

While it is clear that Socrates is demonstrating his own effortless superiority to Callicles by toying with him, we must also observe that he is also setting about making the supposedly shameless youth experience the very emotion he claimed to have transcended. When Callicles accused Polus and Gorgias of succumbing to shame before an audience, his point was that shame was an externally imposed emotion that could not affect one who knew these experiences to be purely conventional. He now feels shame and must wonder if this is because of incontinence, because his will is not powerful enough to overcome external influences. The other possibility is that he feels ashamed because Socrates has made him feel the emotion of shame internally.[7]

We should also carefully note that there seem to be many levels of shame appearing and operating here; beyond felt damage to one's *amour propre*, there

7   Richard McKim gets to the heart of the matter: "our shame about vice is a natural sign that deep down we prefer virtue. What Callicles calls our 'natural' beliefs represent for Socrates the artificial virtues imposed upon us from without by such corrupting influences as a Gorgianic rhetorical education." See "Shame and Truth in Plato's Gorgias" in *Platonic Writings, Platonic Readings* (Routledge, 1988), p. 39.

is a deeper, more intellectual, experience of shame that rises from within Callicles, as he is forced to reflect on his own discomfiture.[8] In other words, when there is objective damage done to the inner self, it is immediately experienced as shame; and furthermore there is additional shame experienced when one reflects on the causes of this phenomenon. Socrates will continue to test and probe the structure of this inner dimension over the second part of this dialogue. By making Callicles feel an interior dimension that he most manifestly cannot control through violent power, a cave whence he cannot storm out like an unchained young lion, the brash youth is being made conscious of a non-physical moral order that willy-nilly has authority over him. We should also bear in mind that the hapless Callicles is not Socrates' only target as he sets about this forensic dialectical demonstration of the real meaning of shame; his intellectual grandfather Gorgias will also certainly feel some no little reflective shame as Socrates silently reveals to him to the deleterious effects of his problematic pseudo-art on Callicles, without exposing him to any immediate first order social shame at all.

This intellectual dimension is now brought explicitly into play as Socrates once again asks Callicles to explain to him who the superior men are. He seems to help his victim out with a "gift of the gods" or a leading question, asking him whether by the superior and stronger men he means those who are more prudently intelligent (*phronimos*) or some other kind. When Callicles swears by Zeus and affirms "most emphatically" that this is what he means (490a), Socrates tests his certainty (and along with it his intellectual discernment or *phronesis*!) by feeding him a temperamentally attractive but quite deceptive expression of the implications of this superiority. We recall that Callicles had earlier painted a caricature of the hopelessly impractical and helpless philosopher in order to support his counter art of practical affairs, an art that he would now obviously like to exemplify with this model of the *phronimos*. Socrates will later show him that *phronesis* must be based on something nobler than a mere knack for practical affairs, but for the present, he tempts Callicles away from this plausible and defensible but ultimately

8   In his suggestively titled essay, "Socrates and the Irrational," Paul Woodruff refers to this "Socratic shame" as "solipsized shame" – described as "the full awareness that one has betrayed values that are entirely one's own." *Reason and Religion in Socratic Philosophy* (Oxford, 2000), p. 144. The problem with this approach is its assumption that these "values" are maxims created for oneself rather than transcendental timeless measures that the well-formed conscience discovers. Woodruff notes that Socrates "seems to assume, however, that the shame he induces is always in tune with the truth . . . even if it as wildly irrational as *Alcibiades* says he feels it to be" (pp. 144–45). He rather dismissively states that "appeals to conscience have no standing in the court of knowledge" (p. 145).

inaccurate account of his real views by suggesting that the *phronimos* is worth more than ten thousand imprudent men and consequently be should both the ruler and have more than those he rules. The hidden implication of this is that if one should rule over ten thousand and have more than those he rules, then he will have more than ten thousand times the property of an average subject. When Callicles eagerly agrees to this, claiming as his own thought this new mantra "that it is just by nature for the one who is superior and more intelligent to rule over and have more than those he rules," Socrates lowers the boom on him and asks him to stop immediately (490a–b).

Callicles is asked what on earth he means by this. This inquiry is strange since he has only been repeating words that Socrates has put in his mouth. On the other hand, it could be said that Socrates has "midwifed" these thoughts out of him because of the younger man's confused incoherence; they certainly seem to express the outlook of Callicles' earlier diatribe. Even before they begin to explore the import of these words, it can be seen that Callicles is quite lacking in the prudent intelligence that he has just lauded. Indeed, to the extent that he is giving and taking away arguments from his inferior, Socrates is ironically exercising the prerogatives of the stronger intellect in this discussion. The ends towards which he will employ this power will soon become evident; like a master-herdsman, he fattens up his cattle before dispatching him.

Socrates asks Callicles to imagine a circumstance where there were many men (*anthropoi*) crammed together in the same place, as they are in their present surroundings, with much food and drink available, being of all sorts and strengths with one of them, a physician, more practically wise about these things, but only of average strength. When Callicles agrees that the physician will be the superior and stronger man – as they understand the latter term – Socrates then asks him whether on this basis he should have more of the food than the others, or distribute it according to his knowledge – not giving himself the largest portion for fear of being unjust to himself but avoiding excess. There is also the possibility that he could give himself the smallest portion if he were physically the weakest (490b–c). Even before we consider Callicles' reply, we can see that Socrates is not supporting the view that the best man will take the least share because he is masochistic or weak-willed. This is the exaggerated view only taken by those, like Glaucon and Polus, who tend to situate the most virtuous man on Job's dunghill. Neither is Socrates advocating strict numerical equality; we could even coin a neologism and call this state one of "equantity." Instead, as we shall see, he advocates geometrical or proportionate equality.

Faced with these possibilities, Callicles again tries to bluster his way out of the trap that he has helped to construct. While he clearly sees that a physician or healer (*iatros*) would not gorge himself to death, Callicles yet seeks to avoid the implication that the practically intelligent man, the physician, respects the order of *physis*/nature. Accordingly, he accuses Socrates of talking of nonsensical matters like food, drink, and doctors that have nothing to do with what he meant. Even though Callicles admits that he holds the man of *phronesis* to be superior, and consequently deserving of more, he angrily rejects the notion that this has to do with food or drink. Socrates' next suggestions – that the best weaver should wear the best cloaks, and the best cobbler wear as many of the biggest shoes as he can – only compounds Callicles' fury (490c–e).

Callicles now accuses Socrates of always saying the same things (490e). Here he echoes the complaint of the exasperated Hippias, recorded by Xenophon, that Socrates kept asking the same tiresome questions over and over again.[9] This leads Socrates to make the same pointed response he gave Hippias, saying that he continued to say the same things about the same things. Then, when Callicles denies that they were discussing cobblers, weavers, cooks, and physicians, he asks what it is that the more intelligent and stronger men take more of, observing that Callicles neither accepts the examples supplied by Socrates nor offers his own (491a).

We must recall here that while Callicles' lack of intellect and imagination are patently evident, Socrates isn't simply flogging a dead horse or tormenting a helpless opponent. The purpose of his debate with this violent and arrogant young man is to suggest, against the dark backdrop of the Peloponnesian War, how these very dangerous qualities can be dealt with in one incapable of apprehending the finer points of dialectic – those employed earlier in the *Gorgias* in defeating the two rhetoricians. The nightmarish scenarios created by Glaucon and Polus may well materialize if Socrates is not able to defeat this kind of opponent. Though Socrates cannot defeat an ignorant mob, he is must at least be capable of neutralizing them in a one-on-one duel; after turning one mob into many men, he seeks to turn their many unruly desires into one unified whole. Also, it is not enough to midwife a man's perverse desires out of him; they must then be defeated. As we noted, the more ignorant his opponents, the harder it is for Socrates to convince them. This is the dialectical equivalent of asymmetrical or guerrilla warfare. Unlike Gorgias, who found pleasure in his ability to defeat few before many and Polus who sought power and admiration from the many, Callicles seeks only to satisfy the many mad desires that have enslaved him.

Because the youth's aims are irrational, Socrates cannot argue reasonably with Callicles; this was not the case with the two earlier interlocutors. There is a regression in the quality of Socrates' interlocutors: from intellectuals, think

9   Xenophon, *Memorabilia*, 4.4

of Gorgias or Pericles, who gain satisfaction from the sheer exercise of their art and defer external gratification; to their power hungry successors, like Polus or Cleon, who value demagogic power over hedonistic pleasure; and ending with those ranging from Callicles or Alcibiades, who have disintegrated into psychic chaos. Looking back on the prior stages of the *Gorgias* we see that rhetoric was first easily discredited as a science, and then shown with slightly more difficulty to be an esoteric but ineffective means of wielding power. Even though power corrupts, dreaming of it is not as corrosive as actually wielding it; this is why Socrates can do business with Polus in the language of realism. Now, finally, rhetoric must be publicly exposed for its malignant influence on democracy; Socrates will display the soul of one who has been corrupted by it. While Callicles believes himself to be a realist, he is both too intellectually deficient and emotionally enslaved to form an accurate impression of objective reality. Exposure to the nihilistic power of rhetoric leads the corrupted soul to lose its powers of self-movement, self-control, and self-knowledge. Callicles' chaotic reality is much like ours; peopled by ungrateful freedmen, it is like Plato's Cave without anyone in charge of the shadows.

Meanwhile, replying to Socrates' suggestion that his superior rulers would be too overwhelmed by excessive profiteering to be able to govern at all, Callicles now protests that he spoke of one intelligently versed in the ways of the polis and its governance; he adds to this virtue a quantity of courage sufficient for him to achieve his objective without softness of soul (491b). This testifies ominously to his increasing frustration with dialectical methods; perhaps his earlier impulse to thrash Socrates was sounder? This was the danger indicated in Book I of the *Republic* when Polemarchus and his spirited cronies blithely contended that they would not listen when Socrates tried to persuade them not to abduct him to the house of Cephalus. Philebus employed a not-dissimilar version of this strategy when he remained silent throughout the dialogue on pleasure named after him.[10] We could imagine a short and deadly, silent dialogue on violence with Callicles as Socrates' only interlocutor.[11]

Clearly Callicles and his oligarchic friends, who have taken an oath of ignorance with him, are most dangerous when they detach themselves from the world of reality and plot to overthrow it. While sophistry represented the first stage of a withdrawal from the world into a skeptical language game, the war

10 Friedlander suggests that this is why the tyrannical must reject philosophy and speech "by entering into a discussion, they acknowledge that validity of a law that must, ultimately, cause their downfall" (p. 261).

11 Eric Voegelin remind us that "in a decadent society the ridiculous intellectual is an enemy of the spirit and . . . powerful enough to murder its representatives physically" (p. 25).

and chaos caused in no small part by sophistic demagoguery led many like Callicles to give up on trying to manipulate conventional *nomos*. Instead, they shamelessly choose violence as an end rather than a means. Socrates will continue to try to use Callicles' penchant for violent speech and desire for recognition to force him to reenter reality, or at least to arrive at a more sober appreciation of the insidious effects of violence and shamelessness.

Accordingly, since Callicles added courage to the practical intelligence that constituted his earlier definition of natural right, but neglected to state where this superiority would be exercised, the philosopher must point out that Callicles himself may be accused of charges that are the very opposite of those he made against Socrates. While "most superior Callicles" was annoyed by Socrates' steadfastness in posing the same questions, the accuser is guilty of great inconstancy in never saying the same thing twice. Like his spokesperson, Zethus, Callicles is a nomad; he conducts linguistic raids on reality, but can never be counted on to stand by his own positions. So Socrates asks him again to define both who is superior and stronger, as well as explain what it is that they will be superior in. Callicles now protests that he has already answered the question, stating that those intelligent with regard to the affairs of the polis are those who are superior, and adding that they will be superior to others in their power over the polis (491a–b).

Now it should be clear that this statement is but another tautology; the character of a regime and its virtues are co-extensive with its ruling class: murderers, sadists, and Jew-haters are ideally suited to ruling a Nazi state, and different traits are to be found in the rulers of democratic and oligarchic political regimes. However, we see why Callicles added the virtue of courage; he means by it something akin to Nietzsche's Will to Power and Heidegger's Resoluteness.[12] Callicles feels that whoever has to ability to wield power ruthlessly in a polis will be superior in the art of statecraft. Now this is far removed from Polus and his partially idealized view of Archelaus, who, despite all of his crimes, did rule in a way that brought no little benefit to his kingdom. Most of the populace of many of the world's nations, even in our day, would be quite happy to be under the yoke of benign and efficient authoritarian rulers who make the trains run on time and maintain order, albeit at the cost of political freedom. It is the combination of paranoid totalitarianism and inefficiency that proves to be both unbearable and cataclysmic in its effects.

What leads one to infer that Callicles is talking about something far worse than an efficient despot is made clear by his single-minded, and quite postmodern, belief that a tyrant can and should do anything he wishes. We recall his

---

12 See "Self Assertion of the German University," in *Martin Heidegger: Philosophical and Political Writings* (Continuum, 2003), pp. 2–11.

words about the young lion breaking out of the chains of convention and ruling according to nature, which he takes to mean the advantage of the stronger. The belief that he can bend reality and nature to his will marks the worst and most dangerous ruler of all. While enlightened despotism was characteristic of the modern age's belief that the human intellect could decipher nature and reconfigure sublunary reality to utopian specifications after God's death, nihilistic tyranny is inherently connected to the very postmodern belief that since God never existed, only reason is absurd and hence prohibited, while everything else is permitted. Unlike modern materialism's view that matter is substance, the postmodernist position that appearance is reality, and matter nothing but flux, leads to the "valorization" of random acts of destructive virtuosity. Though the triumph of technology has aggravated this problem to apocalyptic proportions in our time, the combination of flattery, solipsism, superstition, and paranoia took the tyrannical temptation very far in ancient times also.

Socrates sets out to confirm and confront the grave suspicions that we have just entertained by addressing Callicles in familiarly oligarchic terms as his comrade or partisan (*hetaire*), and asking him how these rulers would stand towards themselves. His fellow traveler is astonished at the question. When asked again if every man would rule himself or only rule the others, Callicles asks him again what this means. Socrates' mild reply, "Nothing spectacular, but just what most people mean: being moderate and having control over oneself and ruling over the pleasures and desires in himself,"[13] successfully provokes in Callicles great contempt. His condescending reply is to call Socrates hilarious (*hedus*) for supposing the wise to be silly or simpletons. When Socrates ironically protests that everyone knows that he is making no such identification, Callicles loftily explains that no human being could be happy while being enslaved to anything (491d–e). A man must be forcibly liberated from himself to be happy!

Callicles now tells Socrates, bluntly, that it is naturally just and fine for a man to let his desires become as great and unfettered as possible. Unlike Polus, he is not ruled by ambition or the Will to Power. The purpose of his courage and practical intelligence, the qualities Callicles earlier used to define a natural ruler, is to serve these desires to the fullest extent when they are as great as could be.[14] However, since this is not possible for the many (who seem to lack

---

13 Stauffer is puzzled and perplexed by Socrates' seemingly abrupt transition from discussing the rights of the superior to talking about moderation and self-control (p. 102). However it is self-evident to Socrates that rulers lacking self-knowledge are a danger to both the city and the soul. Great power and technical mastery are harmful and useless to ambitious political scientists deficient in the philosophic virtue of temperance.

14 Weiss claims: "it is not ruling that Callicles wants for himself, nor does he want,

the necessary manly courage and intelligence), they denounce these real men out of shame at their own impotence and call intemperance shameful as they seek to enslave those with superior natures. Conversely, out of spite and resentment at not being able to gratify their own pleasures, they praise moderation and justice. He believes that nothing would be more shameful than for the born aristocrats of nature, those capable of gaining tyranny or dynastic rule, to impose limits on themselves and enslave themselves to the laws, chatter, and condemnation of the common multitude. He asks Socrates how these fine fellows could not be miserable when forced to share benefits with all equally, even as rulers of their own state. Socrates sought the truth and Callicles reveals it: luxurious excess, overt intemperance, and raw freedom, violently gained and sustained, are the essence of happiness. Normal virtues and vices are unnatural and worthless (491e–492c). Compared to this Glaucon's concealed cave-ruler is a stodgy oligarch.

Acclaiming Callicles for speaking with the frankness of "one not ignobly born," Socrates says that he forges ahead of others in saying what they dare not. This seems to be the very contrary of Socrates' folly in plunging deeper and deeper into philosophy – the very folly for which Callicles chastised him. Callicles is now urged by Socrates to continue speaking without restraint so that the best way of living will finally become clear. After he gains confirmation that virtue, according to Callicles, consists of not restraining the desires in any way but in letting them become as great as possible and in procuring satisfaction for them in any and every possible way, Socrates asks whether it is mistaken to describe those who need nothing as happy. Upon Callicles' curt rejection of this opinion, "For then stones and corpses would be the happiest," Socrates then contends that the life described by Callicles is also uncanny (*deinos*). Quoting Euripides' lines from a relatively unknown play: "Who can tell if life is death and death life?" Socrates entertains the idea that maybe they all were dead. Of course at the time these words were written by Plato, both Socrates and Euripides were dead and perhaps Gorgias also! This not withstanding, the resurrected literary character called Socrates now quotes a saying he once heard from an unnamed wise man to the effect that life is really death and the body a tomb (492d–493a).

Since the sources of this saying are left obscure, and would not mean anything to Callicles, we should perhaps attend to its significance in the *Gorgias*.

> like Polus, to kill and banish at whim. All Callicles wants is to be safe and prosperous" (p. 104). While agreeing with her that he is not attracted to politics or ruled by ambition, I suspect that Callicles does not seek stability; his worldview is too ugly, and his desires are too unruly for Epicureanism to appeal to him. In Weiss's words "what makes men superior in Callicles' eyes is their unrestrained pursuit of . . . their intemperance" (p. 106).

Callicles himself brought up the topic of the upside-down reality when he questioned Chaerephon (the bat) about Socrates' seriousness, and this theme will loom even larger in the final *logos* about the afterlife. Neither can it be ignored that most of those lucky or unlucky few who survived the plague, the Sicilian disaster, the final starving out of Athens, and many other terrifying episodes during the twenty-seven-year-long war, were already men without shadows. It is certainly the case that hyper-realistic and ultra-hedonistic views, such as those espoused by Callicles, could only have been given shameless public expression in post-apocalyptic times. It is also helpful to return once more to the *Republic* and recall that Socrates viewed political life itself as a sort of underworld in which human beings knew themselves only as reputations/shadows/bodies. Consequently, they had no idea, and were literally *a-ides*, of whom they really were.[15] As we shall see, Socrates, through an extension of his familiar *reductio-ad-absurdum* technique, starts to triumph over Callicles the moment he forces his adversary to describe his infinite desires in words.

Socrates also stated in the *Meno*, a dialogue closely related to the *Gorgias* in the Platonic *corpus*, that one who can make another into a statesman, the so-called "political art" that Socrates will soon claim to practice, will be like Tiresias in Hades (100a): "Alone among those below keeping his mind. The rest are but fleeting shadows."[16] By this model, Socrates is alive while Callicles is one of the dead. We have also seen Callicles himself often suggests that Socrates and he belong to different realities; recalling his warning against chasing deeper into philosophy, we may infer that as reason and reality are incompatible, philosophy is in non-being. This means that Socrates is dead to the world while Callicles, the shameless, is thoroughly alive to reality. This clash between conflicting realities was also played out memorably in the *Crito*, where Socrates and his oldest friend each tried to rescue the other from what he believed to be an illusory worldview.

Back in the *Gorgias*, Socrates further states that, according to this saying of the wise man, the part of the soul containing the desires is both persuasive and persuadable; it also "wanders up and down" in its confusion (493a). This outlook makes the desires of Callicles akin to ghostlike and pathetic humors that must be put to rest as soon as possible. He is like the shade of Elpenor, the youngest and least competent of Odysseus's crew, who blundered up to the roof of Circe's house in a drunken stupor only to fall down again.[17] Callicles'

---

15   Benardete suggests that the natures of these men are so devoid of content that they might as well have been dead: "the dead are not miserable because they are dead; they are miserable because they are needy. They are indistinguishable from those Callicles says are the most fully alive. Life then is death" (p. 75).

16   *Odyssey* X. 492–95.

17   *Odyssey* X. 552–60.

inability to adhere to any firm position is clearly consistent with this Homeric link. Because he had not yet drunk of the waters of Lethe, Elpenor, though already dead, could still converse with Odysseus. Now it is clear, even to Callicles himself, that he lacks both the ability and desire to live the life of the unchained lion that he had earlier described so enthusiastically; to this extent, the polis is not threatened by his ambitions. On the other hand, the health of the polity is deeply compromised when men like Callicles allow an anarchic regime to hold sway in their souls. Even though Callicles may be beyond education, he must at least respect the legitimacy of principles that he cannot obey.

Accordingly, Socrates further quotes another unnamed mythmaker from Sicily or Italy who, making a play on the words for persuade (*peithos*) and jar (*pithos*), called the uninitiated the "un-stoppered" (493a–b). Following this playful analogy, which depends on the Cratylus-like magic of the *logos*, one could conclude that every soul needs a restraining *daimon* or guardian spirit to prevent it from going beyond itself into the bad infinite of non-being – what Callicles would call true freedom. It follows also that temperance, moderating self-knowledge, is only gained through awareness of the limits and ignorance of one's soul. There is also a more serious analogy drawn between Pericles' strategy of staying within one's limits or long walls, and the aggressive expansionist spirit pursued in such endeavors as the tragic Sicilian expedition. Socrates himself, following the mythmaker, says that that jar-like part of the soul containing the desires is prone to be leaky and intemperate. Of course even the best jar, if it lacked a stopper, or *daimon*, would lose its contents when held upside-down or nurtured in an unhealthy political *ethos*.

Even if Callicles may not be able to take in any of these rather playful analogies, they are certainly of value in helping us to understand what Socrates understands the soul to be. He now points out to Callicles that the uninitiated – those with "no-idea" – in Hades (literally, *a-ides,* meaning without a "look" or the possibility of being discerned) perform their impossible infinite labors in much the same spirit, with similarly flawed implements. Socrates provides the example of a man condemned to draw and convey water with a sieve to a leaky and perforated pitcher. It also follows that those who follow the un-persuadable and skeptical outlook with regard to truth can neither take in nor retain anything substantial in their fickle souls (493b–c). While Callicles stays unimpressed by all attempts to make him choose order and sufficiency over intemperance and insatiability, and indeed makes Socrates himself superficially resemble one of those souls condemned to pour wisdom into an empty vessel, one final analogy is employed at this point.

Socrates now uses a more provocative simile in a way that will help Callicles to better perceive the absurdity of his ideals and desires. Gathering together most of the salient elements in his previous analogies, he now makes a new image between their respective approaches towards the best life. He speaks of two men, one temperate and the other intemperate, who are both owners of many jars, filled with wine, milk, honey, and many other good things that are said to be obtainable only with considerable exertion and risk. While the temperate man fills his jars to the brim and then is at rest with regard to them, the intemperate man has perforated and leaky jars and is thus compelled to continually devote all his time and effort towards keeping them filled – otherwise he suffers great pains (493d–e). Callicles rejects this comparison, asserting that the man who has filled his jars no longer has any pleasure but lives like a stone. He lives in what Sartre would call a state of being-in-itself.[18] Callicles rejects a way of life where one no longer either rejoices or feels pain. He believes that happiness is keeping as much as possible flowing in (494a–b). By contrast Socrates' model suggests that while justly acquired wealth is a good thing, the education of desire or demand and the art of spending wealth well are at least co-extensive with it.

Callicles' crude account of instant hedonism is *prima facie* inadequate insofar as he cannot even account for delayed gratification, but it must be also recognized that the purpose of life extends beyond consuming or storing large quantities of necessary substances. Socrates does not say very much explicitly on this subject in the dialogue, but the teleology emerging out of his engagement with Polus, his critical view of power that was accumulated for the sake of envy, along with many tantalizing hints about a genuine art of legislation for the good of the soul suggest strongly that the best human beings should not simply bury their talents in the ground or take shelter from political storms by building the little wall referred to in the *Republic* (496d). Indeed. Plato's famed account of the ship of state in that dialogue also suggests that such an art exists; as we know, he is sharply critical of those who are so intent on being popular or powerful enough to command the ship that they either neglect, or are oblivious to, the art of navigation. We have every reason to suppose that his recommendation for the best souls is that they should use their stores of wine, milk, and honey to take care of their body while they study and pursue what is positively good through their soul in this life. We already have noted several indications scattered throughout the *Gorgias* that Socrates did not champion a Stoic policy of voluntary submission to unjust laws or any other masochistic otherworldly fixations. Likewise, the navigator's art cannot be subordinated to ends. How we get there has everything to do with reaching our destination.

Returning to the argument, Socrates points out that the maintenance of a constant state of maximal flow would necessitate that the intemperate man's jars should be very leaky indeed. When Callicles accepts this, possibly revealing an

---

18 Sartre, *Being and Nothingness* (Washington Square, 1956), pp. 24–30.

affinity to the prodigal son of a miserly oligarch of the *Republic*, Socrates says that his ideal man leads the life of a *charadrios*, a messy bird with a high metabolism notorious for its capacity to excrete and eat at the same time. In other words, his various appetites would be as excessive, harmful, and wasteful as his exertions to satisfy them would be long, dangerous, and arduous. Since Callicles states that one who satisfies all his desires, glories in this and leads a happy life, Socrates offers congratulations and urges him not to restrain himself through shame, since he will not do so either in questioning. He then asks Callicles if it is happiness for one who itches to continue scratching all of his life. When Callicles accuses him of crude demagoguery, Socrates urges him not to succumb to shame, like Gorgias and Polus, but to answer courageously. So Callicles must admit that he who scratches lives pleasantly, and by extension, happily (494b–d).

Socrates now asks if this happiness should extend beyond scratching of the head, pointing out that Callicles has exposed himself to other, more extreme, pleasures and extremities. The climax of the path endorsed by this hedonistic approach is the life of a catamite, an insatiable but passive male homosexual. Socrates asks Callicles to deny that such a life is awful, wicked, and shameful, since such persons are happy by his definition of having an unlimited quantity of the pleasure they choose (494e). Callicles' attempts to shame Socrates to silence again fall on deaf ears as this "nobly born" man is told that his own arguments have led him to this self-evidently offensive position. He cannot find the pleasures of a catamite shameful without acknowledging that all pleasures are not equal to each other (494e–495a). When Socrates now challenges him to either assert that the pleasant and the good are the same, or to admit that some pleasures are not good, Callicles says that they are the same but only after admitting that he does so in order to avoid contradicting himself (495a). This admission proves that he is shameless, but self-consistent to the extent that he has already stated that intelligence and courage are only means towards gaining his desires and passions. In other words, his shamelessness is not primarily concerned with speaking the truth without fear; after all he does not believe in objective truth, its independent existence would fly in the face of his *libido ergo sum* philosophy of solipsistic hedonism.

However, when Socrates charges him with contradicting himself, and of no longer following through on his promise to examine the things that are, by speaking at variance with his own opinion, Callicles accuses Socrates of doing the same. Socrates' response is to state that if so, he too is not doing what is correct. He then goes on to point out that the good is not a matter of finding pleasure at any price because shameful consequences naturally result from them (495a–b). This mystifying exchange may suggest that Callicles' intellect and courage (shamelessness) are very much at variance along the lines just indicated and that he sincerely believes that Socrates is also just like him but too ashamed to admit to it. Callicles could also be ashamed of his own shame – believing like Raskolnikov in *Crime and Punishment* that this proves him to be composed of all-too-human clay.[19] Socrates' response reminds Callicles that even an immoralist must admit that certain imprudent shameless acts bring bad consequences; this is why courage or boldness alone is insufficient, the perfect immoralist also needs instrumental intelligence. In other words, the catamite's real sin is imprudence rather than immorality.

Socrates now implicitly challenges Callicles' courage by asking if he would contend mightily to defend his views, and duly receives an assurance to that effect (495b–c). Socrates seems to realize that he is arguing with a damaged and bifurcated soul and proceeds accordingly. His aim seems to be more to make Callicles better aware of the implications of his own views, rather than to claim the victory that he has already won many times over. Callicles must recognize that his hedonistic outlook is based on nihilistic criteria, and can have no connection with moral probity, intellectual consistency, or even reality itself.[20] Accordingly, Callicles is asked to reprise his earlier claims regarding knowledge and confirm his statement that a certain manly courage or boldness went along with it. He is then asked if courage (*andreia*) and knowledge (*episteme*) are different things and, when this is confirmed, he is then invited to make similar distinctions between pleasure and knowledge, and pleasure and courage respectively (495c–e). Socrates will now proceed to speak in the language of legal proclamation and set these threefold distinctions beside Callicles' earlier identification of pleasure and the good as being one.

When Callicles, using similar language, asks Socrates if he agrees with these distinctions, he is told that by the philosopher that not only does he disagree, but also that even Callicles himself will reject them *when he looks on himself correctly* (495e). This language harkens back to Socrates' complicated statement to Gorgias regarding his own efforts to convince himself that he was the kind of person who valued learning above victory. This is worth bearing in mind as we return to our present context, where Socrates gains Callicles' agreement that the experience of doing well is the opposite of the experience of doing badly. It follows that these two states are related as health and sickness are; being mutually exclusive. The same organ, Socrates uses the eye as an example, cannot be simultaneously be healthy and sick. We should note that

19 As Waller Newell puts it "Callicles becomes even more deeply ashamed of *being* ashamed than he is ashamed," *Ruling Passion* (Rowman and Littlefield, 2000), p. 26.

20 As Benardete observes, "Callicles' hedonism is not just what rhetoric sponsors; it is the invention of rhetoric and bears little relation to experience and no relation to knowledge" (p. 79).

Socrates' use of the eye conforms to the logographic economy of the dialogue, since his purpose is to make Callicles see reality in a healthy manner. Callicles now admits that these paired qualities – strength and weakness, speed and slowness – are also related in the same way, as are good things and happiness or bad things and unhappiness (495e–496b).

Socrates now turns to consider things that a human being is released from while they yet describe him. These would clearly not be related to each other as the good and the bad. Perhaps we could include many processes under this heading. Ignorance would be a good example of this, as would weakness, but healthy processes do not account for every possibility here. Socrates does not provide any examples of this matter for Callicles, but urges him to consider the question very carefully before replying. Callicles strongly concurs: "we are enormously in agreement" (496c), thus suggesting that he sees a connection to monstrously excessive hunger – a perverse appetite that grows with feeding. Of course, this is completely consistent with his view of pleasure and happiness. When Socrates takes him back to matters they had earlier agreed to, and asks whether hunger, by itself, is pain or pleasure. Callicles replies that while hunger is painful, eating is pleasant to a hungry man. Socrates agrees, but takes him back to the unpleasantness of hunger in itself. Callicles now agrees that both hunger and thirst are inherently unpleasant states. After Socrates now widens this category and suggests that all needs and desires are painful (496d), Callicles agrees readily. Hedonism swiftly passes beyond the natural needs and lusts of the body to become fixated on impossible, perverse, and contradictory goals.[21]

The discussion now shifts to the satiation of the various natural needs and desires, with Socrates asking whether drinking is pleasant to a thirsty man. It then follows that the unpleasantness of thirst is connected to the "pleasure and rejoicing" that Callicles had earlier spoken of as pleasure kept flowing in and out of the leaky jars. He also agrees that drinking under these circumstances both satisfies a need and constitutes a pleasure. This means that it would not be a pleasure were it not simultaneously based or dependent on an unpleasant need. When Callicles agrees with all this, Socrates then returns to the previously agreed-upon impossibility of doing well and badly at the same time. He concludes that since rejoicing is not the same as doing well, and suffering pain is not identical to doing badly, the pleasant is not the same as the good (496d–497a).

When Callicles complains that he doesn't see the subtle sophistry being

21   Newell points out that Callicles "prefers the possibility of limitless pleasures" (*Ruling Passion*, p. 22). In other words, like Glaucon, his unchecked imagination rules over his desires and deeds in the real world. "Callicles would rather resist clarifying eros than rob it of its grandeur" p. 36.

employed by Socrates, this proudly shameless man is accused of acting like a coy woman in feigning ignorance, when he really understands quite well (497a). Urged to advance further, Callicles is told by Socrates that he is being shown how wise he is in admonishing him (497b). This seems to be exemplified by his next question, as to whether one both ceases to be thirsty and being pleased at the same time by drinking. This suggests that Callicles can't learn because he prefers to be ignorantly un-slaked and shameless; differently put, he esteems chaos and raw power higher than its actualization. In terms of the model of the leaky jars: he values sensual taste above nutrition and would vomit to stay hungry and eat more. While the comparison to the *charadrios* is apt indeed, this analogy also applies to the cynical outlook and nihilistic procedures of Gorgias's art. Victory in debate cannot be pursued at the expense of learning and virtue. Neither should a polity be made more aggressive by the implanting of unnatural and artificial desires and/or paranoid fears in the citizenry.[22]

At this point, Callicles vomits up his lesson again and refuses to proceed further. He is persuaded to continue by the long-silent Gorgias, who urges him to answer for their/his sake also so that the argument (*logos*) may be concluded (497b). Quite apart from Gorgias's famed persuasiveness, we must also pay attention to the request that this be done for his sake. When Callicles complains that Socrates always proceeds in this way of asking petty questions until he refutes his opponent, Gorgias surprisingly replies that it isn't Callicles' honor (*timai*) that is at stake here (497b). Taken along with his earlier request, and our previous anticipations of the trajectory of his dialectic, it may be seen that it is Gorgias who is the true indirect addressee of Socrates' *epideixis* here. This inference is confirmed when Callicles gives in with bad grace and asks Socrates to continue with his small and narrow questions since Gorgias is of this opinion.

It may be a narrow and petty point, but it isn't Gorgias's desire to hear more but his opinion (*dokei*), that Callicles' honor isn't at stake, which counts here. Socrates' response, complimenting Callicles on his happiness or good fortune (*eudaimonia*) in being initiated into the greater mysteries before the lesser, seems to suggest (at least to the reader) that Callicles has seen the broad frame of the dialogue without perceiving the relevance of these issues to his own narrow and petty soul. Since the Greater Eleusinian Mysteries pertained to the glories of the enlightened soul, while the Lesser Mysteries made the uninitiated soul aware of the misery of its present state, it is as though Callicles is the pig being sacrificed for Gorgias's enlightenment!

---

22 Saxonhouse applies the parable of the leaky jar to the city as well as the individual soul. She observes that because "filling the city is like filling the leaky jar . . . (Athens) can never be fully satisfied." p. 166.

Nevertheless, when Callicles is again asked whether thirst and pleasure terminate at the same point, his answers inevitably lead to the general point that pains and pleasures cease together (497c–d). According to this view, pleasure is inevitably regarded as a distraction that is necessarily dependent on the pain of the world. This despairingly solipsistic and negative viewpoint cannot conceive of a positive happiness stemming from a productive relationship between the soul and the macrocosm. Put crudely, while happiness derives from truly being actualized as oneself, pleasure is a shameless and slavish self-forgetting. This remarkable implication is closely connected to Socrates' paradox-filled exchange with Polus concerning the difference between subjectively believing oneself to be happy, as opposed to the objective condition of being happy. The stunning implication is that happiness is not a solipsistic state of Epicurean detachment from reality. We shall return to the question of how Socrates overcomes the three denials of Gorgias – which separate speech from Being – in the final quarter of this work.

It must be seen that the absolute disjunction between good and bad things stands in striking contrast to the symbiotic relationship between pleasure and pain. Even if one way of regarding the problem of evil would hold that what is good emerges out of successfully struggling with evil, the hedonistic view sees pleasure-good as a separation from pain-evil that is yet bound to it. By needing to be visibly detached from others and/or through indulging violently adversarial cravings that refuse to be educated, hedonistic pleasure maintains an essentially parasitic and dependent relationship to the evil of the world. This means that the criterion of pleasure and pain are closely connected to what is bad or evil to the extent that it represents a prideful egocentric perspective that shamelessly refuses to be in solidarity with the rest of reality.[23]

Meanwhile Socrates now shifts the discussion in the direction of intelligence by asking Callicles if people are called good because of the presence of some quality in them. When this is agreed to, it follows that Callicles must find the qualities of intelligence and courage in these men, rather than discovering folly and cowardice. He is asked whether he has ever seen thoughtless men or children rejoicing (*kaironta*); this is then compared to the reaction of a man of intelligence and Callicles admits that there is little difference in the way either kind rejoices or feels pain (497e–498a). Next, when Socrates asks Callicles if he has ever seen a coward in battle (*polemo*), his response "of course" marks him out as a combat veteran – perhaps he served at Delium or Mantinea. He goes on to admit that the cowards both tended to rejoice a bit more when the

---

23   Benardete points out that Callicles' view of pleasure "is not the opposite of morality but derivative from morality. In its reaction from morality hedonism tries to fulfill the posturing of moral freedom. What it puts in its stead is the scratch and the itch" (p. 79). Otherwise put, this Prince of Pleasure's motto is *Itch Dien*.

enemy retreated, and felt a little more pain when they advanced. This established that there was little to choose between foolish and wise men, or between cowards and brave men when it came to rejoicing or pain (498a–c). However, since intelligence and courage are the qualities of the good according to Callicles, it is evident that these qualities do not bring them the greater share of rejoicing, and hardly much less pain. Callicles had earlier defined good men by their skill and daring at obtaining the best things in life for themselves. It follows then that since good men do not gain a greater share of the good things or a smaller share of the bad, Callicles' assertion that good things are the same as pleasant things cannot be upheld.[24]

At this point, Callicles finally gives in and baldly claims to have been joking when he refused to distinguish between good and bad pleasures: "As if you thought that I *or any human being* did not consider some pleasures better and others worse" (499b). Socrates now not so ironically accuses him of being a most resourceful villain (*panourgos*) "claiming at one time that things are one way, and at another time that they are otherwise . . . even though I did not think at the beginning that I were to be voluntarily deceived by you my friend" (499c). Now that he knows himself to have been cheated, he decides to makes the best use of what Callicles has given him. As we shall see, Callicles does not really affirm the qualitative supremacy of the good at all. The whole truth of the matter is that Callicles has also decided to cut his losses here and merely concede that not all pleasures are equally *pleasurable* over the long run; this is how he can speak for all humanity.

Socrates now extracts from Callicles the minimal admission that some pleasures are good and others bad, according to the benefit they provide (499c–d). Good and bad effects thus turn out to be the standard by which pleasure and pain is assessed. Speaking now of the body (it is noteworthy that he does not mention the soul), Socrates states that those pleasures that produce health, strength, and other virtues in the body are good, while those contributing to its debility are bad; pains are also to be classified and pursued or avoided by this measure. Callicles agrees to concur in Socrates' and Polus's conclu-

---

24 Stauffer defends Callicles against the charge of hedonism, suggesting that he was provoked by Socrates to express himself in a more extreme manner than he would otherwise have chosen to express his deepest beliefs (pp. 115–16). While Stauffer denies that Callicles is a "thoroughgoing hedonist" and points to his praise of prudence and courage, it should be seen that both qualities/virtues are instrumental steeds at the disposal of the ruling passion of hedonism. Differently put, courage and prudence are nomadic virtues; they may be contrasted to cultivated virtues that connect us to the cosmos. The contrast between nomad and cultivator runs parallel to asking whether peace or war (*polemou*) is the more natural state of affairs.

sion that all things should be done for the sake of the good (499e); actions do not become good by being performed for the sake of the pleasant. He also agrees with Socrates that not every person is artful *(teknikou)* enough to select, out of the pleasant things, which ones are truly good (500a). The problem with regarding this as a concession is that, for one like Callicles, the distinction between body and soul may simply be the difference between long-term and immediate pleasure. Likewise, intelligence and courage can be seen as potential powers of assets for pleasure. This would account for men with intellect and courage not enjoying more pleasure or less pain; they simply haven't been liberated from conventional justice.

Socrates now recollects the things that he already said to Gorgias and Polus. While some means or schemes *(paraskeuai)* aim only to procure pleasure, and do not consider what is better or worse, others come to know what is good and bad. Socrates claims to have separated the knack of cookery from the art of medicine by following this principle. Now, swearing by Zeus, the god of friendship, Socrates urges Callicles not to joke or speak at variance to the way things appear to him, or to take his (Socrates') words in jest. Their speeches are about the most serious matters: the way one should live. The choice is between living in the way Callicles recommended to Socrates, following the pursuits of a real man – demagoguery, rhetoric, and practicing politics as it is presently conducted – or by living a life of philosophy.[25] The two ways of life should be made distinct from each other and a decision must be made about the way to be followed (500a–d).

At this point, Socrates somewhat surprisingly suggests that Callicles has not understood what he has said. Just as strangely, Callicles agrees (500d). This only makes sense if he still does not really know what the soul is. Socrates then agrees to speak more clearly, pointing out (a) there is a difference between the pleasant and the good and (b) that there are different ways of caring for and

25   This preference for "real men" is the basis for Callicles' patriotic admiration for Themistocles, Miltiades Cimon, and Pericles. Although Stauffer claims that Callicles' admiration for these four men proves his commitment to something beyond glory and hedonism (p. 116), this argument could be reversed. These men could have believed that the greatest achievement of Athens, *qua* school of Hellas, was in winning undying glory and creating meaning. Conversely, a Socratic would attach greater value to the Athenian discovery of the connection between *logos* and the cosmos. In retrospect we see that the lasting cultural contribution of the Greeks to civilization have been derived from philosophy and literature. Homer, Plato, and the tragedians have all helped us to be better cultural critics of power, violence and materialism; they have shown future generations to better appreciate the unchanging features of reality. Likewise, the true greatness of Greek architecture is derived from the discovery of the mathematical beauty sustaining being.

attaining these two divergent ends. He then urges Callicles to agree with his statement that cookery did not seem to be a genuine art but a mere knack, while medicine studies the nature of the patient and the causes of the actions it performs. Accordingly medicine can give a rational account (*logos*) of all that it does. However cookery cares only for pleasure and proceeds artlessly and irrationally, without study of nature or causes, by instinct and experience. It only retains memory of routines that are probably likely to produce pleasure.

Socrates now asks Callicles to first consider whether medicine and cookery can be distinguished as he has done, and next to ponder whether similar ways of proceeding exist with regard to the soul also: some that are artful and proceeding with forethought (*prometheian*) for what is best for the soul, and others which dismiss this concern and care only for the soul's pleasure and ranking these pleasures purely by the extent or intensity of the gratification produced. Socrates tells Callicles that he both believes these two different means or ways of acting to exist, and that he further holds that the way concerned with pleasure is but flattery conducted with complete indifference to what is better or worse (500d–501c). He now asks Callicles whether he supports him in this opinion or disputes it. Callicles replies that he agrees so as to conclude the argument and gratify Gorgias (501c). This almost amounts to saying that the argument has become too painful – in the sense of tiresome – for him to continue. Being openly shameless, he doesn't care that much about being shamed, and he has better things to do with his time. It seems as if Callicles has calculated that he cannot outgun Socrates. It is not that he is incapable of thought or generalization; Callicles' problems stem from knowing too much about his desires and too little about his soul. Because he is both overly and superficially familiar with the bad, Callicles is incapable of attending to what is worth fighting for – either in himself or in the world.

Before proceeding any further, it is noteworthy that Socrates does not take Callicles to task for ranking pleasures on calculative rather than ethical grounds. In other words, when Callicles finally concedes that there are better and worse pleasures, he is merely being an intelligent Epicurean by taking his long-term prospects for the enjoyment of pleasure – and only these prospects – into consideration. Hitler, we recall, was a vegetarian and a non-smoker. Perhaps Socrates does not press the issue further with Callicles because he sees that his interlocutor cannot progress beyond the aesthetic level of enlightened selfishness. He is one of those described by Glaucon in *Republic* II who desist from acts of shameful vice purely because they care for their body and fear painful punishment. Callicles would gladly put on the Ring of Gyges.

Both the intellectual Gorgias and the spirited Polus possessed some awareness of their souls through their respective experiences of, and commitment to, *nous* and *thumos*; this is how they are shamed into becoming aware of the erotic power and *telos* of the *logos*. However, since Callicles functions purely at the level of the desires, he cannot be made to adopt a higher standard. To this limiting extent, self-interest is self-sufficient. It is also self-exclusive, since one who lives by desire cannot see his soul as anything but a nexus for the continued enjoyment of pleasure. To the extent that Callicles is aware of the powers of intellect, spiritedness, or courage, which served to redeem Gorgias and Callicles, he sees them only as external assets, drag-horses, or Greek slaves serving his sovereign barbaric desires. It is as wasteful as Alcibiades abusing his intellect and letting his great captain's heart serve "as fan and bellows of a gypsy's lust."[26]

Still, Socrates has succeeded in making Callicles distinguish, albeit on purely calculative grounds, between exploiting and educating the desires. This distinction is very important because rhetoric, which merely deceives desire, must not be confused with pedagogic arts that give self-knowledge to desire. Socrates then asks whether such a division can also be made between procedures concerned not just with one soul but pertaining to two or more. When Callicles agrees again, Socrates makes a point that could hardly gratify Gorgias – asking if it is possible to give pleasure to many people collectively without any concern for what is best for them (501d). Upon receiving Callicles' assent, we must again recall that they have very different views about what is best, Socrates then asks that he list which procedures do this, or if he wishes, to agree or disagree as they are named. He first mentions flute-playing, asking Callicles if it is the kind of thing that is concerned only with pleasure. Callicles' agreement leads Socrates to ask him to extend this judgment to all of the other skills of this sort, including competitive lyre (*kithara*) playing, and then even further to cover choral and dithyrambic contests (501d–e).

Socrates now makes special reference to two musicians, father and son, Meles and Kinesias. He notes that while the son was concerned only with gratifying or arousing his mob-like public, the father's muse was neither edifying nor pleasant (501e–502a). Dodds tells us that Kinesias was also a notorious atheist and informer.[27] The implicit question seems to have to do with whether abstract technical solipsism is better or worse than flagrant demagoguery. Socrates seems to be suggesting that even though pleasure is not the criterion for aesthetic excellence, good art need not be unpleasant. Boring technical virtue, like that of the miserly Oligarchs of the Republic is very likely to breed Democratic children enthralled to a demagogic Dionysian muse. When the unity of goodness and beauty is lost, their degenerate forms – vulgar utility

26   William Shakespeare, *Antony and Cleopatra*, I i. 9–10.
27   Dodds, p. 323.

and shameless pleasure – are spawned out of the resultant loss of creative tension. Dull fools tend to produce sharp knaves.

This prepares the way for a discussion of the solemn and wondrous art of tragedy. For the reasons mentioned earlier, Socrates is very critical of this high form that is serious only about its intent to impress its audience. According to him, it should strive against the temptation to please by pandering to baseness and instead artfully express what is unpleasant and beneficial to the spectators – regardless of whether or not they rejoice. In other words, sublime awe can replace cheap pleasure. After Callicles then agrees with him that, stripped of tune, rhythm, and meter, tragedy boils down to demagogic flattery. Socrates pejoratively describes it as a "rhetoric towards a many composed of children, men and women all together, both free and slave" (502d). The danger is that appealing to the lowest common denominator necessarily looks to the *anthropos* (common man or *hoi polloi*) rather than to the *aner* (the gentleman), if not to the *barbaros*.

Socrates pointed towards the problem with popular art in the *Ion* where he slyly suggested that the source of the artist's inspiration is frequently the horizontal rather than the vertical dimension of reality.[28] The problem is that many artists practice the pseudo-oracular art of ventriloquism; they are uncannily able at capturing the mood of an audience and tell it exactly what it likes to hear. Obviously such an art is very closely related to the sophists or demagogues. However, though any attentive reader of the *Apology* knows full well that even though Socrates found that inspired artists were often the worst interpreters of their works, there is no doubt that he does believe in the possibility of artistic inspiration from a transcendent source. True art, whether aesthetic or political, appeals to the individual rather than to a collective tribe or mob; it breaks up one mob into many individuals and conversely turns many desires into one man.

It is quite thought-provoking to reflect on the fact that the Greek tragedies we revere so much today owe much of their appeal to the fact that they have been stripped of precisely those musical and cultic elements that would appeal most to the vulgar. This fate is the reverse of what happened to the sea god Glaucus at the end of the *Republic* (611d) – a case where what was originally human became unrecognizably rich and strange. In a like manner, we can only wonder what our reaction would be to Greek sculpture if we were to see those works in their almost gaudily painted original state. The hostile public and critical reaction to the restoration of Michelangelo's Last Judgment certainly makes one pause for thought. The rapt contemplation of splendid ruins and

---

28 See Bloom, "An Interpretation of Plato's Ion," in *Giants and Dwarfs* (Simon & Schuster, 1990), p. 150.

hoary patinas somehow makes it easier for the mind to recollect the pure idea that appeared before the inspired artist; this is why the value of some of the parts often exceeds that of the sum of the parts and the cost of the whole.

The dialogue now turns to explicitly treat of political rhetoric, that which is aimed towards free men in their *poleis*.[29] Socrates asks rhetorically if the orators speak with a view to the best, so that the citizenry may be edified through their discourse. The other possibility is that they merely seek to gratify the *demos*. In order to serve their own private interests, it is necessary that orators should ignore the public good and treat the citizenry like spoiled children. When Callicles suggests that some politicians do care about the citizenry, though others are as he describes, Socrates grants that this competency is potentially twofold. While one part would consist of pandering and base mob-oratory, the other would be noble and aspire to make the citizens' souls as good as possible by saying the right things – regardless of whether they will be unpleasant to hear. However, Socrates tells Callicles that he has never seen a practitioner of this kind of rhetoric, adducing as proof of this claim the fact that he did not name such a man. When Callicles concedes this point, at least with regard to the current crop of politicians, Socrates challenges him to name someone from olden times who improved the Athenians after he began to speak to them (*demegorein*), claiming that for himself that he could not name such a man. When Callicles mentions the storied names of Miltiades, Themistocles, Cimon, and Pericles, Socrates' response is that this would be the case only if true virtue were a matter of satisfying desires: one's own and those of others. If, however, the satisfaction of these desires is not supposed to leave someone worse rather than better, he cannot come up with a name of such an Athenian leader (502d–503d).

Callicles clearly believes, along with Pericles that the undying glory of Athens matters more than the improvement of the souls of individual Athenians.[30] While he would implicitly regard the former enterprise as constituting the meaning of life, the latter would be viewed as little better than a fan-

---

29   Because of his "will to believe" that Socrates wishes to learn something from and/or befriend Gorgias, Stauffer cannot see the fundamental difference between rhetoric and philosophy (pp. 126–27). Gorgias can contribute nothing to this venture because noble rhetoric is erotic and non-manipulative. Dialectical speech is ruled by its ends and cannot proceed by the sophistical devices of exploiting ignorance and creating false certainty. While Gorgias *pushes* ignorance, Socrates' eloquence comes from his being *pulled* towards a cosmic order that he will soon describe. Otherwise put, rhetoric is called rhetoric because it proceeds by speech alone. Conversely, philosophic speech is inspired by erotic awareness of something revealed to it.

30   *Pace* Stauffer, p. 129.

ciful abstraction – better suited for little children than for grown men. Such an undertaking clearly goes beyond mere hedonism; much of the power of rhetoric seems to consist in its power to take men beyond sensual pleasures, which are at least given reality by the body, and towards a vast nebulous empire of words and reputations. While such projects would seem to transcend the body, in reality they only betray it to the vicissitudes of foreign war and civil strife.

Socrates further asserts that a genuine leader would not speak at random but instead have a view of what was best (503d). In other words, he would be cognizant of a certain form or idea that he would seek to bring disorderly human affairs into conformity with. This familiar Platonic theme must be understood to mean that a form is not simply creatively imposed from above but is rather discovered. Socrates' point is that human beings have an inner order or nature that cannot be violated or changed according to someone's desire or plan. He appeals to the arts of the trainer and physician as proof of this. The designers of houses and ships also proceed in a similar manner. Just as proper attention to its nature produces health and strength in the body, we may expect something similar to occur in the soul too. The soul is said to receive order by law. The beneficial results of this ordering are justice and moderation (504a–c). Strikingly, Callicles – for whom efficient causality is sufficient – does not name these virtues but leaves it up to Socrates.[31]

It follows that the good orator will look to these things (justice and moderation) when he applies speeches and deeds to souls (504d–e). Whatever he binds or loosens will be done with these ends in mind. Accordingly, Socrates asserts that he cannot see the benefit in giving a sick or diseased body fine and pleasant food or drink that could quite easily ending up harming the patient (504e). Good health, rather than glory, pleasure, or life, is the appropriate criterion in these cases. We hear echoes of the *Republic* when Socrates states that living with a degenerate (*moktheros*) body only causes one to live wretchedly. This is why physicians generally allow healthy people to satisfy their desires, but do not extend such freedoms to the sick – presumably because their desires are in disarray. It follows that the soul must be treated in the same way; when it is filled with vices, it must not be permitted to indulge its desires and perform actions other than those which will improve it. Following this line of thought, we may also see why just punishment – even including death – may be preferred to living on with a diseased and untreated soul (505a–b).

Socrates finally says that since punishment consists in keeping the diseased soul from the objects it desires, it actually benefits the soul (505b). Even

---

31 Newell points out that while Callicles agrees with Socrates on the worth of courage and prudence, this cannot be said about moderation and justice; *Ruling Passion*, p. 53.

though Callicles has agreed with this chain of reasoning, he rejects its implications once Socrates reaches and refutes the ultimate particular: his opinion that intemperance is preferable to punishment. Here, Callicles becomes hostile again. This response illustrates Callicles' striking lack of self-knowledge; he is ruled by egoism – which kicks in and displaces the argument the moment anything pertaining to him is reached. Once he sees that Socrates is attacking *his* position, Callicles refuses to participate in the questioning, claiming not to know what Socrates is talking about (505c). While he is eager to discuss the art of enslaving others, Callicles refuses to use this very speech to free himself from its deleterious effects.[32] Socrates responds that Callicles cannot stand being benefited through suffering the very thing they were discussing: correction or punishment. Callicles replies that he did not care for the matters being discussed and answered only to gratify Gorgias. Since Socrates claims that it is irreverent and unrighteous to break the argument off in the middle without giving it a head – so that it would not wander around headless – he agrees to Callicles' suggestion that he complete the *logos* by answering himself (505c–d).[33] He believes, *contra* the rhetoricians, that every argument (and arguer) should have a rational justification and not be dependent on the authority of an alien politician or irrational desire.

Callicles' behavior clearly reveals one of the problems with punishment – it is more likely to be resisted if it is seen or identified as such. In other words, it must seem to gratify the desires while actually frustrating them. The *Republic* is certainly most amenable to being regarded in this manner.[34] Additionally, as we have suggested, one of the worst symptoms of moral corruption is the loss of self-awareness. Poverty and physical sickness are far more likely to be recognized for what they are by the person afflicted. Even though the bedside manner of a Gorgias seems to be necessary to persuade a patient to receive treatment, such a flattering approach cannot come to grips with what is most essential to healing of the soul: the patient's recognition that he is diseased. Extending the earlier-mentioned Cretan paradox, there seems to be something about the very categories of speech, a curious moral prohibition, which prevents someone from calling himself bad. This is why the *reductio ad*

---

32 "Again and again . . . Socrates' apparent progress towards agreement is disrupted by Callicles' refusal to follow the *logos* of the craft analogy from a means of producing greater power, wealth and honor for the artisan to the self-forgetting orderliness of soul prescribed by Socrates" (Newell, p. 50).

33 Strikingly, Stauffer suggests that Socrates is exhorting Callicles to a view "that somehow has the character of a myth" and "still does not have a head." He believes that Socrates "does not make a serious effort to discover the arrangement and order of the soul" pp. 132–33).

34 See *The Soul of Socrates*, p. 11.

absurdum is used to make the bad consequences of a proposed course of action evident in speech, before its actual performance corrupts the soul of the doer. Only in this way will he be freed to see the evil objectively and condemn it. Otherwise, the bad consequences resulting from disordered desires are rarely seen by the diseased party to originate in his own soul. It is thus hardly a cause for wonder that many persons with bad characters are also paranoid in projecting the delayed effects of their psychic disorder all around them. Additionally, an attraction to bad things could be clouded so much by the mist of false self-evidence that it may never be seen as a symptom of soul-degeneration; we recall that matters self-evident to Polus were not so at all to Socrates and *vice versa*. Connecting this to our penultimate theme, we see also that bad rhetoric makes prolific use of the false self-evidence of diseased perception, and necessarily advances the degeneration of its victims as it exploits their symptoms.

This problem is made all the more acute in our own day by the postmodern tendency – seen at both ends of the political spectrum – to identify freedom, and indeed establish identity itself, through the unimpeded expressions of one's desires – rather than viewing it through the more positive category of self-mastery. In other words, it surely cannot be the highest expression of our freedom to succumb joyfully to consumerist pressures that we cannot resist. The credit card replaces the soul when we shop for sport and entertainment. The conclusive proof of this depressing state of affairs is provided by the fact that the period between the purchase and its arrival is always happier than that following the taking of physical possession over the desired object. While we are justly shamed by Rousseau's neo-laconic barb, "I do not care to listen to slaves discussing freedom,"[35] our embarrassment could easily lead to even more extreme forms of denial. We need a way of speech that mediates between honeyed lies that corrupt the will and abrasive truths that lack volitional power. This seems almost impossible when one is dealing with a soul like Callicles', which, because it has literally has no idea of itself as anything more than a pleasure center or trash talker, is to all intents and purposes already in Hades.

This is why the dialectical pedagogy of a Socratic dialogue is inevitably triangular and indirect. It most often is the case that the person directly relieved of his ignorance by Socratic midwifery is highly indignant and ungrateful. While the punishment has taken away a dangerous thought that can no longer be used to do injustice, and thereby harm the potential evildoer, the full intellectual significance of the lesson is all too often lost on him. This means that readers and bystanders who are not blinded by *thumos* have a better chance of seeing all that takes place in a dialogue. Like spectators at a tragedy, they will witness how those who tend to understand their identity and

---

35   Rousseau, *Discourse on Inequality*, II. 39.

happiness by catering to their ego and feeding their desires end up cultivating shadows within themselves and expelling their virtues from the cave – or using them instrumentally. While Callicles is a striking example (and whipping boy) of this phenomenon, the real beneficiary of his humiliation may well be Gorgias – the person for whose sake he consented to "humor" Socrates.[36] Nevertheless, Socrates' time with Callicles has not been completely wasted. The man who made a brashly intemperate speech predicting the advent of the blond beast of Zarathustra has now been reduced to a state of confused incontinence; his subsequent indignation at the prospect of a good and noble man being killed by one much baser than he, is but one illustration of his tacit repudiation of this earlier rant. This inference is also supported by the curious way in which Callicles often agrees with Socrates in theory before then refusing to follow the practical consequences of his assent. Even Callicles' sullen reluctance to speak suggests strongly that, like many of Socrates' other interlocutors, our Lion has been forced to abruptly abort his monstrous intellectual offspring. While he still lives for pleasure and self-gratification, Callicles will do so as a natural slave; he longer yearns for the strength to dwell beyond good and evil. Simply put, he sees that his tyrannical dream was unstable and foolish. Socratic idealism is also more realistic.

36   Benardete observes, "Callicles has become the spectator of his own rhetoric, he has through his silence freed himself from being its spokesman" (p. 95). This means that Socrates has reversed time and freed him from the ignorance of self that using the rhetorician's art would otherwise cause.

Chapter IV: The Socratic Cosmos

The dialogue now resumes with Socrates ruefully recognizing that he will have to perform the interlocutor's part as well as his own: "What two men did before me I, being one man, must be sufficient for" (505e). This means that he must re-enact the sort of internal dialogue that was hinted at in comic form in the *Greater Hippias*. Now that he has criticized and purged almost all the fine arts (the exception is comedy – we note that he chooses to quote the great comedian Epicharmus), Socrates will complete the *logos* for us. The tragic trilogy of Gorgias, Polus, and Callicles is rounded off by a satyr play of cosmic proportions recollected from within his own soul. Furthermore, the *agon* of Zethus and Aphion will now become the song of Amphion. Rather than being made to serve antagonistic ends, the love of victory must be placed in service of the common good. Socrates warns that he does not speak out of certain knowledge, but rather places his trust in the self-corrective character of the *logos*; he promises to be the first to recognize the truth in any statements refuting him. He is also willing to bid the argument farewell if they should not be willing to see it to its conclusion. Here again persuasive Gorgias speaking on behalf of all, but especially for himself, assures Socrates of the desire of all those present that he should complete the argument *solus*. Socrates consents but only after expressing regret that he could not have replied to Callicles as Amphion responded to Zethus (506b). Then, after Callicles also urges him again to continue, the philosopher takes up the *logos* from its origin.

Though Callicles is far from silent, Socrates will not have an interlocutor in this final quarter of the *Gorgias*. His accuser serves as little more as an intellectual backboard; even Meno's slave displayed more intellectual energy than Callicles does over this final turn of the dialectic. We should note that by reporting this reference to a self-corrective *logos* Plato seems to invite the reader to both elucidate and develop the fullest meaning of some of the remarkable accounts and myths set forth here. What is self-evident from

Callicles' perspective is no longer highlighted, and we shall see things through Socrates' eyes. This means that while the soul and the ideas will become visible, the mimetic power of appearance and the coercive *ananke* of the body recede into illusion as Socrates, in the spirit of the Age of Kronos, turns reality right-side up. The philosopher will emphasize causes and ends rather than effects and means; he also privileges the recovery of erotic being over the sophistical aim of creative dominion over godforsaken becoming. It is in this spirit that my commentary will aim to explicate the fullest implications of his winged words; instead of gleefully drawing abysmal conclusions from the lack of direct divine rule that allows evil to exist, we must see in this divide an opportunity to practice human virtue for its own sake.

The aforementioned theme of the priority of causes and ends immediately comes into prominence when Socrates points out that Callicles and he had agreed that the good and the pleasant are not the same. The question then is whether the pleasant should be done to serve the good or *vice versa*. It is agreed that the good should be the end and the pleasant be in its service. Also, the pleasant is acknowledged as that through which we are pleased when it comes to be present, and the good is likewise that presence through which we are good. Socrates now proposes that every thing (humans included) becomes good through a virtue being present. He also claims that all things, whether tool, animal, body, or soul, do not come to be themselves most nobly, present or actualized in the finest way, simply randomly (he seems to contrast virtue and pleasure) but by arrangement (*taxei*), correctness, and the appropriate art. It follows then that each thing's virtue comes from its being rightly ordered (506c–e).

What this means – since Socrates surely includes his own *logos* under the category of things that flourish when well ordered, thus suggesting that these very words (and the *Gorgias* itself) are susceptible to very close analysis indeed – is that things have both a given nature or power (arrangement) as well as a further capacity for flourishing through the proper autonomous actualizing of this nature (ordering by arrangement) by art. This formulation makes allowance for the self-evident incidence of both order and chaos in the world. It also reveals the true purpose and meaning of the potential that Polus found to be so attractive *qua* raw power. This is why a tyrant like Archelaus could not bring a perfect regime into existence – even with the help of rhetoric. The very nature of the incomplete but erotic human soul seems to necessitate that it choose and actualize its own virtue *from within itself*, albeit in circumstances that inspire it towards transcendence with a vision of the nobility and beauty of the cosmos.

Socrates goes on to claim that an appropriately ordered soul is better and more moderate than a disorderly, foolish, and intemperate soul. The temperate/

moderate man would conduct himself appropriately by showing piety towards gods and justice towards men. Furthermore, beyond justice and piety, he would also be courageous, "for it is not the part of the moderate man (*sophronos andros*) to pursue or flee [from] things that are not fitting, but only to behave appropriately towards matters persons, pleasures and pains – being steadfast in whatever he does."[1] Moreover, since he will perform all his actions well and nobly, such a man will be blessed and happy (*makarion te kat eudaimona*) – while the base person who acts badly will be wretched. While this base person is identical to the intemperate man who was earlier praised by Callicles (507a–c), Socrates' portrait of the temperate man may be found by many to be more attractive than Aristotle's description of the rather priggish and egocentric great-souled man.[2]

This remarkable statement, which suggests that only virtue can lead to true happiness, must be viewed in the context of Socrates' earlier disjunction between happiness and pleasure. In other words, it must be understood that he is not claiming that the virtuous and temperate man will enjoy a life of painless pleasure. Happiness, as Socrates describes it, is an internal state of flourishing that is not dependent on external events. Indeed our very word "happiness" depends too much on "hap" or happenstance to be able to accurately express the condition of moral invulnerability that Socrates describes. We are reminded of Aristotle's brilliant observation at the beginning of his *Nicomachean Ethics* to the effect that happiness cannot be gratuitously conferred by the arbitrary will of a god because that would make it too ugly to be admired![3] All of this means that the Greek word *Eudaimonia*, literally meaning having a happy guiding spirit, does not translate well into the English "happiness." We should also bear in mind the famous claim of Diotima in the *Symposium* that *daimons* are semi-divine messengers who travel and mediate between the human and divine realms (202e). Lest we do not approach this matter seriously enough, it is worth repeating the brute fact that amazed so many sophisticated Athenians: Socrates, an old, unhappily married, poor, and very ugly man was also widely regarded as the best and "happiest" citizen of Athens. *This* incongruity is truly and timelessly beautiful.

Differently put, while the height of pleasure is conceived as an ecstatic state, an experience of literally standing outside of oneself; *eudaimonia* will be soon shown to come from a condition of the virtuous individuals being precise-

---

1 Stauffer rightly sees that moderation is the foundational Socratic virtue. However, he immediately discounts the value of this recognition by wondering "how closely the virtue Socrates is describing resembles the virtue that most people admire and would like to see defended?" (pp. 135–36).

2 Aristotle, *Nicomachean Ethics*, IV 1123b–1125a18.

3 *Ibid*, I 1099b20.

ly in their proper place in the world – not contradicting their integrity in speech, deed, or character. It can also be said to express a state of unified virtue that allows the *sophron* to dwell both well within himself as well as in the world. This quality is famously exemplified by Socrates' refusal, even when faced with death, to go '*a-topos*' in the sense of deserting his station on earth. Unlike the *Republic*, there is nothing utopian about the topography of the *Gorgias*. Neither is this view either apathetic or deterministic – as the Stoics would have it. Even though the Stoics obviously were tremendously impressed by Socrates' exemplary fortitude and dutiful single-minded dedication to virtue, their masochistic code over-emphasized his scorn for pleasure and imposed a fatalistic and materialistic worldview with no room for *eudaimonia*, freedom, or *eros*. To put the matter very bluntly, Socrates was not an ugly Buddha. He was not happy because he renounced pleasures; he scorned pleasures because he possessed *eudaimonia*. As he put it to Alcibiades, when that notorious young prodigy tried to exchange sexual favors for wisdom, it is a very poor bargain to be persuaded to exchange gold for bronze (218e). It was the tragedy of both Athens and Alcibiades that neither the city nor the soul could find the humility to cash in their great erotic potential and desire for the beautiful.[4]

While beauty is greatly admired in the cave, it is ultimately regarded as something coercively charismatic and irrationally powerful. So, while the beautiful object demands attention, it does not point beyond itself: it demands to be either possessed or worshipped. Likewise, the images of sacred things in the cave point towards divine power rather than goodness. They too have far more to do with vain human desire to be divine, or the pusillanimous wish to submit, than with representing the harmony, ratio, and *logos* connecting humans to the divine. Even though rhetoric uses the power of beauty to sell and persuade, it does not understand the real power or erotic *telos* of the beautiful – that which gathers us up towards the noble but unrealized promise of the heterogeneous wholeness of our cosmos. This vision of the noble affirms the essential and deep unity of the beautiful and the good. However the sophistic art perversely splits transcendental ideas up into the irrationally sacred (Jihad) and the vulgarly useful (MacWorld) respectively and plays them against each other. Consequent to this division, the human soul itself becomes divided on account of its concomitantly conflicting attractions to tragic beauty and comic utility. While this deep, literally schizophrenic, splitting of the soul generates tremendous power that could be exploited by sophistry and rhetoric to offer the kind of satisfaction discussed in Aristophanes' myth of the Circle-Men in the *Symposium*, the self-knowledge of the soul is fatally compromised and its capacity for *eudaimonia* hidden, lost, and forgotten.

4   See Ranasinghe, *The Soul of Socrates*, pp. 159–78.

We are now ready to return to the *Gorgias* just before one of Socrates' most celebrated perorations. He first concludes his account of the Eudaimonic life of the temperate man by reasserting the truth of his belief that the life of the temperate man is both blessed and happy, and stating that one who would be truly happy should flee intemperance as fast as his feet will carry him. Socrates further states that while one should prepare oneself to live so that one should have no need for punishment, if oneself or one's own family, friends, or polis needs it the just penalty must be applied for the sake of happiness. In his opinion the goal that one must always strive towards, straining to point all the elements of one's own life as well as all things of one's polis towards it, is *eudaimonia* gained through temperance and justice. The other way, one of continually striving to satisfy insatiate desires, is the path of *akolasia* – a predatory life (507c–e).

Before turning at last to Socrates' account of the four fundamental principles of reality -what Heidegger called the fourfold- it is vital that we scrutinize the assertion that has been just made. When Socrates spoke of the necessity of believing that justice and temperance are necessary for *eudaimonia*, was he expressing a statement of fact, a noble lie, or something else? It is easy enough to see how some things could be true while not necessary to be known for one to live blessedly (Socrates did not need to know of the existence of North America or the non-existence of Atlantis to lead an exemplary life). Is Socrates claiming that paying continual heed to justice and temperance is necessary for *eudaimonia*, or is he speaking of the great practical value of this belief as a common goal or target? Another dimension to this question is supplied by the ease with which *eudaimonia* and pleasure are confused with each other. Our time uses the words "happiness" and "pleasure" almost interchangeably; at best "happiness" means a long-term state of gratification while "pleasure" is viewed in more immediate terms. However, both words are very much expressive of an egotistical perspective on reality. What Socrates seems to understand by *eudaimonia* is founded on the soul rather than being centered on the ego viewed as an end in itself; furthermore, as evidenced by his emphasis on justice and temperance, as well as his concern that the polis should strive collectively towards these goals, there is a much stronger sense of being active in the world and contributing to its goodness.

This is why the aforementioned way of a predator, which clearly applies as much to the polis as to a soul, is singled out for the strongest condemnation. Socrates says that this way of infinite striving in service of impossible desires is an endless evil and amounts to no more than the life of a pirate or outlaw (*laestou*). Socrates tells his "dear friend" Callicles that such a man would be dear to neither another human being nor to god. This is because he would be unable to live in common or community (*koinonia*), and where there is no community there can be no friendship. Beyond the obvious and profound meaning of this claim, there is also a powerful implication that a man of intemperance cannot be friendly with god or man because there is no friendship within his soul – only a mad tyranny of lust. The word *koinonia* also means integration; beyond saying that such a man cannot integrate with others, Socrates is also suggesting that because he has no integrity within his own soul, he cannot even trust himself. This deficiency is the central element in the paranoia of a tyrant. A man cannot trust others if he cannot trust himself. We are reminded of Nietzsche's poignant description of man as an animal with the right to make promises[5] and his sublime words of rebuke to a former friend: "I forgive for what you did to me; but that you did it to *yourself* – how could I forgive that."[6] These words, uttered by one of his most famous critics, somehow get to the core of Socrates' insights regarding the most deleterious effects of evil.

We must also see how this condemnation of a career of predatory accumulation amounts to the sternest condemnation of the deteriorating quality of the democratic political leadership of Athens over the course of the fifth century B.C. The ongoing Persian War led to the steady erosion of morals and a growing opportunism that was unblushingly justified in the name of necessity, even as it made great material prosperity and cultural progress possible. Indeed we could even say that the rule of Archelaus, with its combination of authoritarianism and cultural hegemony, was a by-product of Pericles' celebrated "School of Hellas."[7] Under the rule of this uncrowned king, the former allies of the Athenians in the war against the Great King irrevocably became tribute-paying members of a de-facto Athenian Empire from which secession was violently discouraged. The most extreme statement of this predatory outlook was famously voiced in Thucydides' account of the Melian debate between the Athenians and the ambassadors of the far weaker island of Melos: "Justice is only enforced among those who are equally constrained by it; for the rest, the stronger take as much as they can, and the weak must accept that"[8]

According to this bleak take on reality, human beings and nations naturally exist in a state of war. It follows from this that all law is conventional and backed by nothing higher than the threat of violence. Under these dark skies, survival and security trump all higher values. Moral compromises are both readily and easily made when the lives of one's loved ones are at stake; differently put, patriotism is only the first refuge of a scoundrel; many other combustible moral accommodations may be found along the path to perdition. It is

5   Nietzsche, *Genealogy of Morals*, II. 1–2.
6   Nietzsche, *Thus Spoke Zarathustra*, II.3 115 17–19.
7   Thucydides, *Peloponnesian War*, III. 41.
8   Thucydides, *Peloponnesian War*, VI. 89.

also easy to see how sophistry and demagogic oratory flourish under circumstances which seem to dictate that many become one. The three-fold denials of truth, intelligibility, and reasoned speech constitute three waves of irrationality that sweep all accounts of reason and natural order before them when war, famine, and plague are seen as the truth of nature. Beneath their baleful influences, the beauty of the world and the self-knowledge of the soul are forgotten and buried.[9]

Given the seeming self-evidence of this view of reality, it seems only natural that rootless raiders and ruthless entrepreneurs should seek to provide for their own security – an unlimited need that could only increases as new enemies are made, chaos widens, and paranoia increases. Furthermore there is also the ever-present and insidious temptation to give oneself a moral holiday in times of emergency and actually exploit the opportunities provided by such circumstances. In other words, when "everything is permitted," many persons disregard unusual opportunities for virtue in favor of thoroughly materialistic and banal forms of vice. Meanwhile Gorgias gained satisfaction through feats of mental agility in a meaningless reality, Polus dreamed of being envied for his power, and Callicles hoped to find happiness through the destruction of morals and the practice of shamelessness. When Socrates destroys the illusions and rationalizations of the corrupt, thus stripping away their false self-knowledge, he does so without necessarily changing their behavior and thus abruptly exposes them to full awareness of their own corruption. This must cause us to assess the value of his interventions and ask whether his conduct has been merely vengeful or genuinely punitive. While we cannot dispute that he has weakened their mimetic power over others, this merely widens the scope of the question. Has he acted irresponsibly in exposing the unspeakable and false knowledge holding Athens together during the desperate times of the Peloponnesian War and leaving nothing in its stead? Are not binding illusions preferable to the maddening terror and chaos that follow our exposure to the primal irrationality of existence?

This is why Socrates now moves beyond the genuine sciences that Gorgias acknowledged, and the economy of soul which refuted Polus, and looks to their source: a transcendental horizon that should be accessible to all souls – however nihilistic – and all times – however chaotic. After praising order and friendship between men, other men, and gods; he now quotes "the wise" who declare that "heaven, earth, gods, and human beings are held together (*sunexein*) by community, orderliness (*kosmiotes*), friendship, moderation, and jus-

---

9   Yet, as Voegelin points out, "The conclusion of the *Gorgias* formulates the conditions under which the community of mankind can be maintained even when on the level of concrete society it has broken down. The condition is the faith in the transcendental community of man" (p. 30).

tice" (508a). After making this statement, Socrates immediately goes on to tell his comrade (*heteire*) Callicles – with the aforementioned suggestive name meaning "called beautiful" – that "it is on account of these things that they call (*kalousin*) this whole (*olos*) a cosmos and not a chaos/disorder (*akosmian*) and intemperance (*akolasian*)." This is a very profound statement indeed. Not only does Socrates make a very fundamental ontological statement that he attributes to the wise, he also uses the word *kalousin* to suggest that the wise men (*sophoi*) not only make this statement about the cosmos but, in a sense, *summon* this cosmic order into visibility. While this daring claim does not amount to saying that the wise, through the *logos*, say "let there be a cosmos" and bring it into existence – although this stunningly mirrors the divine performative lettings be of *Genesis* and anticipates the opening of John's Gospel – it certainly suggests that the *logos* of the wise plays a very crucial and essential role in what one could call the "worlding" of our world. This is possible because the *Logos* at the origin of creation pre-establishes a potential for harmony between human speech and the structure of the macrocosm. Since this structure is revealed and realized by acts of virtue we might also take a deeper look at the status of Socrates' own words here.

All these audacious inferences are certainly supported by, and connected to, Socrates' earlier statements regarding the necessity of the polity believing in justice and temperance as essential conditions for *eudaimonia* and flourishing. There is also a very interesting play between the words *cosmos* and *cosmetikos* – which means orating and embellishing – the origin of our word "cosmetics." In other words, while the pseudo-art of cosmetics gives the deceptive appearance of beauty and flourishing, while only contributing to forgetfulness and degeneration, wisdom and the *logos* play a vital role in summoning this cosmic "well being" into activity. This cosmic flourishing is neither a divinely granted revelatory dispensation – an *ereignis* as Heidegger would put it – nor is it a wholly human creation.

Let us now return to consider the list of elements making up the cosmos that is held together by the five virtues. It is quite obvious that heaven, earth, gods, and human beings can be combined and opposed in two different ways. We can either place the gods in heaven and humans on earth, or relate heaven to earth and gods to human beings. While the first set of relationships would occasion a sort of Epicurean separation between the human and divine realms, the second tends to be too deterministic in the sense of imposing form over matter, being over becoming, and quintessential perfection over ephemeral imperfection. However, this list of four elements held together by anthropomorphic virtues strongly suggests that they define a field where meaningful interaction between the four could take place. They seemingly cannot exist apart from each other.

In other words, while the first pairing (gods and heaven, men and earth) allows for sufficient separation for freedom of action, the second pairing (god and man, heaven and earth) provides a non-coercive erotic authority that would allow these actions to be meaningful and valuable. Since the higher elements do not occupy the same existential plane as the lower elements, this allows for the formal perfection of what is higher to be meaningfully emulated by the material freedom of what is lower. Differently put, instead of coercive efficient causality imposed by the higher on the lower so that only our ignorance protects us from the ugly truth of our un-freedom, the non-deterministic inspirational power of what is beautiful and noble is permitted to work its magic in the region of flux and freedom. The earth, stirringly described by the dying Keats as "the vale of soul-making,"[10] is neither abandoned by heaven nor overshadowed and eclipsed by it. Likewise God is neither dead to the world nor a double-predestining, doom-dealing puppeteer. We must also see that while the space between these four elements – the *metaxy*, where participation occurs – cannot be over-determined, neither form nor matter can totally abandon it.

It should now be readily apparent that what Socrates has described is a partnership between the human and the divine that allows god to be god and man to be man. However, since he has further suggested that extraordinary human activity of a certain kind prevents both common humanity from becoming another generic earth species (the last man) and also keeps the gods from receding out of disinterest or disappointment into Epicurean aloofness, our task is to comprehend what this art could be. We have already observed in the speeches of Gorgias concerning his pseudo-art, the amazing power that the *logos* has to legitimize, influence, and all but compel human actions. Yet we also noted disapprovingly that this knack only has the effect of turning many individuals into a mob, and reducing single souls into raging snake pits of desire.

Even though Gorgias's false art operates through mobilizing the desire of souls for the beautiful, it does so in an entirely cosmetic manner – by creating a terrible disjunction between image and reality. Indeed, as we noted earlier, rhetoric visits the greatest damage on the soul of the deceiver; these far exceed the quite substantial injuries inflicted on the desires of the deceived. Of course, all this bears out the truth of Socrates' discovery that it is worse to be a predator than a victim. Furthermore, the deep skepticism that oratory actively incites in its practitioners, and produces as a kind of lasting hangover in its victims, concerning the inaccessibility of truth and reality to human speeches and deeds, turns reality itself into a kind of living Hades. The many parallels with the cave of the *Republic* are also too clear to need any further elaboration.

---

10 John Keats, "Letter to George and Georgiana Keats," Feb 14th–May 3rd 1819 in *John Keats: The Major Works* (Oxford, 2001), p. 473.

We must now turn briefly to another dialogue – the *Symposium* – for a supplemental account of how the disparate elements of the cosmos are held together. Socrates' celebrated contribution on this occasion was a speech on Eros – the one subject he ever professed to know anything about. Here Socrates identified Eros as one of a mighty race of daimons, "half-way between god and mortal, messengers shuttling back and forth between the two, taking prayer and sacrifice to the gods, and bringing gifts and commands back in return. Being in the middle of the two, they round out the whole and bring it all together. Through them all divination passes . . . Gods do not mix with men; they talk with us through daimons instead. He who is wise in any of these ways is a daimonic man. But he who is wise in any other way is merely a technician" (202e–203a).

Socrates acquired this wisdom from Diotima (whose name means god-honoring), a woman wise in many matters – who was also said by him to have postponed the plague for ten years by telling the Athenians what sacrifices to make (201d). It may be seen that Socrates, who resembled Gorgias in his pessimism with regard to the unassisted human capacity for wisdom, overcame the nihilism that could come through considering the inaccessibility of cosmological scientific wisdom through his pious and "god-honoring" belief in the possibility of divine inspiration. This strikingly contrasts to Gorgias's far less pious remedy of denying the accessibility, intelligibility, and communicability of being and instead creating a wholly human *logos*. We learn from Diotima and Socrates that daimonic activity mediates between the human and divine realms (202e). This means that the space in between the four cosmic elements is where this daimonic shuttling activity occurs.

A daimon is clearly identified by Diotima as one who is wise in the sense of being a channel for divine wisdom (204a–b). We can safely infer that, as a precondition for this capacity to pass on divine wisdom, daimons would have to be "humanly wise" in their awareness that scientific knowledge of ultimate reality is not available to mortals. They would also, by seeing through the heteronomy of technique and public opinion, have self-knowledge to an extent unsurpassed by other mortals. We may now see how the authority of Gorgias, who presumed to supplant the God of Delphi, has been radically challenged by this account of daimonic mediation. Somebody like Socrates takes one great step for mankind when he simply refuses to accept the hubristic and/or nihilistic accounts of reality that rhetoricians and politicians take for granted. Indeed it should be noted that the very catastrophes and injustices that give rise to despair almost invariably originate either from bad theology or from the acceptance of prior, sophistically inspired, acts of rhetorical hubris. Conversely, uncorrupted awareness of the erotic and gracious reality beyond the artificial and chthonic structure of the cave bridges the three gaping discontinuities between being and human speech that Gorgias sought to exploit. Differently put, knowledge of the goodness of reality is necessarily refracted through the human soul. A psyche warped by rhetoric and ruled by envy becomes quite incapable of either perceiving or dwelling in the fullness of reality.

However, this account (*logos*) of the four-fold order of the cosmos provided in the *Gorgias* has even deeper implications. Since the structure of the four-fold order makes human freedom both possible and desirable, it follows that scientific wisdom in the sense of (a) perfect knowledge of all that ever will be, along with (b) perfect technical power over human souls – two powers that must be seen to be inconsistent – cannot be available to *any* being. This is so for the simple reason that absolute wisdom and power of this kind (omniscience and omnipotence) cannot be wielded over humans as long as they are defined as beings meaningfully possessing soul, mind and freedom. In other words, either the possession of such wisdom or the exercise of such power would destroy the very qualities that make human beings rational animals. Thus, the four-fold cosmic order is structured so that divine omniscience and omnipotence cannot overwhelm the ratio between gods and men. This being the case, any *human* claim to possess such wisdom or power – the ability to answer any question or sway any will – must be seen to be palpably absurd. Moreover, this model accounts for the gaps between the divine and natural realms, the very discontinuities that sophistry attempted to turn into nihilistic abysses, and shows how the absence of monistic truth and deterministic necessity are essential for the flourishing of the cosmos.

It may also be seen how this account of the daimon supplements and clarifies Socrates' well-known account in the *Apology* of the inhibiting influence that his own daimon exerted over his actions.[11] Socrates' daimonic voice never positively recommended that he do anything, but only held him back from a course of action he was about to embark upon. In a sense this is akin to the ancient legal maxim that what the law does not forbid, it commands (40a–c). Daimons can be seen to be essential to the very structure of the four-fold cosmos to the extent that they brake and constrain the very basis of the imperatival and expansionistic hubris of efficient causality: the belief that every problem can be solved through the exertion of technical power. In other words, the daimon limits and ridicules the vain delusions of sovereign omnipotence, and the hopes of omniscience, two blasphemously inaccurate fantasies constantly entertained by the will to power.

11 See also my account of the daimon in "Inspiration, Interpretation and Interdependence: Gods and Men in Plato's Euthyphro," *Skepis* XVI (2), pp. 269–77.

In an important sense the concept of the daimon does more than simply bring the belief in human technical prowess into disrepute and ridicule; it also challenges the authority of those disguised practitioners of rhetoric who claim to represent omnipotent and omniscient gods. In so doing the daimon performs the very important function of restoring the authority of transcendental ethical standards based on the soul's integrity – these are otherwise discredited by the invocation of divine *force majeure*. Thus, by guardianship and "policing" of the respective limits of human and divine power the daimon helps avert situations where the piously hyperbolized power of an omniscient God is used to deny both the freedom of finite minds and the virtue of imperfect individuals.

By resisting the power of mimetic heteronomy and rhetorical manipulation, the daimon reasserts both the ability and the obligation of the individual to know, love, and do what is right. Although, in an important sense, the idea of human freedom is immeasurably strengthened and enriched by the denial of omnipotence and omniscience, this in no way means that anything goes and/or that absolute right and wrong do not exist. True moral autonomy is not asserted in a vacuum or an abyss. The daimon's role seems to strip away every calculation of egotistical advantage, and each temptation towards coercive overstepping, that could exert a malefic or distracting influence on the workings of the human conscience. The ability to see things clearly, unimpeded by fear and desire, is greatly increased by the belief in the moral categories that Socrates has introduced.

In this context, the full meaning and greatness of Socrates' axiomatic but seemingly preposterous claim that doing evil is worse than being exposed to the unpleasantness of being victimized by evil shines forth. Socrates' point is that instead of being based on selfish calculations regarding probable events in the future quite beyond man's (or god's) control, human actions should instead be ruled by the ideas of justice and temperance. The state of soul in which an action is performed generates happiness by bringing the individual into harmony with the cosmic order; as such, it will prove to be of far greater moral and practical consequence than whatever ephemeral sensations of pleasure and pain that may be supposed to expectedly or unexpectedly result from it. From such a perspective, it is clearly not enough to be just towards others in the sense of not lying or cheating; it is very much harder to be completely just towards oneself in the truest and fullest sense of being equal to one's potential for virtue. This potential is only fully expressed by the daimonic activity (*energeia*) of bringing out the wonderful beauty of the cosmos.

It follows then that someone playing the role of a daimon experiences *eudaimonia*, the supreme satisfaction of being a good daimon, through his bringing the four elements of the cosmos closer together through genuinely erotic and unselfish speech and deeds. This means that in contrast to pleasure-happiness, which as was noted earlier, is found from being separate and in a sense opposed to the world, genuine happiness comes from the virtuosity of fully being oneself; there is teleological fulfillment from giving fully of oneself to the flourishing of the cosmos. This view of *eudaimonia* solves the problem created by selfish pleasure-happiness: how can a moral person be happy when there is so much unhappiness in the world? The Socratic reply is that happiness in the sense of satisfaction can only truly be experienced in knowing that one is doing the best one can to actualize the goodness, truth, and beauty of the cosmos. True happiness – in the sense of *eudaimonia* – can only be experienced when one actively participates in the quickening cosmos after transcending the *amour propre* of an ego that can never be fully in harmony with the world.

It is noteworthy how Gorgias created a simulacrum of this happiness through his pseudo-art of bringing people together, as a great and seemingly invincible hedonistic demos, though words alone; of course, as we have noted, the grandiose word structures he built were fatally vulnerable to reality itself. Genuine rhetoric should address the individual soul; it should urge us to be true to our destined character. When Heraclitus remarked that one's *daimon* is one's fate,[12] he could be understood to suggest that it is through embracing our *daimon* that our microcosmic psychic elements become as harmoniously ordered as the macro-cosmos we dwell in. Furthermore, the ordering of the microcosm helps it to both perceive and participate in the macrocosm. Socratic dialectic is the best example of how this daimonic activity of bringing the beauty of the cosmos into sharper definition occurs. Both through the miracle of own uncanny happiness and by his ability to "midwife" the erotic soul out of the hedonistic ego, the life of Socrates serves as one of the best models of how the kingdom of heaven within us may be brought into being on earth.

Unlike rhetoric, which sets out to "save the world" on a grand scale, the *daimon* preserves the cosmos one soul at a time. It does this through saving individuals from becoming enslaved to their egos and desires by reminding them of their soul's capacity for temperance and justice. As the great German Idealists have reminded us, what we believe isn't as important as what we want to believe.[13] Implicit in this statement is wry recognition that all people want to believe in the same virtues and ideals but seldom see much evidence of their existence in the world. They must learn to "recollect" these ideas from within. Daimonic activity is sustained by the trust that those who are exposed to genuine virtue will be far less likely to be seduced by false mimetic images. They will be emboldened to leave the caves of rhetoric and return to the surface of the real world.

---

12   Heraclitus fragment B 119.
13   These words are frequently attributed to Fichte.

Likewise, we must descend from these sun-lit heights of *Poros* to discuss matters of geometry and justice in the vale of *Penia*. After having eloquently defended the idea of a cosmic order, Socrates now warns Callicles that the idea of geometric equality has great power over both gods and human beings (508a). We have already studied some of the more audacious implications of this idea in discussing daimons and limits; it can now be brought into yet sharper focus by our trying to understand what Socrates means by geometric equality. We have already seen good reasons for unfavorably regarding both infinite power and numerical equality (e-quantity). In Leibniz's terms, while the former denies and destroys the integrity of the ability of the soul or microcosm to relate to the macrocosm, the latter cannot account for the fact that different monads or souls can reflect the macrocosm in more and less adequate (better or worse) ways. By saying that the idea of geometric equality has great power over gods, Socrates is suggesting subtly but clearly that the divine side of the cosmic four-fold respects the integrity of its opposite number – the human soul. However, he just as clearly states that the divine and the human are not and never should be *equal* partners. They play very different roles in the cosmic economy.

The concept of geometric equality means that things are divided between unequal partners in proportion to their powers and needs. This idea is definitely opposed to Callicles' earlier claim that justice is an artificial imposition since, according to nature, the strong take all they can. But it also opposes the romantic-democratic view that brutish animality and/or un-judgmental divine love reveal the artificiality and viciously elitist quality of the categories "better" and "worse." The use of geometrical equality suggests that power is not the ultimate category because reality is not a divinely abandoned chaos; in the cosmos, all gain when each element contributes to the common good in its own distinctive way. The best proof that Socrates can provide of the truth of this grand statement is by appealing to the immanent order of the individual soul. The soul's mysterious capacity for maieutic recollection of its own microcosmic order points beyond itself to a higher macrocosmic order sustaining this possibility. Indeed, the very experience of the soul recollecting itself explains a great deal about why the *kalon* cannot be imposed from above but must rise out of the microcosmic unit's free reflection, and awe-filled recollection, of the beauty of the cosmos. Indeed what is perhaps most beautiful about the cosmos for us consists precisely in its being a place where true happiness necessarily arises out of human virtue only.

Socrates' words reveal a synergistic relation between reason, diversity, and friendship that is crucial to the cosmos; ratio-nality holds many partial accounts together in due proportion. We could even speculate that a fully realized life is possible only through weaving together rationality and friendship.

The ability to graciously and playfully entertain different mythic and rational *logoi* from past and present makes it possible for humanity to gain a coherent take on reality while remaining open to learning, with wonder and openness, about what is beyond us. This ratio of friendship between many partial truths and perspectives, each striving willy-nilly for the good, also informs the Socratic dia-*logos*; for this reason any attempt made in the name of manipulative science to supplant the ethical and erotic aspects of reason betrays Socrates' account of cosmos.

Socrates has also tried to show Callicles that intemperance is temporarily permitted but not supported by the cosmos. Those like Callicles believed that because the gods fail to visibly punish injustice – they either do not exist or do not care. Socrates' alternative model of the cosmos shows how divine justice is both indirect and consistent with human freedom. Indeed, the very fact that a direct proof cannot be provided shows that everything depends on how our character, or *daimon*, disposes us to view the world: as cosmos or chaos. Socrates' model of the cosmos comes from the experience of order and moderation within his soul. This is why he claims that happiness cannot be seen as egotistical pleasure; the inherently unsatisfactory quality of hedonism leads to the infinite, self-destructive cravings of dis-eased intemperance and a warped take on reality.

Callicles is now warned that injustice must be punished precisely because it can otherwise visit great misery on one who practices it. We have seen that what he means by punishment has little connection to the punitive model and prison system of the present day. Indeed Athenian law did not even provide for incarceration as punishment! Socrates views justice as a process through which "rehabilitation" and "atonement" can occur. Quite literally this means that a wrongdoer is supposed to come home to, and become one with, himself. In other words, it pertains to the soul rather than to the body. Like daimonic activity, just punishment should be seen to be something that takes place between individuals. A wrongdoer is cured only when he has become "individual" again, and no longer lives in a soul divided against itself – by conflicting desires, loyalties, and needs. This is why an individual must be swift to accuse his nearest and dearest of injustice, and participate in their punishment. This is also why those who use rhetoric, and seek to make matters apparent to the many in a short time, must first learn the truth about justice and injustice.

Socrates now responds to Callicles' contention that his shameful inability to defend himself and his friends and relatives against the greatest dangers is proof of the absurdity of his position concerning the best way to live (508c). His response is to deny that these things are the most shameful, we can see how both his model of the cosmos and his disjunction between pleasure and *eudaimonia* support this case. Socrates reiterates that performing evil is worse and more shameful than suffering pain and injustice. He claims that these theories he has offered are "bound down by iron and adamantine arguments" and unless they are weakened, no one else will be able to make a speech disagreeing with him that will sound *kalos* or fine (509a). A lesser-known Delphic maxim, "the most beautiful is the most just," is most apposite here. Moreover, while Socrates cannot, and ought not according to his own model of the cosmos, give demonstrative proof of the superiority of justice over injustice, he is claiming to occupy the moral and aesthetic high ground. It is quite suggestive that, like bound-and-tortured Prometheus, he is looking down on unjust Zeus from his lofty Caucasian mountaintop and foreseeing the end of the Power-God's reign. We can also more playfully observe that Callicles could no longer be true to his name and "be called noble" while disagreeing with Socrates on this matter. Even though he cannot explain it, Socrates further claims that, while his own speech is always the same, those who contest him always end up sounding ridiculous (509a). It follows then that a life of injustice not only appears to be most unjust, it is also – quite shamefully – unable to defend itself or its friends and loved ones from the very evil and corruption that its conduct infects them with.

Callicles is now asked whether one should not endeavor to make preparations to be protected from both doing and suffering injustice. He seems to believe that it is possible to provide against suffering injustice by procuring sufficient power, but when asked whether one can protect oneself – through power and art – against *doing* injustice, he is reluctant to answer (509c–e). Socrates further reminds him of the earlier agreement with Polus that nobody seeks to do injustice for its own sake, but only does so involuntarily. Callicles agrees with even greater reluctance, but soon brightens up when Socrates, after again mentioning the possibility of a power and art against suffering injustice, suggests that this is gained through becoming either a ruler – even as tyrant – or a comrade of the existing regime. This strategy Callicles is pleased to call fine; he even calls Socrates' attention to the alacrity with which he praises any statement of his that is fine (510a–b).

Promethean Socrates then gets Callicles to agree that the strongest degree of friendship is that between persons similar to the greatest possible degree. He next proceeds to claim that when a savage and uncultivated man is tyrant, he would only fear and could not be friends with one better than he. But neither could a tyrant befriend one much lowlier than himself. Only one of the same character as the tyrant could be his friend: one who will praise and blame the same things and is willing to submit to the ruler in all matters. Such a man will have great power and enjoy immunity from suffering injustice. It follows that a young man (like Callicles) desirous of gaining great power and avoiding suffering injustice will accustom himself to imitate that ruler in every way possible. However, even though he avoids suffering injustice, such a man will not be able to avoid doing injustice; indeed he will be just like the ruler – in seeking to do as much injustice with impunity. Thus the greatest infirmity, a degenerate and wounded soul, befalls him (510b–511a).

The paradox revealed here is quite striking. The very art of seeking protection from pain, externally inflicted evil, transforms a fearful person into a tyrant who will seek to eliminate all possibilities of doing harm to him. This inevitably leads to the inflicting of great injustice and pain on others. However, the efficient causality employed by tyranny cannot operate outside the pleasure-pain continuum to exchange or transmit evil between bodies, let alone souls. Since the greatest evil of all consists precisely in doing injustice, by seeking to avoid the lesser evil of pain, a tyrant ends up visiting the greatest evil of all upon himself! Socrates' point is that the soul is damaged by evil rather than pain, the affliction of the body. Someone who does evil actually only visits pain on another's body; meanwhile, the evil stays and grows deep within his own soul. Leibniz's thesis that a monad is windowless[14] is a different way of expressing the fact that evil cannot be spread without the active consent of the soul being exposed to it. Evil can only inflict involuntary damage on the body of its victims; the soul of a good person cannot be touched by it.

When Callicles angrily accuses Socrates of ignoring the most salient fact, that he who imitates the vices of the regime will despoil and kill the man who refuses to imitate them, Socrates responds that it will be a base man killing one who is noble and good (*kalon kagathon*). Now asked by Callicles whether this isn't infuriating, Socrates denies that this is so to a man of intelligence and asks whether one should devote one's life to living as long as possible and learning those arts – such as rhetoric – that will be most supportive of this goal. Upon Callicles' swearing by Prometheus' enemy Zeus that this is indeed his view, Socrates asks him whether he finds the art of swimming to be noble. Callicles doesn't think so, but Socrates points out that this art preserves life too. So does the ship-pilot's art, which saves soul, bodies, and property from being lost. Yet, the pilot charges very little for his expertise and does not think too highly of himself because he does not know which passenger's souls were actually harmed by being kept alive; neither does he believe his voyage to have benefited their souls in any way. Curiously, the pilot is said to know that it isn't better for a bad man to live longer, because he will only live badly. Socrates points out that the both the physician and engineer (*mechanopoios*) are in the same category; even though their arts give them great power over life and death, they are not considered worthy of marriage into the ranks of the *kalos*

14 Leibniz, *Monadology*, #7.

kagathos of Athens (511a–513e). We should note Socrates himself was born into another banausic craft, that of stonecutting. We also know, from his description of it in the *Theaetetus,* that his mother's art of midwifery was far more pertinent to decisions concerning suitability for life and death than we would expect today (150d).

This means that nobility and goodness are not about devoting all one's energies to staying alive, or saving the lives of others, at any cost. Socrates states that a real gentleman (*alethes andra*) must scorn living for the sake of life. We should not be lovers of life (*philo-psuche*); instead one should put these matters in the hands of god, and believing the old wives tale that nobody can flee from his destiny, reflect instead on how best to live one's life (512d–513a). In other words, instead of seeking to escape from something that was often equated with one's destiny: one's *daimon*, one should instead seek to be equal to it. This stands in stark contrast to the rhetorical strategy of telling people what they want to hear. This power, once used, only ends up holding one hostage to deeds and positions that were not one's own to begin with. Socrates' own use of the *reductio-ad-absurdum* strategy is far more prudent.

Socrates warns Callicles against trying to become as much like the Athenian regime as possible for the sake of gaining power; he warns that this would make one like the witches of Thessaly, who were said to gain power sufficient to draw down the moon by sacrificing the life of a loved one. Likewise, Callicles is told that it would not profit him to obtain hegemony over the polis in exchange for what he should hold most dear (513a). He must not emulate Archelaus in selling his soul to gain evil powers that will end up controlling him. This is why he will gain genuine friendship only with his two loves: beautiful Demos and the Athenian demos, by being equal and true to himself – and not by practicing falseness and imitation (513b–c). This was the same point made in the *Republic*; true political success is not gained through simply learning how to pander to all the passions of that great beast – the multitude. Both demos and demagogue are weakened by this mindlessly mimetic exercise, and the latter even loses his very capacity for friendship.

Now Callicles makes a very striking admission. Though he cannot explain how it is possible, he grants that he believes Socrates' words, yet shares the common feeling (*pathos*) of the many (*polloi*) concerning Socrates – he is not persuaded (513c). In other words, the false self-evidence of public opinion outweighs reason in his mimetic soul and also commands his will. This surely represents the sentiments of the jurors at Socrates' trial. Callicles' psychic state is the exact opposite of Socrates' – we recall the philosopher being unmoved by Crito's efforts to mobilize private emotions and public opinion against his deliberate decision to face death. In Socrates' temperate soul, the inner self-evidence of morality drowned out the irrational passions. Socrates is not surprised by Callicles' minority report – he has just addressed him as "dear head," thus recognizing that he was not reasoning with the part of Callicles that ruled his actions (513c). This also completes the earlier argument that Socrates was unwilling to leave headless (505d). At least Callicles now knows what Socrates was talking about, even though his body is un-persuaded by this non-rhetorical reasoning. By forcing Callicles' reason to testify against himself, Socrates has helped the younger man to weaken his fragmented, intemperate, and demagogic psychic regime; he has turned Callicles away from admiring intemperance and left him merely incontinent.

Now suggesting that Callicles could yet be convinced if they searched further and better, Socrates goes back to the earlier distinction between the two ways of taking care of body and soul. While the one used pleasure as its goal, the other fought for what was best – as Socrates is doing now. Callicles then admits – letting Socrates achieve his wish – that the way given to pleasure is but ignoble flattery. He more readily concedes that the aim of the other "therapy" is that its target object, whether body or soul, be the best it could be. Socrates then asks whether this should not be the task of rulers, to attempt to tend the polis and its citizenry in such a way as to make them as best as possible (513d–e). Here he is clearly harnessing the *logos* itself to publicly articulate what is self-evident – in speech that the *demos* could hardly dispute. This goes back to his earlier claim that anyone refuting his position had to discover ground above his Promethean mountain crag.

Since the task of the rulers is to aim for excellence, the question of their authority and credentials becomes paramount. This is not an issue in the case of a democracy, since it equates the pleasure of the many with the truth. The contrast is between the collective subjectivity of the many and the objective authority of the few knowledgeable persons ruling in the interests of all. Socrates has already suggested that these rulers should be men of justice and temperance; thus they would not be tyrannized by insatiable desires for pleasures and wealth. Socrates raises the question of how prospective rulers would prove their competence in the matters they make proposals about. In the case of building projects, he suggests that their advocates present the people with evidence of having successfully undertaken projects of this kind in their private capacity (514a–515b).

It is clear that we are not merely speaking of suitability for executing a project; it is also a matter of whether it represents the best use made of the resources available to the polity. While Socrates does not make this point explicit, it is clearly essential to his criticism of the Athenian leaders of the past. In other words, it is not sufficient to be a successful war leader if the prior question of the necessity of the war had not addressed in a non-demagogic manner. The most obvious example of this distinction is the great Sicilian expedition; even though Alcibiades was arguably the Athenian best suited to lead it, Nicias – who turned out to be the worst possible general – was yet perfectly correct – albeit rhetorically ineffectual – in advising Athens against going to Syracuse in the first place.[15] The other intriguing question raised by this proposal concerns the extent to which public projects entered into *en masse* substitute for private virtues and friendships. This issue was strikingly raised in the *Republic*: can the city reproduce and replace the processes of the soul? In other words, should someone unable to rule his own soul have hegemony over a polity? Can engineering replace ethics? Xenophon's *Memorabilia* hints that the *Republic* is founded on Socrates' indirect teaching of this lesson to a Glaucon made wiser and more beautiful.[16]

Regardless of his willingness to be a ruler, Socrates has shown some ability to practice the true political art by his successful efforts at moderating the souls of several of the young men he came into contact with; he is critical of the political value of rhetoric precisely because its hubristic claim to have irresistible power to persuade all its addressees. Such a combination of ignorance, ambition, and violence is most dangerous to both city and soul. By contrast, the philosopher's best claim to authority is his own psychic regime; as we know Socrates – the least physically attractive man on Athens – was proud of his beauty. Just as Gorgias was especially pleased by his ability to outsmart the most competent specialists in their own field, Socrates' ability to exert erotic attraction despite his ugly appearance calls attention to another dimension of *to kalon*.

This is why some form of these questions regarding personal prudence and maturity ought be asked of prospective rulers; looks, wealth, connections, and/or demagogic charm should not take the place of temperance. The *Republic* suggested that the best rulers would be among those most reluctant to rule and further implied that those with private virtues would be best suited to serve as daimons and guardians. Their role would surely be to dissuade the polity from hubristic projects that seduce citizens away from justice and temperance. This, after all, is the basis for Socrates' criticism of the great figures from the recent past (another list of four): Miltiades, Themistocles, Cimon, and Pericles (515d). Asking Callicles if any of them made the people better or worse, Socrates points out that since two of these hegemons were ostracized, and the other two were heavily fined at the end of their rule, the evidence hardly suggests that the Athenians were grateful for the benefits received from these men – most of whom were wildly popular at the beginning of their ascendancy. The fact that Miltiades and Themistocles, as well as Cimon and

15 Thucydides, *Peloponnesian War*, VII. 8–14, 20–24.
16 Xenophon, *Memorabilia*, III.6.

Pericles, were bitter political rivals hardly speaks well of the collective virtue of this great "four-fold." Neither could witnessing and emulating vicious struggles of this kind edify the demos. Aeschylus' words "The dead are killing the living" irresistibly come to mind.[17]

Speaking specifically of Pericles, Socrates damningly remarks: "A caretaker of asses, horses, or oxen of this kind would seem bad if when first taking over he was neither kicked, butted or bitten but then left them doing all these things out of wildness" (516b). Even though one could contend against Socrates that the Athenians repented of their anger towards Pericles and restored him to office in the last year of his life, it is still the case that he manifestly failed to curb their hubris and left after him a political order that no one could successfully rule. Socrates adds, "It cannot be that good charioteers at the start don't fall out, but only do so after they have the chance to train the horses and become better charioteers" (516e). The suggestion is that Pericles and the rest, all the way to that most extravagant of charioteers – Alcibiades – were reckless drivers of men. They displayed their virtuosity to Greece at the expense of their demotic horses. Soon, both riders and horses came to confuse hubris with health, boldness with courage, and pandering with politics.

Bluntly put, the skill of winning elections and holding office is a matter of pandering. It has little or nothing to do with the far more serious task of statesmanship – which aims to actually improve the polity and citizenry over the long run. Indeed, the two techniques are inversely related since an artful politician corrupts and weakens his constituency to stay in power longer. Conversely, while a slim majority of his jurors chose to convict Socrates when he ensured that a vote for his innocence would also indict the Athenian way of life for its shallow materialism, the glorious memory of his moral Thermopylae continues to bathe the deepest roots of Western Civilization.

Socrates now goes on to say that none of the present politicians or those of the past displayed excellence in political affairs. When Callicles suggests that the achievements of the older generation still far surpass the shabby records of the politicians of the present day, Socrates replies by pointing out that while the older rulers were terribly good at pandering to the desires of the demos, and supplying such things as ships, walls, and dockyards (517c), they failed to educate these desires in a different direction that would improve the citizenry. In other words, while these great men of yore plied the Athenians with political confectionaries and cosmetics, they neglected the equivalents of the medical and gymnastic arts – which alone provide for the virtue and freedom of the body politic. Their rule brought immediate pleasures of body and appearance at the risk of long-term debility, envy, and corruption. While

---

17 Aeschylus, *The Libation Bearers*, 886.

Socrates' harsh indictment of past rulers does not factor in the role played by fortune and contingency in human affairs, this very recognition argues against those who see politics as a craft of irresistible persuasion and ignore civic temperance.

The harshest indictment of these leaders was that they made a free people into a *demos* – intent on defeating shadows and preserving appearances, but incapable of ruling (or knowing) themselves. This leads the unschooled many to praise those cooks, bakers, and hucksters who corrupted them, and recall them with nostalgia when they grow weak and diseased – by these very indulgences (518c–e). However those who happen to be in charge when the results of over-indulgence set in will be blamed and harmed for evils that were reaped on their watch, though sown by their heroes. He chides Callicles for "praising those who feasted the many lavishly with what they desired. They said that these men made the polis great, when it was actually swollen and festered with disease through their vices. Ruling immoderately and unjustly, they filled Athens with harbors, dockyards, walls, tribute and other drivel [*phluarion* – Callicles' favorite word] (519a)" He goes on to warn Callicles and Alcibiades about the danger of being blamed by the corrupt citizenry when the polis loses not only the things it unjustly acquired, but also its original inheritance. In reality, however, these present-day leaders will only be accessories after the fact.

Nevertheless, Socrates finds it strange that when a politician is accused of injustice, he complains bitterly of being punished despite having done many good deeds for the polity. According to Socrates, it is impossible for the leader of a polis to be unjustly condemned for bad leadership. They are just like the sophists, who set themselves up as teachers of virtue but sue their students when they do not pay for their lessons. The truth of the matter is that the very fact that the student is dishonest proves that the teacher has not taught him virtue. Similarly a politician who claims to have done the polity much good cannot complain with justice. This is because the ingratitude of the *polloi* proves them to be vicious, and thus to have received no such benefit from him (519b–e). In this context we note that because Socrates himself held public office for only one day, all his deeds were of a private and negative character. As the tripartite action of the *Gorgias* suggests, Socrates never claimed to impart virtue; he only tries to deter his comrades from vice and folly by exposing the illusions and temptations preventing them from rightly seeing their moral condition.

We could anticipate and explain Socrates' claim to be the only living practitioner of the genuine political art by attending to the difference between politics and philosophy. When Aristotle says in *Ethics* I that politics is the highest art,[18] this is because it establishes the conditions for the other peak,

---

18   Aristotle, *Nicomachean Ethics*, I.1094a25.

personal/philosophic happiness, considered in the last book of the same work.[19] While Socrates clearly has a more erotic understanding of philosophy, he would certainly agree that politics has to do with collective potential for, and philosophy with private actualization of, excellence. Decent public mores, or an ethos of habitual orderliness, can never do more than provide necessary conditions for virtue; they are never sufficient and substitutable for private deliberation and action. This why *Eudaimonia* cannot be imposed upon a people; as Aristotle suggests, the polis itself is an extension of friendship and civic concord.[20] It also follows that *thumotic* justice is not a sufficient basis for a city; we saw why the originally apologetic skill of rhetoric, that expands to cover the rallying of friends against enemies in the name of justice, cannot make the necessary qualitative leap to teach the true happiness of soul or city.

When Socrates then tries to make Callicles criticize those who falsely claim to teach virtue, he is asked instead what he has to say of "those who are collectively worth nothing" – meaning the many. Callicles means that the orators and politicians are not to blame for the crassness of human nature. This request is also the mirror image of Adeimantus's approving account of the bad opinion popularly held concerning philosophers in the *Republic* being responded to by Socrates' asking him "why the many were so bad?" (487). On that occasion, Socrates' account of how the many came to be corrupted by democratic politics and poetry culminated in the celebrated myth of the cave. Here Socrates will provide a *logos* of a purgative anti-cave in the afterlife that will undo the effects of the cave, but he does so only after denouncing the politicians for projecting their own baseness on the polity: "what do you say of those who claim to govern a polis to make as good as possible, and then accuse it of being most base when the fault is theirs?" (520a). This is akin to the abominable Nazi practice of humiliatingly dehumanizing their victims in every way possible before righteously declaring that they were merely ridding the world of vermin.[21]

Socrates says out that while orator-politicians and sophists practice practically the same art, on account of ignorance, rhetoric is praised while sophistry is denounced. In truth, sophistry is to rhetoric what legislation is to justice, and gymnastics is to medicine. This means that while political sophistry exploits corruption in souls through evil temptations, the cosmetic skill of rhetoric defends or justifies it. Socrates further points out that the very fact that rhetoric charges for its services means that it does not promote or

---

19   *Ibid*, X.1179b20.
20   *Ibid*, VIII.1159b25 ff.
21   Tzvetan Todorov, *Facing The Extreme* (Henry Holt, 1996), p. 160.

reveal justice – both of which would naturally evoke justice in their beneficiaries – but only creates a false impression of it.

We could add here that it was precisely for this reason that it was considered disgraceful until very recently for legislators to receive salaries or offices of profit for their services. This is also why Socrates had earlier harshly criticized Pericles for corrupting the many by offering payment for what was previously considered honorable public service (515e). We recall Kant's brilliant insight that the best way to corrupt a virtuous man is by offering him a reward for acts that he formerly performed for their own sake. Kant predicted that these deeds would inevitably end up being performed for the sake of the reward, rather than for their intrinsic worth. The proof will consist in the man's altered attitude towards the action after the incentive is taken away.[22]

Socrates now returns to the basic choice that faces any honest man in dark times, asking Callicles to state frankly whether it is better for him to struggle against political corruption like a physician, or to flatter and serve the Athenian *demos* like a servitor who cares only for his own profit (521a). Despite Socrates' urging that he speak well and nobly, Callicles continues to advocate the way of the servant or deacon. When Socrates asks bluntly if this means that should turn to flattery, the formerly shameless Callicles finds this crudeness distasteful and attempts once again to warn against the other path of life. Socrates responds by asking him not to waste his time with talk of death and confiscation. Socrates then cryptically adds that one who unjustly takes his property will be ignorant of how to use it properly, and only make unjust, shameful, and bad use of it (521b–c). Perhaps this warning best applies to hubristic readers of the *Republic*! More seriously, the merely curious or power-hungry cannot expect to grasp Socrates' ideas or ethical precepts.

When Callicles suggests that Socrates seems too confident that his circumstances make him immune from prosecution by a complete degenerate, someone like Meletus, Socrates replies by saying that only a thoughtless (*anoetos*) man would think that anything could not happen to anyone by chance in present-day Athens (521c–d). This is a glancing reference to the theories of Anaxagoras – who placed his spiritual substance Mind *(Nous)* amid a chaotic mixture of everything in everything[23] – and his fate – of being tried for impiety by the Athenians and escaping death through Pericles' intervention. Still we must note that this prosecution was probably politically motivated, stemming from Anaxagoras's close ties with his *deus ex machina,* Pericles.

Socrates goes on to state that if he did face prosecution it will not be unlikely that he would die. He goes on to explain this probability by claiming

22   Kant, *Religion within the Limits of Reason Alone,* vol. VI, p. 37 of Akademie Edition.
23   See *The Presocratic Philosophers* (Cambridge, 1983), p. 362.

to be one of the few Athenians, if not the only man, to attempt the true art of statesmanship (*politike tecne*). He claims further that he alone of the men of the present time does so, insofar as he speaks not to gratify but with care only for what is best (521d–e). This is also why, as Callicles foresaw, he would have nothing to say in a law court accustomed to flattery. This unlikely Cordelia compares himself to a physician standing trial before a jury of children. He would stand accused of corrupting the youth by exposing them to pain, hunger, bitterness, and suffering. His accuser would be a wildly popular cook or confectioner who promises to stuff the jurors with all kinds of pleasurable experiences. The doctor's defense, that he did all these things for their health, would be met with great derision from the boy-judges. Speaking no longer by analogy, Socrates further states that were he to go before the Athenians he would not be able to list the pleasures he has supplied, or even to state that he envies either the purveyors or recipients of these pleasures. Moreover when accused of corrupting the youth by making them feel perplexity (*aporia*), and of slandering his peers by speaking abrasively to them in private or public, it would do him no good to tell these self-styled judges that his speeches and deeds are just and in their best interest (521e–522a).

Since these words were clearly written after the actual trial of Socrates, it seems that Plato wishes us to see that they are not prophetic but said with a clear-eyed recognition of the issues involved. Socrates knows that his judges would be for the most part too corrupted by demagoguery to see beyond the false self-evidence of bodily self-interest and immediate pleasure. Consequently they will be compelled by this corrupt self-evidence to believe that Socrates is guilty – both of introducing dangerous and impractical ethical standards and of slandering the ancestral pieties of his fatherland by being critical of the achievements of its greatest men. This is probably the substance of Aristophanes' charge of father beating and potentially outrageous intentions towards the other parent. These similarities between Socrates and Oedipus are hardly accidental. Socrates has brought the patriarchy into ridicule, sought to recover the sacred origins of morality, and voluntarily blinded himself to values that the polity angrily holds to be self-evident. Socrates' refusal to leave Athens makes him both like and unlike Oedipus – who visited fraternal strife on Thebes and gave the Athenians the benefit of his uncanny daimon.[24] It is noteworthy that the words used by Socrates to claim to practice the true political art, claiming that he was the only one of the present age to do so and one of few to attempt it, parallel his reference to his *daimon* or divine sign in *Republic* VI. He claimed that this came out of the corrupt quagmire of Athenian politics, adding that it had perhaps occurred in some other man before him (496c).

---

24   See Sophocles' *Oedipus at Colonus,* 1393–94, 1533 ff.

Upon Callicles asking him if he thought this state – of being a powerless man in the polity – is noble (*kalon*), Socrates replies that he would at least be not guilty of any injustice towards men or gods (522a). It is only for such an outrage that one should be ashamed, since Callicles has already agreed many times that it is the greatest security of all to be a just man. He would indeed be ashamed to be found guilty of being unable to help himself or another in this way, whether his accusers were many, few, or even a single man. But he would face his end lightly were he merely convicted of being a bad flatterer. Socrates contends that only the unreasonable and cowardly fear death *qua* death; people only fear death out of a guilty awareness of injustice. This is because it is the worst evil of all to arrive in the house of Hades with a soul filled with injustice. He then offers to provide Callicles with a rational account (*logos*) of this point if he so wishes. Callicles agrees, in his last words of the dialogue, granting that since Socrates has completed every other account, he should finish this one too. It is most noteworthy that this final speech of the *Gorgias*, which is composed of four equal quarters, each ending in a long monologue, is described as a *logos*. In other words, Socrates explicitly claims that he is not practicing poetry or rhetoric. How are we to understand his elaborate *logos* about Hades in a way that isn't in contradiction with his claim in the *Apology* to be wise only in knowing that he is ignorant about transcendent matters? What genre can this *logos* belong to if it cannot be fact and is explicitly said not to be myth?[25]

Let us first begin with Socrates asking Callicles to listen to a very fine *logos* (*mala kalou logou*), which he will regard as a myth, but Socrates considers a rational account because it will reveal what he regards as truth. Claiming to quote Homer, Socrates speaks of the time when Zeus, Poseidon, and Pluto succeeded Kronos and shared up power (523a). He tactfully omits to mention that this division of spoils occurred after a violent struggle against their father. Homer's account also emphasizes the supremacy of Zeus over all the other gods. Poseidon irately mentions this division in a context that makes clear that he is no longer an equal partner in the triumvirate.[26] Yet we shall see that Socrates has his own reasons for emphasizing this division. In the earlier account of the four-fold cosmos, the principles are gods, man, sky, and earth. While Zeus is both the king of the gods and sky god, Poseidon – the earth-shaker – is the god of the natural elements of earth and sea. The third son Pluto, also called Hades, seemingly has no place in this cosmos.

25 For what it's worth, we note Stauffer's claim that the *Gorgias* ultimately does not provide an adequate account of the Good for which Socrates made himself vulnerable to the angry city. He adds that Callicles probably would not have been receptive to such an account anyway (p. 167).

26 *Iliad*, XV.222 ff.

The *Republic* most memorably depicted the current Athenian political order in Socrates' famous image of human nature in its education and lack of education: the Myth of the Cave. This cave or chasm was an underground cavern lit artificially and ruled by false image-making poets, orators, and politicians. It is strikingly similar to the Homeric Hades in that its denizens have "no-idea" (*a-eidos*) of who they are, but see and know themselves only as shadows. The process of education is represented as the task of helping these self-imprisoned men to leave their artificial habitation and gaze upon what is true and beautiful. Socrates is suggesting that there would be no need to fear Hades like Achilles, and prefer living as a slave to a landless man on the harsh earth, if people led their lives as though they were already in Hades – living as shadows in a cave with all of their thoughts and perceptions completely manipulated by orators, poets, and politicians.

The *Republic's* depiction of the plight of uneducated humanity is bleak indeed. Everything depends on educated and enlightened individuals performing the daimonic service of individually liberating their fellows from the bonds of chauvinistic convention and taking them out to see the beauty of the real world. These daimons would not stay out in the open very long because their vocation required them to keep returning to the cave and continually helping their comrades to free themselves. We see that these daimons perform the task we have already seen described in the *Symposium* – that of holding together the divine and human realms. This scheme could also be transposed on to the earth-sky axis with equal ease since the cave is deep in the earth and the transcendent beauties seen outside of it are set in the inaccessible heavens. It is also noteworthy that the bliss of the daimons is derived from ethical virtue and exceeds the merely human intellectual happiness of those who gaze at the big sky like the cicadas of the *Phaedrus*, by as much as they are happier than the dwellers in the cave. Differently put, the daimons are in a state of *eudaimonia*, the liberated prisoners know happiness, and the prisoners feel pleasure and pain.

Speaking in a dialogue set symbolically at Delphi, the navel and womb of the universe, Socrates describes a law that still applies to gods and used to pertain to mortals in the days of Kronos. According to it, those who dwelt justly and piously would at the end of their days depart for the Isles of the Blessed to enjoy perfect bliss. Conversely, the unjust and godless would go down to the prison of retribution and punishment, Tartarus. This suggests that even the gods are subject to a higher destiny that cannot be avoided. This claim is not inconsistent with the theology of such works as *Prometheus Bound*, where the titan warned that even Zeus's tenure would end.[27] We also recall Zeus's lament

---

27 Aeschylus, *Prometheus Bound*, 755 ff.

upon recognizing that he could not reverse the fate of his son Sarpedon.[28] The mysterious distinction between the sky and the gods is better understood when we take the sky to represent a realm of eternal unchanging ideas to which even the gods are subject; this issue was notably examined in the *Euthyphro* – where the virtues are recognized by the gods and cannot be whatever the arbitrary deities happen to fancy. The further implication of this is that the gods themselves are but time-bound representations of the Platonic forms or ideas. These anthropomorphic deities are made more accessible in parochial terms in such places as the cave. We now remember Diotima's statement from the *Symposium* that the gods do not communicate directly with man (203a). This is another way of explaining why poetic representations of gods, along with daimonic philosophers, must mediate between the hollow earth and the distant sky.

However it would appear that just as the gods are different from the sky, so too are men distinct from the earth – their womb. The point seems to be that it is through shared representations of the gods and virtues that humanity rises out of the earth to play its part in the four-fold cosmos. In other words, Socrates would agree with Aristotle's definition of man as a political animal[29] – even though his unique political art is surely more erotic than Aristotle's mimetic model of politics. While Heaven and Earth serve as ontological pillars, gods and men play a more time-bound, though no less essential, dynamic role in the cosmos. This model further clarifies the part played by daimonic men in mediating between gods and mortals through *logos* and mythos. More specifically, by seeing the connection between this *logos* and his previous account of the four-fold we can also understand the authority exercised by Socrates in giving this account (*logos*) of transcendent reality. Consistent with the *Antiope*, Socrates replaces the authority of Zethus the shepherd or herdsman – who represents his father Zeus – with the speech of the intellectual poet and builder of Thebes: Amphion, whose lyre, unaided by physical power, will move stones and trees. He starkly contrasts the former leaders of Athens, who Gorgon-like turned cities of men into stone walls, and this truly political music or art of drawing souls out of the cave or womb.[30]

Following the older laws from the Age of Kronos, mortals could foresee the time of their death. In the time of Zeus however this law had to be changed because deceptive appearances caused its abuse. Many potentates would

---

28   *Iliad*, XVI.512–48.
29   Aristotle, *Politics*, 1253a1.
30   Saxonhouse summarizes this political art: "Philosophy abhors the concept of conquest, of masters and slaves. The best person, made best by the activities of the true politician, would be a complete whole, not a ruler over others, just as the best city . . . would not need to have hegemony over other cities" (p. 168).

appear in all their finery accompanied by a coterie of henchmen and sycophants so as to sway the judgment of the living men who would judge them –
presumably on the basis of appearance and reputation (523c). This is clearly a
representation of the Homeric warrior ethic – which attached great importance
to appearance and reputation among men. It was following these rules that
Achilles chose a short glorious life and practically engineered the manner of
his death: struck down from afar at the height of his glory by a coward. By the
time of the *Gorgias* however things had changed. This is why we see Socrates'
logos has Pluto and the unnamed custodians of the Isles of the Blessed angrily complaining to Zeus about the quality of these judgments. Many of the dead
were unjustly exalted or punished; the quality of their lives was assessed purely on the basis of appearance and reputation. In other words, their souls were
judged by democratic public opinion; the last judgment on a human life was
literally conducted according to the rules of the famous underground chasm or
Cave of the *Republic*. The parallel is subtle but devastating. We must see that
just as subtly as his *logos* avoids drawing attention to the violent deposition of
Kronos by his sons, Socrates is himself effecting the overthrow of Zeus.[31]

If the Greek heroic age began with the Trojan War, it ended with the
Peloponnesian War. This was why Thucydides said unequivocally that the later
war was the greater motion of the two; it was from this grim vantage that he
re-interpreted the earlier conflict and went on to draw new and disturbing conclusions about the place of providence, chance, and necessity in human
affairs.[32] Socrates had earlier drawn a causal link between the Peloponnesian
War and the perfected rhetorical art of verbal deception. By this *logos* he now
implies that once Gorgias can claim greater glory than Achilles, in keeping
with the arch persuader's boast that he could verbally defeat the best in the eyes
of the ignorant *demos*, the Homeric era was over and its gods overthrown.
Socrates is not introducing strange deities in their stead; rather, he is uphold-
ing the higher timeless principles that the sky represents in his model of the
four-fold.[33] Pious Socrates sees that the transcendent signified matters far
more than its discredited Olympian signifier.

This is why the *Gorgias* cautiously inaugurates a moral revolution that
distinguishes between bodily appearance and ethical reality. Human life is no
longer to be eked out in an underworld pervaded by myths and presided over

---

31 See Alessandra Fussi, "The Myth of the Last Judgment in the Gorgias," in *The
    Review of Metaphysics* vol. 54 (2001), pp. 540–42.
32 Thucydides, *Peloponnesian War*, I. 1 & 9–12.
33 See Strauss, "On the Euthyphron," in *The Rebirth of Classical Political
    Philosophy* (Chicago, 1989): "Meletus erred grossly in speaking of Socrates'
    introducing novel things. For the ideas, being prior to any beings which imitate the
    ideas, are prior to any gods. They are the first things, the oldest things" (p. 200).

by sophists and rhetoricians; rather, the *Logos* of Plato's Cave decisively exposes the soul-killing values of opportunistic politics. Following this outlook, superficial qualities such as popularity, envy, cosmetic appearance, and destructive power would no longer be the criteria of excellence. When Callicles denounced the Athenian shame culture, he did so in the name of a moral code based on the nihilistic will to power. By contrast Socrates sets out to make moral virtue the focal point of authentic human experience. Also, consistent with his previous profession to have provided the most beautiful account of the cosmos, Socrates' *logos* claims authority by virtue of its self-evident justice and beauty. Since the *Gorgias* never took place in historical time, it is as though Plato's dialogues are enacted in a revolutionary Age of Kronos. The truest causes of human actions are depicted for our edification in this timeless space where the *Gorgias* provides a *logos* of psychic interiority to support its after-worldly *mythos*. This power is also what makes it possible for twenty-first century readers of Plato's *Gorgias* to successfully return to the timelessly renewing sources of the Western intellectual tradition.

The moral order suggested by the *Gorgias* also covertly overturns the manipulative theology of the Cave. Ostensibly ordered by Zeus, this new way of judging the lives of men represents an understanding of the gods based on values that are transcendental not mimetic, and interior rather than external. Socrates will neither derive the "ought" from the "is" nor allow human passion and envy to serve as the source of all value. The anthropomorphized gods of Homer permitted the power of warlords to be legitimized and sanctified, following the pious belief that all power came from above. Still, as the *Euthyphro* shows, attempts to reverse time and literalize mythic piety produce absurd results. By contrast Plato's texts redeem time and refute the capricious power of *ananke* by revealing the possibilities for virtue available throughout human history. While Plato's reluctance to use demonstrative proofs has to do with his preference for free moral deliberation, this has far-reaching theological implications. As I have suggested, Socrates' account of the transition from Kronos to Zeus is nothing less than an invisible deposition of the latter god. Going far beyond changes in judging the dead, his *logos* signals the end of a piety-based economy (based on Homer's willful power-hungry gods) and its replacement by a moral cosmic order.

The Socratic account of the four-fold cosmos provides a new model of reality that could account for both the human experience of freedom and our inner awareness of transcendent moral ideas needed to regulate it. Without the latter term, the heady experience of freedom would soon see moral nihilism coexisting with the manipulative and cynical processes of demagoguery described in the Myth of the Cave. As the *Republic* foresaw, anarchic

Dionysian freedom – once unleashed – inevitably terminated in tyranny. Indeed the *Bacchae* of Euripides, which exposed the dark side of Dionysus, the demi-god of drunken democracy, was written in the court of Archelaus, tyrant of the very nation that permanently destroyed Greek freedom scarcely ten years after Plato's death.

Speaking with Zeus as his mouthpiece, Socrates now sets forth a morally authoritative vision of judgment incorporating all the various ethical positions that he has defended in the *Gorgias*. According to it, men will no longer be ruled by false appearances or mortally damage their souls trying to defeat justice by deceptive rhetoric and flattery. This new order of justice is designed to promote virtue and prevent humans from being deceived and condemned by the cosmetic arts. It will not be possible to deceive the judges because everyone at this court will be completely naked and dead to the seductions of appearances; it was in this sense that Socrates famously described philosophy as a constant preparation for death in the *Phaedo* (64a). The judgments of this court would not be influenced by fleshly, mimetic, or parochial factors. The judges will only see the soul of the dead man, stripped of adornment and flesh.[34] Strikingly, the judges who would deal with Athenians, though renowned for their justice on earth, would hardly be well-disposed to them on partisan grounds; even though the Athenians claimed descent from him, Aeacus, who would first judge those of European descent, was the fabled king of Aegina, the hereditary enemies of the Athenians. Aeacus was also the grandfather of two great heroes of the Trojan War, Achilles and Ajax; we are prompted to wonder how he would regard the actions of his heroic but bellicose grandsons.[35] It is also striking that Minos, the great foe of Athens, will hear appeals against Aeacus's decisions.

Yet in an important sense, the judges are almost as redundant as Zeus. This means that Socrates is not illicitly providing a positive account of matters above the sky; the moral character of the soul appearing before the judges is self-evident because, just as the body of a corpse reveals the physical damage it had sustained while alive, the soul of the dead man serves as a record of the deeds it performed – both good and evil – over its tenure on earth. Socrates has consistently held throughout the *Gorgias* that while rhetoric and sophistry make it possible for a person to deceive others, and visit great pain upon them, the greatest deception and psychic damage is self-inflicted. While the judges

---

34 We recall that Gorgias was stripped of all his flowery speeches before being examined by Socrates.

35 Legend has it that Aeacus disinherited his two sons, Telemon and Peleus, for killing their half-brother. In Aristophanes' *Frogs*, we find that Aeacus is sufficiently courageous to whip Heracles (the disguise assumed by Dionysus) for stealing Cerberus from Hades.

merely witness that the soul of an evil man is scarred by false oaths and injustice, crippled by lying and bragging, and filled with ugliness from intemperance and hubris; the real jurors are his incorrigibly corrupted desires passing sentence on themselves as he lives.

We also noted earlier the truly deleterious effects of the invulnerable "armor of the lie" donned by a truly vicious man. Far from being a "gift of the gods" this armor only has the effect of causing an evildoer to believe his own lies concerning the necessity of vice and thus lose both his conscience and his connection to the *logos*. Mighty Achilles was reduced to a bestial state when he was forced to see what he had done to his best friend while enjoying divine protection; likewise, Hector himself succumbed to hubris when he donned the accursed armor of Achilles. The terrible pattern continues when, after Ajax commits suicide upon failing to gain them,[36] Achilles' son, Neoptolemus, is involved in some of the most heinous atrocities of the Trojan War (brutally killing aged Priam at the temple of Zeus, sacrificing Polyxena to the shade of Achilles, and throwing Hector's infant son from the walls of Troy), once he receives these blindingly invulnerable arms from Odysseus.

It is in this context that Socrates pointed out that since poverty leads a person to work, and a sick man goes to a physician, it is necessary for one who is unjust to seek out punishment and rehabilitation. Of course very few men do this; indeed the seemingly self-evidently absurdity of such conduct to persons like Polus and Callicles reveals the truly grievous and insidious character of the damage caused by vice. A wrongdoer who is no longer incontinent (regretting his lack of control over his sinful impulses), but intemperate (placing his reason fully at the disposal of his now insatiate appetites and believing himself to be beyond morality), has truly lost awareness of his soul – even though it still continues to register his career of evil. Differently put, his conscience and his consciousness have parted company so that his sensual and aesthetic enjoyment (consciousness) of his depredations may be unclouded by moral reservations and misgivings (conscience).[37] Accordingly he does not feel guilt, even though the state of disease in which he lives is clearly not one of happiness but only drives him further away from it and himself. In a sense we could argue that since his bodily consciousness has become detached from his soul-dwelling conscience, his soul has already died and resides in Hades. This is because he has "no idea" of himself beyond the dis-eased experience of an infinitely painful, insatiable and laborious quest for pleasure. As Aristotle

36   *Odyssey*, XI.620 ff.
37   See Arendt, *Thinking and Moral Considerations* in *Responsibility and Judgment*, pp. 180–89.
38   Aristotle, *Nicomachean Ethics*, III, 1118b30 ff.

suggested with reference to *Akolasia*, the absence of an impossible imagined pleasure itself becomes the cause of incurable pain.[38]

Differently put, incorrigible evil is like an advanced stage of spiritual diabetes; the inevitable loss of moral sensibility, while vainly welcomed as a sign that one has progressed beyond Good and Evil, is but a sign of the advanced progression of the dis-ease. Indeed, just as the lack of sensation in one's extremities indicates that they are very badly damaged to the point of requiring amputation, the soul of a sociopath will necessarily be incapable of common moral experience. It will eventually seek death as a form of liberation once belated awareness of the full extent of the self-inflicted damage finally and roughly comes through reality. After falling (or hubristically jumping) off his wall, the aforementioned Humpty Dumpty would doubtless ignore his very dire predicament and proclaim that he is flying, almost up to the moment before he metamorphoses into a raw omelet. Part of the dire punishment exacted by evil on us is that awareness of the results of vice, and our responsibility for it, comes only after the process has become irreversible.

Homer vividly depicted Hades as a kind of Alzheimer's ward, where the dead lacked any abiding awareness of who they really were, or what they had been. His moving depiction of the afterlife must surely have been derived from observation of the sad plight of dementia and senility, states in which the aged patient's occasional flashes of seeming lucidity only add to the suffering of their loved ones and compounds the confusion of the sufferer himself. The Homeric warrior ethic was also reinforced by this frightening account of the fate awaiting almost all men; the only immortality available was gained through turning one's life into an unforgettable story that would, one hopes, be remembered over the ages.[39] It is obvious that in such circumstances the tools of rhetoric and boasting were far more valuable than the doughty deeds of a hero falling like a tall tree without a witness in a forest of lies. The less renowned of the two grandchildren of Aeacus, Ajax was probably the bravest man and most reliable fighter among the Greeks. Yet he was perpetually overshadowed, first by the tragic glamour of his cousin, Achilles, and later by the poly-tropic guile of Odysseus – who soon figured out that the right to tell the best stories belongs to the last man standing. This alternative even enabled the grandson of Autolycus to gain the last laugh over Achilles – who supposedly told him that life under any conditions was preferable to being prince over the dead.[40] The only immortality available to Homeric man resided in the collective memory of the tribe; it is small wonder that the Greek shame culture found little use for individual integrity, which posed a dire threat to its mythic

39   See Arendt, *The Human Condition* (Chicago, 1958), p. 192.
40   *Odyssey*, XI.488–91.

solidarity. And yet, under these insecure circumstances, would the truth really be preferable to an elaborate lie? Or does the memory of your name matter more than the survival of *your* story? Only rhetoric would say so.

In Socrates' *logos* of the afterlife, Homer's pessimism is overthrown along with Zeus's power-hungry schemes. While in the *Odyssey* the arbitrary favorites of the gods (Menelaus and Helen!) went to the Elysian Fields,[41] and blasphemers against the Olympians were excruciatingly tortured in Tartarus, the vast majority of the dead languished perpetually without self-knowledge, desire, or wit. This makes earthly existence completely meaningless from any moral or intellectual standpoint. It is striking that Socrates rejected the option of the Blessed Isles offered him by Zeus's *doppelganger*, Archelaus; this murderous fratricide, who extended his patronage to a veritable Who's Who of Greek former intellectual luminaries, and who also tellingly presided over his own Olympian games. Yet Socrates scorned the attractions of this sanctuary and preferred living as a poor man in Athens to being a princely favorite among the dead souls in Olympia. By his new *logos* of Hades and his refutation of power-dazzled Polus, Socrates overthrows the blood-stained Olympian tyrant and replaces him with a regime of virtue.[42] He provides a new account of the proper relationship between the divine and mortal that rejects Zeus's arbitrary will; however, human virtue and freedom are quite compatible with the new emphasis upon divine goodness.[43]

This new emphasis on morality is why the judges in this new Hades have very little to do beyond seeing whether the damaged soul is incurable or not. Good and evil lives are treated accordingly; the latter go to Tartarus, described as a prison of punishment and justice, and there is now a purgatorial zone between Tartarus and the Blessed Isles, where the dead are rehabilitated for virtuous life. There are three moral types in this reformed afterlife: the already good, those capable of rehabilitation, and the incorrigibly evil. While the Socratic *logos* is more just and hopeful than Homer's, suggesting that the virtuous will be rewarded and the incontinent may be straightened-out towards virtue through self-knowledge, there is also a stern warning that those who deliberately give themselves up to careers of intemperance cannot be reformed. According to the view of rehabilitation set forth here, someone pun-

---

41   *Ibid.*

42   Voegelin sees that "the transfer of authority from Athens to Plato is the climax of the *Gorgias*" (p. 39). Furthermore, the transition from the Age of Cronos to the Age of Zeus is actually a symbolic representation of "the new order of the soul inaugurated by Socrates" (p. 41).

43   Here again, Voegelin is right on target: "The order of the soul as revealed through Socrates has, indeed, become the new order of relations between God and man" (p. 43).

ished is either personally improved or serves as an example so that others may amend their ways by witnessing his sufferings. Persons in this sorry category are simply shown as they suffer the greatest, most painful, and fearful pain.

Are these sufferings caused by demonic tortures too gruesome to be described any further, or do they simply consist in the evildoers being stripped of the lies they told themselves and being forced to view their own monstrous souls from within? The trajectory of the *Gorgias* strongly suggests the latter possibility. It is as if Hades has been privatized, and the damned are self-tormented by being stripped of the lies that had protected them from moral self-knowledge.[44] For sinners and hypocrites no longer able to avoid psychic self-awareness, the disparity between their former glory, deformed state, and daimonic destiny would be torturous indeed! The very *logos*-driven structure of consciousness would then be sufficient for them to hate themselves in ways that resembles the infinite self-renewing sufferings of Homeric villains like Sisyphus and Tantalus. Since evil consists in the illusion of self-sufficiency, there is a rough economy of justice in this solipsistic inferno of suffering. The tormented souls echo the terrible words of Milton's Satan: "Myself am Hell."[45] Or, put differently, a soul ruled by *thumotic* anger, and driven by lustful appetites, could not participate in a cosmos bound together by eros, beauty, and friendship.

This state of affairs may be understood better by viewing the soul as the moral equivalent of an atom. The physical atom is defined as being un-splittable by its very name "a-tom" – it is regarded as the basic unit of reality. Although we know today that the atom may indeed be split, we also understand the literally apocalyptic consequences of this event. Likewise, while the soul can be split, by the sophistic seduction of desire discussed earlier, it would never be its best interests to be disintegrated. Despite huge amounts of energy and destructive power being released by such a psychic explosion, this does not benefit the diseased husk of a dead soul in any way. Despairing of Gorgias's parasitic cleverness and Polus's radical creativity, a psychic consumptive like Callicles looks for happiness by cannibalizing his immortal faculties to gain a false nirvana of hedonistic, albeit self-destructive, ecstasy. Hesiod famously warned that mankind would be terminated in an Age of Iron when men would be born grey-haired and cruel.[46] This perverse tendency persists in our era of postmodernity where, while everything is permitted, it is known to everybody and no one that meaningful human interaction is impossible. This leads to prodigious waste and apathy; while mankind is oblivious to

---

44 For a contemporary rewriting of this inversion of Hades, see Sartre's brilliant play *No Exit* (Vintage, 1989), pp. 1–46

45 Milton, *Paradise Lost*, IV.75.

46 Hesiod, *Works and Days*, 176 ff.

irreversible environmental degradation, our restless concupiscence and desire for deathlessness, the unconscious stirring of our repressed spiritual nature, lead us – as though by *ananke* – to conduct biotechnological experiments that will result in the spawning of humanoid monsters and the permanent fragmentation of the human species.

Callicles, the literary forebear of this postmodern tendency to regard *homo consumo* as the warped measure of meaning, employed Gorgias's discovery of the disintegrative power of rhetoric to conclude that the meaning of life is nothing more than deception, exploitation, and hedonism. He used this nihilistic revelation to anticipatively celebrate the splitting of a moral atom, his soul. In effect, he boasts of his absolute autonomy *qua* spiritual self-cannibal. While such a person has a great deal of raw power at his disposal, most notably in our age of sybaritic technology where every man can be his own tyrant, the incredible torment and self-loathing eventually caused by this process of psychic suicide – which cannot destroy the soul but merely causes it to feed on itself eternally – exponentially exceeds whatever temporary pleasures that may be gained over a gaudy career of envied intemperance. Worst of all, such a person will not be able to enjoy any genuine happiness. We may imagine a judge in Hades asking a badly scarred tyrannical soul if it wants to enjoy *eudaimonia*; while a damaged incontinent soul will gladly accept such an offer, even at the cost of painful rehabilitation, an incorrigibly intemperate soul would feel so much pain at the prospect of actively giving love that it would not be able even to feign assent. The incompatibility between hedonism and *eudaimonia* is seen when such a soul prefers excruciating psychic pain to participating in the cosmos. It will say: "Here I stand, I can do no other." By abusing its mysterious freedom, it has crossed a moral Rubicon and predestined itself to Hell.[47]

Socrates tells Callicles that tyrants like Archelaus will serve as examples of incorrigible cruelty for incontinent souls whose desires will be purged and enlightened by these rare examples of vice (525c). This process will be quite similar to that undergone by Glaucon in the *Republic* where, once he was shown the paranoia and melancholy madness of a tyrant, the prospect of living an invisible and perfectly unjust life became self-evidently undesirable. Indeed, even the Ring of Gyges would not be sufficient to disguise an intemperate evildoer's eventual internal self-awareness of his acute state of dis-ease. Socrates reaffirms to Callicles the very point that was made to Glaucon in the *Republic*: the only thing worse than having an intemperate soul is being an

---

47 Voegelin claims that "In the symbolism of the myth eternal condemnation is the correlate to the refusal of communication on the level of the myth of the soul: eternal condemnation means, in existential terms, self-excommunication . . . the criminal can achieve nothing but the perdition of his soul" (p. 45).

intemperate tyrant. Even Homer bears witness to this, since all those tormented in his Tartarus were kings and potentates.[48] By contrast no private men, not
even the ugly and foul-mannered Thersites, serves as an example of incorrigible vice in Hades; Socrates explains that these men lacked the (political) power
to be truly incurable (525d–e). While ugly Thersites is identified in the
Republic as one of those ready to return to earth, no mention is made of beautiful Achilles.[49] This suggests that his soul suffered irreversible damage seeking glory at Troy at the expense of others. Though Callicles' idealized self is
severely punished (as incorrigible) in speech, Socrates intends this vicarious
experience to partially rehabilitate him by quickening his self-knowledge.

The aforementioned extended power of self-deception accruing from
power has much to do with Socrates' striking distinction between the tyrant
and the natural slave; the latter is far more aware of reality – as he suffers in
alienation from it. While postmodern technology has made a life of solipsism
far more widely available to those desirous of escaping reality, true evil is the
result of sadistic cruelty. Such a soul overflows virtual reality and seeks to torment live victims – trying vainly to find proof that other lives are unhappier
than its own. Sadly, our technology has also granted the power to torture and
destroy to more petty tyrants than ever before, even as it creates a much big-
ger pool of incontinent natural slaves and other hapless potential victims.

Now Socrates grants that nothing can prevent a king or potentate from
becoming a good man, and indeed states that such persons are to be admired
greatly since it is exceedingly hard to lead a just life when having license to do
injustice with impunity (526a). Yet while he clearly believes in the general tendency of power to be spiritually corrosive, very much at variance with the
famous statement in the *Republic* that polities will never have respite from ills
until philosophers become kings or *vice versa*, Socrates does not neglect to
mention an exceptional example of a virtuous Athenian statesman: Aristides,
famously titled "the just" by the very people who ostracized him. Normally,
however, when these just judges view the souls of rulers or politicians, they are
far more likely to be harshly punished. Socrates also asserts that Rhadamantus,
the judge assigned to Asiatics, would send philosophers who minded their own
business to the Isles of the Blessed, beholding their pious and truthful soul
with admiration (526c).

But, unlike the timid thinkers of the *Republic* who hid behind a little wall,
and perhaps showed puppets above it, we could conclude that, since the true
business of philosophy in the reversed Socratic cosmos has to do with continually bringing the four-fold together, Aeacus (the judge of the West) will per-
mit an erotic philosopher's daimonic soul to return once more to the breach

---

48   *Odyssey*, XI.576–600.
49   See Allan Bloom, *The Republic of Plato* (Basic Books, 1991), p. 436.

between heaven and earth. This inference is consistent with Socrates' refusal to live a spoiled life of luxury at Archelaus's court; the contrast between *nirvana* (the blissful enjoyment of non-being) and a *bodhisattva* (one who won't enter heaven until all souls have been saved) is striking. Since in our times the gap between humanity and the other elements of the four-fold has widened, it also follows that more daimonic activity is necessary to repair and bridge this abyss.

Back in the *Gorgias*, Socrates summarizes the reasoning (*logon*) that persuades him to present as healthy a soul as possible to those who will truly judge his life (526d). These are the very judges he hoped to go before the *Apology,* This is why he won't concern himself with the honors of the many, but strives instead to live in the truth and be as good as he can be, both in his way of life and in his way of death. Socrates urges all human beings, but especially Callicles, to choose the same way of life. Otherwise, he fears that Callicles will experience the same humiliations that he expected Socrates to face in a democratic court when he meets the judges of Hades. We must see that, by stripping their souls of glib rationalizations and forcing them to examine the implications of their way of life, Socrates exposes Callicles, Polus, and Gorgias to these healing humiliations.

In conclusion, Socrates admits that while his *logos* could easily be scornfully dismissed as an old wives' tale, one first needs to find a better and truer account of these matters. Indeed the problem with popular Athenian piety was that it had come to consist of little better than old wives' tales that were either scornfully dismissed or used for spiritual blackmail by the likes of Euthyphro. As we noted, this is one reason why Homer and the Trojan War were supplanted by Thucydides and his account of the Peloponnesian War. In this context, *Socrates'* daimonic vocation consists in renewing reified old myths that no longer point transcendentally towards the beauty of the cosmos and the goodness of the gods.[50] Meanwhile, although Gorgias, Polus, and Callicles are as wise as any three Greeks of their day, they have not been able to show a way of life better for this world than that described and defended by Socrates. All their fine speeches are refuted while his position is fixed and unchanging (527a–c). Socrates summarizes its tenets: one should (a) fear doing injustice more than suffering it, (b) value being good in private and public over seeming good, (c) see that goodness comes first with just punishment next, (d) flee all flattery, and (e) take care that rhetoric should be used only to serve justice. Callicles is told that only this way of life leads to happiness, both in this life and the next. Moreover, even if one is despised, trampled in the mud, and struck humiliatingly, he will suffer no real damage as long as he practices

50   See Ranasinghe, *Inspiration, Interpretation and Interdependence*, pp. 271–77.

virtue while remaining noble and good (527d). Regardless of the fate of the soul after death, these propositions remain at the level of myth on our side of death; it is in this world that Socrates' *logos* of the death and corruption of the soul must resonate deep in our souls.[51]

Socrates has not merely provided a likely account of the soul's fate, he has also anticipated the punishments supposedly deserved by injustice in the after-life by his practicing of "the true political art" – something that has everything to do with the medicinal procedure of restoring self-knowledge to the soul. Even though this very *"logos"* of the afterlife is part of his therapy qua "mythos," its claim to be a rational account is amply justified by Socrates' practice of psychic self-recollection and "at-one-ment." In other words, the truth of his *logos* is corroborated in this life by his "political art."[52] Socratic dialectic restores the self-knowledge and integrity of the psychic regime; this is the alternative to corrupting the soul by pandering pleasure and pain. The this-worldly significance of his *logos* is that we must eventually descend into our souls and live with the psychic consequences of our own misdeeds. So too must Athens deal with the delayed effects of the grandiose imperialism of Cimon and Pericles. This is the real reversal from the Age of Kronos to Zeus. Like Kronos vomiting up his children, and the supposed master-art of Gorgias renouncing its claim to supersede all the other arts and sciences, Athens must disgorge her vast imperial acquisitions; she will pay dearly for her reliance on coerced tribute and trade. Yet she will gain in self-knowledge – immeasurably more than what was lost in pride. The future of the School of Hellas must be found in thought rather than deed. While Gorgias defends Hellenic promiscuity, Socrates comes to shrive Athens – not to apply cosmetics to her faded beauty.[53] The torch of Prometheus is passed from Pericles to Plato. It will soon blaze open a path that will carry the imperishable *logos* from Jerusalem, through the Hellenized World, all the way to Rome.[54]

---

51   As Fussi points out, the foreknowledge of death supposedly taken away by Prometheus really amounts to Socrates' destruction of the prevalent beliefs that (a) appearances were the reality of a person and (b) the gods were as easily persuadable as human witnesses. This has the result of forcing men to come to terms with their own mysterious psychic interiority (pp. 535–39).

52   Cf. Newell. "Socratic philosophy is indivisibly political philosophy. Founding the city in one's own soul means a devotion to the good that will guide one's personal and civic friendships. The core of this mission is erotic satisfaction rightly understood.

53   Voegelin tersely observes that "the *Gorgias* is the death sentence over Athens" (p. 39).

54   See Rémi Brague, *Eccentric Culture* (St. Augustine's Press, 2002).

Epilogue

What final conclusions are to be drawn from this dialogue? Socrates has just told Callicles that the opportunistic way of life followed by sophistry is worth nothing and leads nowhere (527e). This path must be traced back to Gorgias's famous triple denial of Truth's existence, its know-ability, and its speak-ability. While Gorgias suggested that the way out of this abyss was by the persuasive manipulation of democratic opinion, Socrates exposes the ruinous consequences of this strategy. Differently put, Callicles' nihilistic outlook was shown to follow inevitably from Gorgias's denial of the conditions for the possibility of both knowledge and non-manipulative speech and Polus's attempt to reform reality through speech alone. Socrates refutes them by showing the irreversible results of nihilism. He does so both directly – in tracing the trajectory followed by Gorgias's progeny – and indirectly – by showing unjust souls being punished by the involuntary restoration of self-knowledge to them in his reformed Hades.

Self-knowledge is both the cure and the punishment for evil. This may be illustrated through the mythic account of the slaying of the Gorgon Medusa. It is as though Socrates, as Perseus, slays Gorgias the Gorgon by forcing him to look at himself. Like the Gorgon's head, seductive sophistry has the power to kill souls by placing them in a this-worldly Hades. Here, without any idea of themselves, morality, or the beauty of the cosmos, the many desires of the demos are manipulated by the murderous beauty and false self-evidence of images, opinions, and reputations. The Socratic remedy for this spiritual malaise is the individual liberation of souls from this cave-like state of false consciousness through his rough dialectical magic. On this side of the Styx, he recommends that men be judged according to virtue and vice by impartial judges who would replace the easily corrupted juries of Athens. This idea along with the belief in just otherworldly judgment, a fate also determined by moral criteria, still remains at the foundation of Western Civilization. It is striking that these concepts arose out of a primal encounter with violence and deception during the desperate years of the Peloponnesian War; they provide a basis for cautious optimism that the resources of civilization are equal to confronting both the apocalyptic violence of fundamentalism and the more insidious violation of humanity through technological seduction.

Since Christianity has altered Socrates' model by externalizing good and evil and placing the complementary concepts of an omnipotent merciful God and original sin, like a good and bad angel, on either side of us, the resultant synthesis is unequal to the task of confronting the problem of evil unless the soul's power to choose between good and evil is taken very seriously. Socrates' literal excavation of the soul goes deeper than Rousseau's; the latter attributes all evil to nurture and cannot see the line separating good from evil that runs through the soul itself. Neither can liberal Christianity account for the soul's historically well-demonstrated power to perversely reject grace and make itself the center of an atomized reality; the austere doctrine of Double Predestination is but a futile effort to claim divine sanction for this terrible human capacity.

Once the dangers of rhetoric and sophistry are recognized, the need for an account of reality that neither falsely affirms the monistic One nor too easily accepts the other extreme of ontological nihilism cannot be denied. Otherwise put, while man cannot live meaningfully under the crushing yoke of omniscient and omnipotent divine rule, authentic human existence is just as impossible when we attempt to exercise these sovereign powers ourselves. Gorgias was too swift in gleefully deriving nihilistic conclusions from the unavailability of certain and objective knowledge of Being. Indeed we have gone so far as to say that the real presence of human freedom necessitates that stifling divine omniscience could not exist alongside it; indeed even theological thought only proceeds meaningfully if it presupposes that humans possess rational and volitional freedom.[1]

Yet, as is seen through poor Callicles' predicament, meaningful freedom of thought and action must also be informed and limited by something higher and nobler than spontaneous preferences and arbitrary decisions. While Socrates helped Polus to see that human speeches, thoughts, and actions must follow a rational teleology, and navigate under a sky of starry ideals, Callicles' view that these directions were selfishly created led to the study of human desire and the chastened recognition that naked self-interest had to be limited and cultivated by qualitative judgments and prudential factors. While this led

---

1   In Pope Benedict XVI's words, "God does not become more divine when we push him away from us in a sheer impenetrable, voluntarism; rather, the truly divine God is one who has revealed himself as *logos* and, as *logos*, has acted and continues to act lovingly on our behalf." *Regensburg Lecture*, p. 138.

to the discovery of the soul, the mysterious microcosmic substance underlying human passions and desires, Callicles' precociously corrupted will could not make the qualitative leap from lusting after the "called-noble" to living by what is truly *kalon*.

So the final quarter of the dialogue saw Socrates complete his account of these matters *solus*; he conducted an internal discussion with his *daimon* that leads to a complementary macrocosmic model being projected out of the human wisdom gleaned from pondering the soul's microcosmic economy. While the words of the *Gorgias* are surely Plato's rather than Socrates', and represent part of his extraordinary efforts to account for the conditions of the possibility of Socratic virtue, their enduring quality testifies to the common human experiences of *Logos* and *Eros*. These great gifts of the gods are believed sufficient to overcome the skepticism of Gorgias and his spawn regarding the possibility of truth, our knowledge and its communication. Socrates suggests that it is within the power of the human soul to deliberate well and prudently when confronted with the many dyadic categories (freedom and necessity, good and evil, nobility and vice) that operate on it.

Even though these claims are made indirectly – in the space between the four-fold – and amount to my own interpretation of Plato's own take on Socrates and his overcoming of the false necessities of fear and pleasure, this discussion of the *Gorgias* has tried to show how sophisticated skepticism concerning the possibility of knowing and sharing the goodness of the world may be overcome philosophically. The ultimate basis for this trust in *Logos* and *Eros* lies in the timeless charisma of Socrates: his ability to lead a virtuous and happy life despite being old, poor, and incredibly ugly, especially against the potentially nihilistic backdrop of the Peloponnesian War, suggests that he lived in a state of *eudaimonia*. Socrates' life exhibits a wondrous capacity for moral resilience and erotic self-transcendence that continues to speak and inspire mankind over the two and a half millennia that separate us from him. The enduring power of this image, which Plato conveys by this dialogue, itself serves as testimony of the indissoluble ties by which our microcosmic souls – spread out over time and space – participate in a macrocosmic order.

Unlike most so-called wise men, Socrates never claimed to have any scientific knowledge of divine or transcendent matters. One does not gain truth by submitting to the rough *ananke* of human power. Neither is this knowledge gained by those who violently force the hand of fortune through manipulative speech and unspeakable deeds. Rather, Socrates reveals that the truth is revealed when we discover its authority over us – and find through it the power to perform free and deliberate actions; we become aware of axiomatic verities higher than ourselves by our inability to command or destroy them. This is why the claims of value-free science to be sole arbiter of truth must be rejected.

Man is more than an analytic machine, and the end of life is not to make humanity machine-friendly; indeed, as we have seen, such a process is far more likely to end in the proliferation of natural slaves. All human wisdom is based on self-knowledge and shared reflection on the conditions for the possibility of virtue and vice. While all of the dialogues give us a deepened awareness of the human condition, the *Gorgias* in particular provides us with a *logos* of psychic interiority along with a *mythos* of transcendence that Plato seems to proffer as the cosmic model that his mentor implicitly lived by. These graciously added dimensions to reality confer beauty, dignity, and meaning to human life. They make it possible for human beings of good will to transcend those oppositional and adversarial contexts that breed strife and spite.

Human wisdom understood in an appropriately Socratic manner also gives rise to an experience of transcendental *eudaimonia* that far surpasses the equivalent connection between the desire for manipulative power over reality and hedonistic satisfaction sought therefrom. While there are several reasons why the experience of participating in the coming together of the cosmos is very much unlike that gained through the pursuit of power and pleasure, the most important distinction is between the *thumotic* "zero-sum" character of power politics and the power of the *logos* by which many human beings bring out the best in each other as they participate in common erotic strivings. Perhaps Plato's most compelling argument in favor of the cosmic model elaborated here is made in his characteristic *reductio ad absurdum* fashion. Socrates demonstrates through closely questioning Callicles how a life led shamelessly for self-gratification collapses under the weight of the consequent existential and rational contradictions; this *epideixis* complements the account in the *Republic* of the melancholy misery of even the most successfully disguised tyrannical life.

While happiness in the strong sense of *eudaimonia* is self-liberating rather than grasping, giving not receiving, the life spent endlessly seeking pleasure is continually in flight from itself; it has nothing to give and nowhere to enjoy it. Such a career culminates in the tyrant's belief that he can derive pleasure only through sadism: by vainly trying to prove to himself that his victims are even unhappier than their tormentor. While such a demonstration refutes itself, to the extent that it is based on a negative rather than positive definition of happiness, the *Gorgias* also claims with no little authority that the life of a sadistic tyrant is always worse than that of its victim because the inner shame of knowing oneself to be evil, or the blind pain derived from successfully hiding the source of the violation from oneself, is qualitatively beyond that suffered through the heaping on of pain and humiliation on the dunghills of just men. The corrupted soul's vain effort to escape itself, in violation of its own psychic integrity, is the culmination of a career spent in an activity as tragic as the sight of a dog chasing its own tail is comic. These furious and infinite exertions can be seen as the basis for the absurd labors depicted in Homer's Hades and Dante's *Inferno*.

Such grotesqueries explain why the soul could be viewed as a moving chariot where urgent personal judgments regarding virtue and vice are continually made – as we journey in and out of the cave.[2] While Athenian democracy recognized the dignity of the individual, it falsely treated the soul's power for good and evil as if the potential for virtue was already actualized in, and measured by, the sovereign ego. Yet the *Gorgias* reveals the strong convictions of its hero and author that while virtue and vice may not be imposed on the soul, they cannot be acquired or expelled merely by an act of will. When this is read beside Socrates' claim in the *Apology* that a just man cannot be harmed by persons morally worse than himself (30d), we're almost irresistibly led to conclude that such an entity cannot be purely physical. There is every reason to suspect that it participates in a moral order with no little authority over our conscience and consciousness.

Not the least among the benefits accruing from virtue is the resultant ability to escape the this-worldly state of Hades and see things as they are. We could call this "leaving the cave" or it could simply be seen as gaining a richer take on reality. The evildoer by contrast literally has "no idea" of the beauty of the cosmos because his consciousness is warped by insatiable desire, blind anger, infinite need, and chronic vice. Yet the beauty of the cosmos lies precisely in the recognition that reality is so structured that true happiness can only result from virtue. This is why Socrates plays an essential role, *qua daimon*, in both bringing together and revealing the beauty of the cosmos.

Meeting the objection that we have employed the *daimon*, like a *deus ex machina*, and emulated the errors of Anaxagoras and Euripides, it should be noted that this concept merely represents the state of mature self-knowledge and spiritual enlightenment that Socrates celebrates in many contexts as being worthiest of the friendship of the gods. While a daimonic man is a practitioner of the true political art, the paradoxical basis for this wisdom is his ability to remain skeptical of all human claims to possess divine knowledge or power. As exemplified by Socrates' conduct, the public deeds performed by this art are primarily negative: it merely deters foolish beliefs and vain acts. Certain wisdom and destructive power are most often sought by credulous and fearful persons – they have lost the ability to live in reality and see the beauty of the cosmos. Socrates' ability to resist the artificial *ananke* of oratory and refute the

2   Implicitly identifying *catharsis* as the content of the Socratic Political Art, Voegelin explains that "the curable soul is permanently in the state of judgment" adding that "to experience itself permanently in the presence of the judgment . . . is the criterion of the curable soul" (p. 45).

foul flattery of rhetoric reminds us that it is possible to defeat false fears and resist toxic pleasures while learning about, and constantly nurturing, the power of virtuous men to live in goodness, truth and beauty.

A daimonic individual is not merely a deterrent against false and toxic pleasure; his life is an example of true happiness. Ruled by self-knowledge, such a person lives among men like Tiresias in Hades. A moderate life of *eudaimonia* helps one's fellow citizens to see that power over others (and limitless pleasures and riches) cannot give true, lasting happiness. Simply put, the good are freed to practice this true political art by their ability to see things as they are. This contemplative power, praised in Hesiod's *Works and Days*,[3] brings with it both the faculty to judge for the good of all and the ability to act accordingly. It is the basis for Socrates' famous claim that no one would deliberately choose evil. Good humans do their polity a priceless service by constantly proving that virtue is immune to the false necessity of vice. This proof of freedom helps virtuous men to live in a way that both celebrates and actualizes the beauty of the cosmos. A genuine polis comes about as an extension of these friendly associations.[4] Conversely, Gorgon-like rhetoric turns a living polis into stone buildings as surely as it reduces public men to brazen statues.

Perhaps the best way to conclude this reading of the *Gorgias* is by returning to its first word: "*polemou*" or battle, and Socrates' apt rejoinder that surely Callicles meant to say "*heortes*" or feast. The first question raised in this dialogue, and the basis for the conflict between the School of Gorgias and Socrates, pertains to reality itself and the proper stance we should take towards it. Is Being itself bellicose, or is it a feast for those who can contemplative it – and so participate appropriately? While rhetoric inflames our passions with paranoid accusations and dreams of destructive glory, Socrates insists that the beauty of reality cannot be known by adversarial opportunism; friendship holds the cosmos together in vertical, horizontal and internal relations: it exists between gods, daimons, and mankind; among humans; and within the soul itself. Instead of the ego striving to be called as beautiful as self-destructive Achilles, the temperate soul can become beautiful by participating in the best of all possible beauty – that of the cosmic order.

While it is not made out of words, this "festive" cosmos requires both erotic speech and heroic deeds to become fully actualized. The *Logos* of Socrates is about the sheer "talk-ability" of the cosmos in all of its beauty – only through loving words and generous acts of friendship may it be seen, conveyed, and realized in its greatest glory. Conversely, a brooding preoccupation with power, accumulation, and display, all part of the warlike mentality that came to plague Imperial Athens, leads men to view reality as resentful

3   Hesiod, *Works and Days*, 293–97.
4   See Aristotle's *Nicomachean Ethics* VIII.9.

creditors – rather than knowing themselves to be its grateful and humble debtors. Such predators obsessively seek to rape, loot, and pillage the world as they vainly crave admiration and pleasure; the blind need to conquer the gratuitous given-ness of reality leaves them oblivious to the fact that they are knee-deep in paradise. Accordingly, the easily seduced desires for respect, happiness, and community – the cause and effect of both war and social aggression – have to be educated and rehabilitated in the soul by the true political art.

Once we learn to dwell temperately in our souls, Socrates' paradoxical moral axioms will be self-evident to us. Waging war against divine law and natural order only visits deeper pollution on our true self and damages the fabric of common reality itself. So ugly a life is clearly worth nothing. Socrates' inspiring example suggests that true happiness is gained neither through 'spinning' vain fabrications in the void nor by being envied in the cave-like abyss of non-being. Rather, *eudaimonia* can only be earned by using the 'enduring power' of the human soul to participate in the beauty of the cosmos.

Index